Indian Companion
to
D.H. Lawrence

Indian Companion to D.H. Lawrence

Mallikarjun Patil

AUTHORSPRESS
Publishers of Scholarly Books

Worldwide Circulation through Authorspress Global Network
First Published 2011
by
Authorspress

Editorial
Q-2A Hauz Khas Enclave,
New Delhi-110 016
e-mail: authorspress@yahoo.com

Marketing
E-35/103, Jawahar Park
Laxmi Nagar, Delhi-110 092
e-mail: authorspress@yahoo.com

Indian Companion to D.H. Lawrence
ISBN 978-81-7273-587-6

Printed in India at Tarun Offset, Delhi.

Preface

D.H. Lawrence (1885-1930) is a fine yet controversial English novelist, short story writer, poet and essayist. He comes from a low socio-economic background of a coal mining community of the Midlands. His education was not adequate for a writer. Ford Madox Ford helped him publish his first novel *The White Peacock* (1911). He often drew his themes from his own life and relationships. *Sons and Lovers* (1913) is a clearly autobiographical novel about working class family life. In 1914 he married a German woman, Frieda Weekley. The object o: hostility and suspicion during World War I was because of his pacifism and her origins, and the couple lived in various countries after 1919, never returning to England.

The Rainbow (1915) and its sequel *Women in Love* (1920) trace the sickness of modern civilization to the effects of industrialization upon the human psyche. *Kangaroo* (1923) describes the persecution he experienced during the war. *The Plumed Serpent* (1926) was inspired by his fascination with Aztec culture.

Lawrence's writing is notable for its intensity and its erotic sensuality; several of his works, including *Lady Chatterley's Lover* (1928) were banned as obscene. He died of the tuberculosis that had plagued him for an early age.

The present comprehensive and critical monograph is a study of Lawrence's entire works — fiction, poetry, plays, travel accounts, essays, and letters. It is a great work of survey, study and compilation. The companion aims at educating the Indian readers about D.H. Lawrence.

Mallikarjun Patil

Introduction

D. H. Lawrence attracted an enormous amount of commentary during his life. After the suppression of *The Rainbow* in 1915 he rapidly acquired a certain notoriety to which he responded by being defiant and often contemptuous of his critics. Towards the end of his life he ran into further notoriety through *Lady Chatterley's Lover* and *Pansies*, his paintings met with outright hostility, and at his death the obituarists wrote about him with an animosity rarely displayed on such occasions. In spite of the heat thus generated some interesting and perceptive criticism was produced.

Lawrence's very first publication was *A Prelude,* entered for the Nottinghamshire Guardian's Christmas competition in 1907, under the name 'Rosalind.' The story won first prize, and two other pieces that Lawrence submitted were also given honourable mention. *A Prelude* had a simple theme "handled with a freshness and simplicity altogether charming"; and one of the other stories, "Legend," was praised for its vivid realism.

For the winning entry Lawrence had used the address of his early sweetheart, Jessie Chambers (the Miriam of *Sons and Lovers*), and it was she who helped him to his first appearance in print under his own name by sending some of his poems to the *English Review*. These attracted the attention of the editor, Ford Madox Hueffer (Ford), who prided himself on his ability to spot new talent.

Another reason for Ford's interest was that he saw in Lawrence a spokesman for the working class. Violet Hunt, who was also on the staff of the *English Review*, and later became the wife of Ford Madox Ford (although their marriage was never properly legalized), found a similar significance in Lawrence's first novel, *The White Peacock* (1911).

Ford and Violet Hunt both helped to smooth the way for the publication of *The White Peacock*. Heinemann's reader accepted it with alacrity, but some changes had to be made to meet the prudish taste of the time–a foretaste of the greater difficulties which were to come with *Sons and Lovers* and *The Rainbow* (published in England by Duckworth and Methuen respectively).

Once out *The White Peacock* "took the town," according to Violet Hunt, and Catherine Carswell, the novelist and later close friend of Lawrence, calls it 'a succes d'estime.' These phrases probably refer to its reception in literary society.

Lawrence worked on his next novel, *The Trespasser*, very carefully, paying special attention to its form. To the author and critic, Edward Garnett, who was at this time acting as publisher's editor to Duckworth's, Lawrence wrote anxiously: "I hope the thing is knitted firm-I hate those pieces where the stitch is slack and loose." When the book was published several critics again attacked its lack of construction, but the *Morning Post* reviewer, praised its "unusual artistic unity," thus showing a second time his friendliness and perceptiveness with regard to Lawrence.

The Trespasser, more so than *The White Peacock,* was an erotic book, and according to Ford Madox Ford the unrevised version "much more phallic than is the book as it stands." If published, he told Lawrence, it would damage his reputation perhaps permanently.

Lawrence's first volume of poetry, *Love Poems* (1913), met, on the whole, with more judicious response than his earliest novels. Two poets, one English, Edward Thomas, and one American, Ezra Pound, welcomed him as an ally in the cause of a new kind of expression that should be modern in subject-matter and independent of the jaded poetic diction inherited from late nineteenth century verse. The *Nation* also placed Lawrence in the ranks of the moderns, and praised his "vivid, unexpected images." Above all, Lawrence was seen as a poet of strength and individuality—for better or for worse, a force to be reckoned with, and distinctively modern.

It is usually supposed that with *Sons and Lovers* (1913) Lawrence arrived as a major novelist. How many copies of the original edition were printed is unknown, but the book does not seem to have sold as well as Lawrence hoped. It was not reprinted until 1922, but from then onwards new editions were frequent, and sales figures for the early 1930s indicate that it was by that time the most popular of Lawrence's novels.

Reviews, however, were plentiful, and Lawrence himself said that he liked them. But, if the tone was laudatory, much of the detail was unfavourable, and few critics showed real understanding of the novel's theme. It was, for example, thought fortunate for Mrs. Morel that Paul supplied her husband's place, and admiration for "the heroic little mother" often led critics to miss the significance of her destructive influence on her sons. The complaints made about Lawrence's previous novels were also repeated with regard to *Sons and Lovers*. He was again criticized for neglect of form and his treatment of sex was found even more distressing.

Duckworth's accepted the novel, and published it in May 1913, but not without making several cuts. The book, however, still remained too erotic for many critics. The well-known essayist and literary critic, Robert Lynd, referred to "the hot-houses of amorous writing" and said that Lawrence had an exaggerated sense of the physical side of love.

Slight as it was, perhaps the most influential comment on *Sons and Lovers* was that made by Henry James in "The Younger Generation" (TLS 19 March 1914, reprinted in *Notes on Novelists*, 1914), where Lawrence was said to 'hang in the dusty rear' of Hugh Walpole, Gilbert Cannan and Compton Mackenzie. Kuttner interpreted the novel as the struggle of a man to free himself from allegiance to his mother and transfer his love to a woman outside the family circle, a struggle which in *Sons and Lovers* ends tragically.

Lawrence's next major work was *The Rainbow,* but before that appeared *The Widowing of Mrs. Holroyd,* in April, and *The Prussian Officer*, in November 1914. Lawrence's first play was well received in 1914. It was not produced, however, until 1926 by which time it was still admired, but Lawrence's reputation had changed, and the play was thought to show how well he might have written had he stuck to the working-class life he knew, instead of theorizing about relations between the sexes. The only other of Lawrence's plays to be produced in his life-time was David. As Sean O'Casey says, he never received the sort of encouragement from the theatrical world that would have enabled him to develop his dramatic gifts, and it was not until the revival of his plays at the Royal Court Theatre, London (1965) that his achievement as a playwright was fully appreciated.

Some of the short stories collected in *The Prussian Officer* belonged to Lawrence's early period, and these, particularly "Odour of Chrysanthemums" and "Daughters of the Vicar," were much praised, but the reaction to the more recent tales, "The Prussian Officer" itself and "The Thorn in the Flesh," was puzzled and even hostile.

Critics were beginning to find Lawrence's work strange and unnatural. To one reviewer it seemed that his characters were almost unconscious of right and wrong; and the misgivings to which this aspect of *The Prussian Officer* gave rise were greatly increased by the appearance of *The Rainbow*. The jingoism and moral cant which had begun to afflict war-time England also provided a climate peculiarly ill-suited to the sexual emphases of the novel, producing a note of hysteria in some of the critical reactions. Robert Lynd, for example, denounced *The Rainbow* as "a monotonous wilderness of phallicism." Shorter professed not to be an "opponent of frankness and freedom in literature," but the 'viciousness' of the book was beyond justification, while Norman Douglas saw in it "a greater menace to our public health than any of the epidemic diseases which we pay our medical officers to fight...."

Among the few who tried to retain critical sanity were Catherine Carswell, the reviewer for the *Standard*, and, more doubtfully, H. M. Swanwick, but even these were uncertain in their interpretations and assessments.

On 13 November Methuen's were summoned to answer a charge made against *The Rainbow* under the Obscene Publications Act of 1857. As a result of the ensuing court case all copies of the novel were ordered to be destroyed. The novelist, John Galsworthy, was revolted by its "perfervid futuristic style" and Lawrence's treatment of sex left him with the "painful impression of a man tragically obsessed." The literary critic, John Middleton Murry, and Katherine Mansfield, the short story writer, both close friends of the Lawrences at this time, were doubtful.

James and Wells also seem to have been adverse. Lawrence, in reply, recognized that the difference between himself and James went deep: "subtle conventional design was his aim," he said of James; but of Wells he could say, "He admires me really, at the bottom...."

Lawrence had thus to be supported mainly by his own belief in his work-which was considerable.

Although he was working on *Women in Love*, Lawrence published no further novels during the war. Apart from *Twilight in Italy* (1916), his books were all verse: *Amores* (1916), *Look! We Have Come Through!* (1917), *New Poems* (1918), and *Bay* (1919). It was the second of these which reviewers found hardest to accept, partly because of the nature of its contents, described by the *Athenaeum* as consisting of "dialogues of the passionate, but not always harmonious pair, self-communings, morbid ecstasies, repulsions, and ravings," but also because of its seemingly loose, undisciplined free verse.

Already in private correspondence with Edward Marsh, the editor of *Georgian Poetry*, Lawrence had argued his case for more flexible rhythms even in traditional verse forms, emphasizing instinct rather than the mechanical rules of scansion dictated by "craftsmanship" and "the hidden emotional pattern" rather than "the obvious form" (L 19 November 1913); and these views led on quite naturally to the defence of free verse as the appropriate medium for poetry of the "immediate present," as expounded by Lawrence in his 1920 preface.

Among more favourable critics of Lawrence's verse were the American poets, Amy Lowell, Babette Deutsch and Louis

Untermeyer. Amy Lowell had tried to recruit him to the Imagist movement, of which she was a leader, but in her review of *Look! We Have Come Through!* she admitted that "Mr. Lawrence, in spite of his inclusion in the Imagist Anthologies, cannot be confined within the boundaries of any school." Untermeyer singled him out as the most notable of a group of poets, including Hardy and Rupert Brooke, who spoke of love with a new frankness. The English critic, Francis Bickley, in a review of *Amores*, similarly linked him with 'the militant honesty of some contemporary poets'; but it was another American poet, John Gould Fletcher, who, in possibly the most intelligent appreciation of Lawrence's poetry at this time, explained why this "fine, intolerant fanatic" was to be regarded as a major figure.

From about 1914 comments began to appear taking account of Lawrence, not only as a subject for reviews, but also as a recognized modern author with a number of works to his credit. Garnett made some sensible observations, and his distinction between "the morality of nature and the morality of man" has affinities with Lawrence's *Study of Thomas Hardy* (written 1914, but at that time unpublished).

The novelist, Arthur Waugh, Louis Untermeyer and the novelist and playwright, Douglas Goldring, tended to emphasize Lawrence as poet—which, paradoxically, led Untermeyer at least to a higher estimate of *The Rainbow* than most novel critics were prepared to make. In his view it was "possibly the most poetic and poignant novel of this decade." Such surveys were a tribute to Lawrence's growing reputation.

The Lost Girl and *Women in Love*, both published in November 1920, were partly the work of an earlier Lawrence, *Women in Love* having been written in 1916, and the first half of *The Lost Girl* in 1913. After the affair of *The Rainbow* none of the regular publishers was willing to run the risk of printing its sequel, and so *Women in Love* had to be privately printed in New York (1,250 copies, 50 of which were issued in England). The first trade edition, of 1,500 copies, was published by Secker in London, 1921, and the American firm of Seltzer issued an edition of 15,000 copies in 1922, since then it has been quite steadily reprinted. *The Lost Girl* was published in the usual way, by Seeker, to whom Lawrence confessed some uneasiness about the public's likely reaction to it. Only the award of the James Tait Black memorial prize in 1921 made the novel financially rewarding for Lawrence. This was the only public recognition Lawrence got in his life time. The Nobel Prize committee did not consider both Joyce and Lawrence.

Reviewers were split in their opinion of *The Lest Girl.* It was generally recognized to be indebted to 'the Bennett manner' and Garnett compared it to the tales of the *Five Towns.*

The smaller number of reviews of *Women in Love* may be due, as Martin Green suggests, partly to its being at first privately printed, and partly to an attempt by the New York Society for the Suppression of Vice to get it banned. Two other books were prosecuted along with *Women in Love,* but Magistrate George W. Simpson, who presided over the case, declared that he could find no obscenity in any of the three books: "On the contrary, I find that each of them is a distinct contribution to the literature of the present day."

The best of the reviews were those written by the American critic, John Macy, and the American novelist, Evelyn Scott. Macy, the more conventional of the two, saw affinities between Lawrence and the earlier generation of poetic novelists such as Meredith and Hardy.

In the early 1920s Lawrence's output was prolific. He had no less than twelve books published in the three years from 1921 to 1923. These included two collections of short stories, *England, My England* and *The Ladybird* (published in America as *The Captain's Doll*) which attracted some of the most complimentary reviews to be published in Lawrence's lifetime. In general the shorter form was thought more suitable to Lawrence's genius than the novel, and was judged to act as a brake on his theorizing.

By the same law the theoretical works were damned. The pseudo-technical terms used in *Psychoanalysis and the Unconscious* and *Fantasia of the Unconscious* provoked reviewers either to laughter or disgust.

Critics of the novels (*Aaron's Rod*, 1922; *Kangaroo*, 1923; and *The Boy in the Bush,* 1924) were equally unwilling to take Lawrence seriously as a thinker. H.W. Boynton, reviewer for the *Independent*, described Aaron's Rod as an attempt "to knock up a nice new world for us on the spur of the moment," and with regard to Kangaroo Raymond Mortimer of the *New Statesman* considered that the philosophy had stifled the more worthwhile poetry. Lawrence's mistake, according to the novelist, Alyse Gregory, was in trying to turn himself into a socio-political commentator like H.G. Wells. His insistence on male domination, wrote the American critic, Louise Maunsell Field, was rooted "in the well-known complex of male sex-fear-the man's fear of the woman and of her power." Even Lawrence's travel writing was deplored when it betrayed this note.

Lawrence's own venture into literary criticism with *Studies in Classic American Literature* (1923) was received as a partly stimulating, partly presumptuous and annoying, but essentially amateur effort. Seligmann, author of the first book on Lawrence (*D.H. Lawrence: An American Interpretation*, 1924), for whom *Studies*, and the whole of Lawrence's work to date, was a highly relevant challenge to an America that lived "off the top, thinly." Seligmann's, however, was an exceptionally favourable opinion.

Lawrence was in Mexico in 1925 to 1927. During this period, he carried to the furthest extreme his rejection of conventional Western values. *The Plumed Serpent* (1926) especially seemed devoid of normal human interest—Katherine Anne Porter, the novelist and short story writer, called it a 'catastrophe'—but the reviewer for the *Manchester Guardian* also found St. Mawr disturbingly indifferent to the world of "decent folk who do a considerable amount of honest work, enjoy their lives, and try to behave themselves," and the Scottish poet and critic, Edwin Muir expressed the same.

Lawrence, however, took little interest in criticism. His books were meant to disturb. "Do you think," he wrote to his friend, Carlo Linati, "that books should be sort of toys, nicely built up of observations and sensations, all finished and complete?—I don't.... A book should be either a bandit or a rebel or a man in a crowd. People should either run for their lives, or come under the colours, or say how do you do?"

Lawrence had his own consuming purpose, and he spoke of the religious experience which he had encountered among the Indians. But Wyndham Lewis said that Lawrence merely attributed to the Indians qualities which derived from the "evolutionist, organic philosophy" of Bergson, Spengler and Whitehead, who were foolish enemies of the white man's superior intelligence. Murry, for example, comparing Lawrence with Proust, James Joyce and E.M. Forster, concluded that Lawrence was the most significant because he possessed the quality of religiousness and was "in permanent rebellion against a society and an age that has it not." From another point of view the Cambridge University lecturer, I. A. Richards criticized Lawrence, along with Yeats, for failing to face the problem of maintaining attitudes without the support of the traditional beliefs which had been eroded by scientific truth.

In 1927 E.M. Forster and T.S. Eliot made the first of their various comments on Lawrence. In *Aspects of the Novel* Forster grouped Lawrence with Dostoevski, Melville and Emily Bronte as 'a novelist of prophecy.' After Lawrence's death Forster became involved in an exchange of letters with Eliot and Clive Bell, who disputed his claim that Lawrence was "the greatest imaginative novelist of our generation," and in April of that year Forster gave an obituary talk on Lawrence for the B.B.C. The posterity admires Forster for this.

Eliot, in an article for *La Nouvelle Revue Prancaise*, used Lawrence as an example of the false seriousness and limited sense of reality produced in the English novel by the fashionable preoccupation with Freudian psychology. Like Wyndham Lewis, Eliot represented Lawrence's interest in the primitive as a betrayal of civilization. Yet Eliot also confessed that Lawrence was a figure about whom his mind would "always waver between dislike, exasperation, boredom and admiration," and that his antipathy to Lawrence remained, on the ground of what seemed to him "egotism, a strain of cruelty, and a failing in common with Thomas Hardy the lack of a sense of humour."

Lady Chatterley's Lover, the most celebrated, or notorious, but neither the best nor the worst, of Lawrence's novels, was first published privately at Florence in July 1928. As trouble was expected from the English police, this edition of 1,000 copies priced at £2 each, was distributed mainly through Lawrence's personal friends; by December, however, all copies had been sold, and a cheaper edition of 200 copies was printed in November 1928. The book soon appeared in several pirated editions, and in an attempt to compete with these Lawrence issued the Paris edition of 3,000 copies in May 1929, which was also sold out by August 1929. The expurgated editions published in 1932, after Lawrence's death, consisted of 3,440 (English ed.) and 2,000 (American ed.). Not until 1959 was an unexpurgated trade edition available in America (15,000), and in England it was thanks to Penguin Books, who in 1960 deliberately tested the revised obscenity law by publishing the complete text of *Lady Chatterley* (200,000), that the novel became generally available. With the publication of this novel Lawrence brought down on himself the fury of British public outrage, exemplified in the fulminations of John Bull under the sensational headline, 'Famous Novelist's Shameful Book.'

Lawrence's purpose was not just pornographic, and in several letters written during the composition of the book, and, more fully, in 'A Propos of *Lady Chatterley's Lover*' (1929), he stated that he was fighting on behalf of "the phallic reality, as against the non-phallic cerebration unrealities." And when, in 1932, Frieda Lawrence authorized the expurgated text, most reviewers endorsed Lawrence's view (see Nos. 77-9). Most interestingly of all, W. B. Yeats, in a letter to a friend (No. 81), wrote that the coarse language of Mellors, accepted by Connie "becomes a forlorn poetry uniting their solitudes, something ancient, humble and terrible."

Murry also welcomed the novel, calling it "a cleansing book," but for him it represented only a half-truth. Andre Malraux said that Lawrence attempted to revise the Western myth of sexuality, substituting impersonal passional awareness for the consciousness of personality on which modern love is based.

In 1928 Lawrence's *Collected Poems* were published and in 1929 *Pansies*. The first of these was widely reviewed without adding anything new to the judgments already made on Lawrence's poetry.

In 1929 there was also an exhibition of Lawrence's paintings at the Warren Gallery which shocked some people, and was raided by the police. The exhibition was withdrawn soon.

Lawrence died at Vence, 2 March 1930, and the news was printed in most English papers on 3 March. The image presented by the obituaries was, as Catherine Carswell complained, that of "a man morose, frustrated, tortured, even a sinister failure." The critics were too inhuman. Even his positive qualities were presented almost as the liabilities rather than the assets of genius. The monthlies and quarterlies were more restrained, more favourable.

No distinction has been made between Lawrence's reputation in Britain and America, since his work from the very first was published in both countries. In other countries, judging by translations, interest in his work began in the 1920s.

The subsequent history of Lawrence's reputation can only be sketched briefly. In the 1930s the pattern of Lawrence criticism was set partly by Middleton Murry's seemingly definitive study, *Son of Woman* (1931), given the influential endorsement of T.S. Eliot in his *Criterion*, and partly by the changing political climate. Murry offered the portrait of an artist whose life-long obsession with his mother distorted his entire treatment of sex and invalidated his art. Aldous Huxley's edition of the *Letters* (1932), which included his own excellent introduction, did something to counteract this view, but the spate of reminiscences between 1932 and 1938, useful though several of them were in themselves, confirmed rather than changed Murry's emphasis on the biographical-subjective approach to Lawrence. To critics who were increasingly preoccupied with the political and economic problems of the 1930s it was this approach which made Lawrence seem virtually outmoded. To specifically socialist critics like John

Strachey and Christopher Caudwell the significant thing about Lawrence was that he was a critic of capitalist society.

But in 1930 the man who was later to become Lawrence's best advocate and critic, F.R. Leavis, also published his first essay on Lawrence, emphasizing the correctness and relevance of Lawrence's criticism of modern industrial civilization.

In 1936 appeared *David Herbert Lawrence et les ricentes ideologies allemandes* by the French critic, Ernest Seillere, which made Lawrence sound like a proto-fascist. In the 1950s, however, Lawrence's reputation revived, and today he is widely read, his tales have been very successfully dramatized for television, and even his plays have begun to receive the attention they deserve. Detailed biographies have been produced, the most notable being H. T. Moore: *The Intelligent Heart* (1955) and Edward Nehls: *D. H. Lawrence, A Composite Biography* (1957-59), and collected editions (not always, unfortunately, complete) have been published of the letters (1962), poems (1964) and plays (1965).

So much criticism has appeared since 1950 that one hears complaints of a Lawrence industry. Frank Kermode's "Lawrence and the Apocalyptic Types" which also revives Malraux's theory of Lawrence as a mythologizer. To some readers Lawrence is now, as Kermode says, 'dated' in the sense that he belongs to what can be recognized as a distinct period in English literature. This period is modernism in literature.

Lawrence's overriding concern with wholeness of being makes his own work something which must be read and enjoyed in toto, not in 'residual' parts. All this shows that Lawrence is a deeply disturbing writer.

Contents

1

D.H. Lawrence's Life and Works

D. H. Lawrence was a great and an influential writer, but opinions vary as to whether his greatness lay in his theories on human relationships or in his undoubted technical skill as a writer. David Herbert Richards Lawrence, was born on 11 September 1885 in Eastwood, a hill town in the Nottinghamshire coalfield. His birthplace was a small brick house in Victoria Street. The front room of the ground floor of the house had for a while been a shop where Mrs Lawrence had sold linen and the lace for which her native Nottingham, a few miles away, was famous.

Lawrence's background has a special interest. He had two forceful grandfathers. On the paternal side there was John Lawrence, a Nottingham man who had gone to Eastwood in the 1850s to be company tailor at the Brinsley colliery. In his youth he had been an outstanding rower and boxer. The other grandfather, George Beardsall, also from Nottingham, was an engineer who for a long time had been employed at Sheerness. He was also fervently religious, and often preached in the Methodist chapels.

The Lawrence parents married at Christmastime in 1875, when Arthur Lawrence was 29 years old and his wife Lydia six years younger. She had been a school teacher, and she was 'a superior soul.' One of her sisters, Lettice, made a distinguished marriage to Fritz Krenkow, a German scholar of oriental languages who became a lecturer at Cambridge. Lydia's grandfather on her mother's side, John Newton, had worked in the lace factories and he was a noted hymn writer. Sovereignty is still sung in the Non–conformist chapels.

D. H. Lawrence, who was brought up in his father's Congregationalist faith, has in his essay "Hymns in a Man's Life" told of the influence, upon his vision and writing.

When Lawrence was a young man he left Congregationalism, took up Unitarianism for a while, then gradually developed his own religion of blood knowledge.

Early Life

Lawrence had two brothers and two sisters, and was the next to youngest in the family. He was from the first a frail child, with brownish hair that turned red as he grew up. He was never very athletic, and often played with the girls of his age. His mother encouraged him in his studies at Beauvale Board School, where one of his older brothers, William Ernest, had had a good record before becoming a successful young businessman in London. Lawrence, who disliked his first name, David, was always known as Bert to his family.

Lawrence's earlier childhood had been a mixture of joy and misery. He was happy when he could walk through the country about Eastwood, of which he was later to write so intimately. There are many memorials of the past. Annesley Park, Newstead Abbey, and Hucknall Torkard are all associated with Byron. Close to Eastwood, the ruins of a fourteenth century castle stands up jaggedly at Greasley. The shattered Beauvale Abbey provided the background for Lawrence's medieval story *A Fragment of Stained Glass*.

He also frequently drew upon High Park Wood, in which the Abbey stands; Moorgreen Reservoir, next to the wood; and the nearby manor house, Lamb Close, home of the Barbers, who for centuries had owned the Eastwood collieries. Lamb Close figures prominently in Lawrence's *The White Peacock* (1911), *Women in Love* (1920) and *Lady Chatterley's Lover* (1928).

The country always seemed wonderful to the boy, when he could get out of sight of the mines. The colliers came home at dusk, their faces masked with coal; dust, singing as they walked along the streets. When they were home, they stripped off their upper clothing, and their wives washed the dust from their backs. This process seemed to fascinate and horrify the young

Lawrence, who was later to describe it in several stories and to put it on the stage in his play *The Widowing of Mrs Holroyd* (1914).

Parents

Lawrence's unhappiness as a child was caused by the fierce quarrels between his parents amid their grinding poverty. His father was a robust, black bearded little man who sometimes stopped at the pub on the way home and spent part of his wages, on which the family lived, drinking with his friends. This infuriated his wife, who was of the temperance persuasion. She would nag him, and he would shout back, sometimes striking her; once, when she was pregnant, he pushed her out of the house and locked her out for the night. Lawrence described these lacerating quarrels in his work, particularly *Sons and Lovers* (1913), of which he said that the first half, the childhood part, was based on real events. The children took their mother's side when they were small. Lawrence later said that he felt he had been wrong in this because he had failed to realize his father's worth as man intensely alive, with a relish for living. He always bore many spiritual scars from those savage fights between his parents. His mother battled, and successfully, to keep her sons out of the mine and her daughters out of domestic service. But it was at terrible cost. The mines themselves were always in his consciousness, perhaps providing the symbol of darkness.

Mrs Lawrence, disappointed in her marriage, turned her strong love upon her sons, first upon Ernest, who was the brightest. But in the autumn of 1901 he died at 23, in London, of pneumonia. For a long time after the funeral his mother was dazed and half alive. Then her son Bert became ill, and she turned her fierce love on him as she nursed him through an attack of pneumonia. He had finished high school and had continued to go into Nottingham daily, walking as a clerk in an artificial-limbs factory. Afterwards he became a teacher of other colliers' sons at the British School in Eastwood.

During these years, the Lawrences had moved several times. In Lawrence's infancy they went to live in the miners' quarters at the bottom of the hill to the north of Eastwood, a place called the Breach (the Bottoms of *Sons and Lovers*). It was a dismal area, soot, soaked, though it was at the edge of open country; and Mrs Lawrence disliked it. At the beginning of the nineties, the Lawrences moved to the hill above the Breach, to a house in Walker Street from which they could look out on the sloping farmlands, the smoking mines, and the patches of Sherwood Forest. Lawrence lived in that house from the age of 6 to 18.

In that landscape there was a small farm just north of Moorgreen Reservoir and Lamb Close: the Haggs farm at Willey Spring, where the Chambers lived. Lawrence had met them just before his illness at 16. He became a fast friend of one of the boys, Alan, and established one of the most important relationships of his life with Alan's sister, Jessie, who was to be the Miriam of *Sons and Lovers*. A year younger than Lawrence, this farm girl was a dreamer, and she became obsessed with the slim youth who so often walked out across the fields to the Haggs. Jessie and Lawrence began to read together. George Eliot meant much to them because she had written of Derbyshire, only a few miles away; even Jane Austen had set some scenes in her fiction there.

Lawrence sometimes helped Jessie's father and brothers in mowing hay. As Mr Chambers said, "Work goes like fun when Bert's here." Lawrence was lively, imaginative, playful, and for years the Haggs was his second home. His mother disapproved of these friends, particularly of Jessie, in whom she saw a rival. The conflict between Mrs Lawrence and Jessie provided Lawrence with one of the principal themes of *Sons and Lovers*. In the book, as in life, the girl eventually lost because the boy was too closely bound to his mother. But Lawrence's relationship with Jessie lasted nearly a dozen years. Jessie was by then in her middle twenties, and she wanted to make the attachment permanent. He had a love affair with an older woman, Alice Dax, who was married, a relationship on which that between Paul Morel and Clara Dawes in *Sons and Lovers* was partly based; but this too came to nothing.

When Mrs Lawrence died of cancer in 1910, her son was unable to shake himself free from his emotional ties with her. It was not until 1912, when he met his future wife Frieda, that he found himself able to consider a permanent attachment.

Teaching Career

Meanwhile, after teaching for a year at Eastwood, Lawrence was reassigned, as a pupil teacher, to the school in the nearby borough of Ilkeston, in Derbyshire. A number of Lawrence's friends were also pupil teachers there. Except for the rather solemn Jessie Chambers, who liked to have Lawrence to herself, they were a merry group, calling themselves the Pagans. At this time Lawrence was extremely interested in Louise Burrows, a girl from a town near Ilkeston Cossall, the Cossethay of his novel *The Rainbow* (1915), in which he drew upon Louise Burrows for part of the portrait of the heroine, Ursula Brangwen.

Lawrence attended the pupil-teacher centre from 1903 to 1905. He spoke later of the savage teaching of collier lads, and in describing Ursula's experience in *The Rainbow* he showed how rough the boys could be. But in December 1904, new horizons began to gleam brightly before Lawrence: in the King's Scholarship Examination, he came out first in all England and Wales. He received a scholarship grant to what was then Nottingham University College, though he had to wait a year before entering because he lacked the 20 pounds required for advance fees. He spent that year as an uncertificated teacher at the British School in Eastwood, saving what money he could. And his mother skimped to help him. In September 1906, he again began taking the daily train to Nottingham, to attend college there.

Lawrence and Jessie still went for long walks and read books together. The Lawrences had moved from the Walker Street house in 1902 to what is now 97 Lynn Croft, the last family home they were to have. Lawrence had begun painting, chiefly copying such then popular artists as Maurice Greiffenhagen and Frank Brangwyn. At 17, he had started to write poetry, later taking up fiction. He spent about four years on his first novel, *The White Peacock*.

In the autumn of 1908, Lawrence went to teach at Croydon, south of London, at the fairly new Davidson Road School, at a salary of ninety pounds a year. He remained there for about three years, until ill health forced him to retire in the winter of 1911. He was a highly successful teacher at Croydon. Lawrence frequently went home to Eastwood. Away from his mother's influence, he became engaged to a fellow teacher.

Agnes Holt. But he was soon far more interested in a girl who was an instructor in another school in the area, Helen Corke. He virtually brought her back to life after she had been through a shattering experience: she had run off to the Isle of Wight with her violin teacher, a well–known musician, H.B. MacCartney of the Carl Rosa opera company, who was a married man. In spite of the idyllic surroundings—a moonlit summer coast—the relationship turned out to be an unhappy one. After MacCartney returned home, he killed himself. Lawrence with his permission based his second novel, *The Trespasser* (1912), upon her prose account of the Mac Cartney affair.

Meanwhile, in December 1910, Lawrence's mother died. The poems he wrote immediately after this show how intensely the event affected him. These poems remind us Hardy's "Poems of 1912" written soon after his first wife Emma died. He could not enjoy the appearance of *The White Peacock* in January 1911 because his mother had been too ill to appreciate the significance of the advance copy.

Lawrence had made his professional debut as a writer in the November 1909 issue of the *English Review*, with some poems Jessie Chambers had sent its editor, Ford Madox Ford (Hueffer). Lawrence became known in London literary circles and met H.G. Wells, Ezra Pound and others. It was Hueffer's friend, the writer Violet Hunt, who took the manuscript of *The White Peacock* to the firm of Heinemann, which published it. But *The Trespasser* went to the house of Gerald Duckworth, whose reader was Edward Garnett, the discoverer of W. H. Hudson and Charles Montague Doughty, and the friend of Joseph Conrad. Garnett encouraged the young Lawrence and was his friend and mentor for several years.

The White Peacock

The White Peacock had been a mild critical success. Lawrence in this book wrote idyllically of the Eastwood area, not describing the mines and the lives of the colliers, but placing the story in a farm and country-house setting. The young narrator, Cyril Beardsall, has a Lawrence-like sensitivity but comes from a more refined background: his mother lives in a lodge in a wooded park. His sister Lettie, the proud peacock of the title, is in love with a youthful farmer named George Saxton; but she passes him over to marry the young squire Leslie Tempest. George loves Lettie and also feels an affection for Cyril that reaches its high point in the chapter 'A Poem of Friendship', in which the physical contact of the two young men, in an episode that seems more athletic than erotic, foreshadows a somewhat similar scene in Lawrence's fifth novel *Women in Love*. Having failed with Lettie, George marries his cousin Meg Cyril, returning to the area on several visits after he has left it, watches George deteriorate into drunkenness and a general stupefaction. There is much literary chatter in *The White Peacock.* The language of the narrative is also too literary at times, though it is always lucid.

In the spring of 1912, after Lawrence had given up teaching at Croydon and had returned to the Midlands, he wondered whether he might not try for a teaching position at a German university. To enquire about this he went into Nottingham to see his former French teacher at the University College, Prof Ernest Weekley, and at his home met Mrs Weekley. She was German, the daughter of Baron Friedrich von Richthofen, a government official at Metz. The mother of three children, Frieda was restless in her marriage to a linguist fourteen years older than she was, whom she considered dull. Frieda at 32 was vivacious and life-hungry; she was having extra-marital love affairs in Nottingham. When Lawrence, a 26 year-old poet with a red moustache, appeared, she was attracted to him and he to her. She tried to draw him into the orbit of her love affairs, but Lawrence refused to play her game. He wanted to attempt a durable union.

In London, Lawrence had not managed to create such a relationship with Helen Corke. And Agnes Holt had married someone else. Lawrence's love affair with the married woman in Eastwood had dissolved. He had apparently become engaged, in a half-hearted way, to Louise Burrows, but this relationship failed to last. He had kept in touch with Jessie Chambers, who had apparently expected to marry him; but for all their mutual sympathy he found her too possessive. It was the very qualities she had in common with his mother that drove him away from her, though throughout his life he was fatally drawn into friendships with will-motored women. Jessie, who never again spoke to Lawrence after reading the proofsheets of *Sons and Lovers*, a book for which she had provided some notes and important narrative passages, was deeply hurt by the portrait of Miriam, which Lawrence had drawn with the necessarily cruel detachment of the artist.

Germany

Lawrence and Frieda left for Metz on 3 May 1912. Frieda had not broken completely with her husband; she was ostensibly going to attend the jubilee celebrating the fiftieth anniversary of her father's entrance into the army. Lawrence stayed quietly at a hotel in Metz, where Frieda secretly introduced him to her two sisters. Later, when Frieda and Lawrence, in one of their clandestine meetings, were walking about the fortifications in Metz, the German authorities arrested him as an English spy. Frieda had to ask her father to use his influence to get her lover released, so Lawrence met the shocked elder von Richthofens. He went alone to Waldbrol in the Rhineland to stay with some of his Aunt Lettice's relatives, but constantly wrote Frieda love letters. One of these was from Hennef, where he was "sitting like a sad swain beside a nice, twittering little river, waiting for the twilight to drop, and my last train to come.... Now for the first time during today, my detachment leaves me, and I know I only love you. The rest is nothing at all. And the promise of life with you is all richness. Now I know."

These sentiments were repeated in the poem 'Bei Hennef' which was included in *Love Poems* (1913), and also later in *Collected Poems*:

The little river twittering in the twilight,
The wan, wondering look of the pale sky,
This is almost bliss.

And then, exactly echoing his letter to Frieda, Lawrence ended the poem:

You are the call and I am the answer,
You are the wish and I the fulfillment,
You are the night and I the day.

What else? It is perfect enough.
It is perfectly complete,
You and I,
What more—?
Strange, bow we suffer in spite of bliss!

The lonely Lawrence flirted with one of his relatives, Frau Hannah Krenkow, a lively little Rhineland housewife. But within a fortnight Frieda had joined Lawrence at Beuerberg in Bavari. They settled at Icking, below Munich, in the peak, in a roofed house of a friend of one of Frieda's sisters, and lived on the upper floor which had a balcony that looked out on the Isar. They were happy, but Frieda at times missed her children. The ecstasy of affection and conflict between the two lovers appears in Lawrence's series of poems "Look! We Have Come Through!" (1917).

Early Work

During Lawrence's residence at Icking, *The Trespasser* came out, telling the story of Helen Corke's experience with the musician H. B. MacCartney. Lawrence's second novel is his poorest, though there are some fine descriptions of the Isle of Wight, to which the music teacher and his girl-student had gone. There is, however, a good deal of fervid imitation-Wagnerian symbolism in this part of the book and, as in *The White Peacock,* the conversation is strained and unreal.

In August, Lawrence and Frieda began walking across the Tyrolese Alps. David Garnett joined them for part of the trip. Lawrence's destination was Lago di Garda, associated with the Roman poet, Catullus; the upper part of this lake was then in Austrian possession. Lawrence and Frieda settled in Gargnano, a little town on the western shore of the lake, in Italian territory. Lawrence's descriptions of the village life appear in articles he sent to journals at the time, later collected in his *Twilight in Italy* (1916). It was at Gargnano in November 1912 that Lawrence completed *Sons and Lovers*.

Yet their relationship went on, through quarrels and dismay and poverty. Writing *Sons and Lovers* helped Lawrence, and so did Frieda, who was strong enough eventually to overcome the beyond-the-grave influence of his mother. As she once said of the situation, "I think a man is born twice: first his mother bears him, then he has to be reborn from the woman he loves." Of course, Lawrence, with his brilliant imagination and reverence for every manifestation of life, made his own contribution to their existence together. Of course they quarrelled through the rest of their lives, all through their subsequent marriage; as Frieda said in court after Lawrence's death, when there was a question about his will and estate, "We fought like hell!"

Sons and Lovers

In April 1913 Lawrence and Frieda left Italy and went back to Bavaria. *Sons and Lovers,* published in May, received several good reviews, but the sale was not large, though more encouraging than that of *Love Poems*. The novel was the first clear indication of Lawrence's stature as a writer: for those with discernment, his third novel placed him among the significant authors of the day, indeed of the entire English tradition. Unlike *The White Peacock,* this book did not idealize the author's childhood and youth, but presented a grim picture of his early life as a collier's son: the heavy drinking father, the long suffering mother and the depressing environs.

The most important conflict in the novel, however, is not between the mother and the father, but between the mother and the son, over the girl. In the story, Mrs Morel dominates her son Paul and brings about the condition summed up by the title of the chapter 'The Defeat of Miriam'. In the chapter 'Passion,' Paul tries to find release in a love affair with a married woman, Clara Dawes; but this relationship is also a failure. When Mrs Morel dies, Paul has the urge to follow her into the darkness, but resists the call of death and turns back towards the glowing, humming town, quickly. This ending, this turning towards life, is prepared for throughout the book, in the very character of Paul. Although his mother dominates and destroys his relationship with Miriam, he is a young man of great spiritual strength who will survive and certainly grow beyond Mrs Morel's influence. H.T. Moore and Warren Roberts think, "*Sons and Lovers,* coming after the somewhat latinized poetic prose of Hardy and the somewhat attenuated poetic prose of Meredith, was a poetic book of a different kind-Anglo-Saxon and strong. Its rhythms had begun to take on a distinctive Lawrencean identity, its landscapes vibrated with colour."

Now Lawrence and Frieda returned to England. Frieda twice saw her children, then staying with their father's parents in Hampstead. She waited for them in the street near their school, and on the first occasion they happily asked her when she was coming back to them. After this they were told not to speak to her, and the next time she saw them, "little white faces looked at me as if she were an evil ghost."

During this London visit, Lawrence and Frieda met John Middleton Murry and Katherine Mansfield. Mansfield was a New Zealander, not yet known for her neat and vivid short stories; she was a slim girl with dark large eyes, who wore bangs and was ahead of fashion in having bobbed hair. Murry remembered the first meeting with Lawrence and Frieda, when they all went off to lunch, straw hats, and sunshine, and gaiety. Mansfield on Frieda's behalf went out to see her children in Hampstead, bringing them messages of love from their mother. Of her relationship and Lawrence's with "the Murrys", Frieda said years later that she thought "theirs was the only spontaneous and jolly friendship that we had."

For part of the summer Lawrence and Frieda went to Kingsgate, on the Kentish coast. Edward Marsh, to whose annual *Georgian Poetry* volumes Lawrence had become a contributor, took him and Frieda to nearby Broadstairs to meet a couple who were to be their friends for a number of years: the Herbert Asquiths. 'Beb' Asquith was the son of the Liberal Prime Minister, H.H. Asquith; he had married Cynthia Charteris, who was to become Lady Cynthia. From the attitude Lawrence expressed a number of times, in his letters and his fiction, he undoubtedly fell partly in love with the glowing Cynthia Asquith. But Lawrence made barmecide love to her through his stories *The Ladybird* and *Glad Ghosts*, and when he chose the name of the heroine of his most famous book, he picked one—Constance Chatterley—suggesting Cynthia Charteris. Lawrence in his writings often played with names in this manner.

In that summer of 1913, Frieda made little progress in her efforts to obtain a divorce. Her husband was firm and bitter. Early in August she and Lawrence returned briefly to Germany. They found a little house at Fiascherino, Lerici, on the Gulf of Spezia, where they remained until the beginning of the next June. Lawrence was working on a novel he then called 'The Sisters.' He was to complete one part of this as *The Rainbow* in 1915 and another as *Women in Love* in 1916 (1920).

When Frieda's divorce came through at the end of May, she and Lawrence planned to travel north again. Once more she took the train and visited her family in Germany, while he walked over the Alps and across France. Frieda and Lawrence were in London before the end of June, and lunched with Edward Marsh and Rupert Brooke. On 13 July Lawrence and Frieda were married at the Register Office in Kensington. At this time they met several new friends who were to be important to them, including Catherine Jackson, soon to become Catherine Carswell, who after Lawrence's death became one of his first biographers (with *The Savage Pilgrimage*, 1932). They also became acquainted with a relative of Ivy Low, and the psychoanalyst Dr David Eder. And the American poet Amy Lowell bustled into London and insisted on having some of Lawrence's poetry for her anthology of *Imagists*. Murry and Katherine Mansfield were a little jealous of these new friends.

At the end of July Lawrence went walking in Westmorland with several men, including the Russian-Jewish refugee, S.S. Koteliansky, who was to be his friend over the years. At Barrow-in-Furness, in early August, they learned that the First World War had broken out. Later that month the Lawrences moved to a cottage at Chesham, Buckinghamshire, where they remained until the following January. During a period of illness there, Lawrence grew the beard he was to wear for the rest of his life.

Anti-war Feelings

Lawrence, shocked by the war, said that at this time his soul was in a tomb and "nobody existed, because I did not exist myself." The title story of his volume which came out in November 1914, *The Prussian Officer*, showed that while he was in Germany he had observed some of the brutal mechanization of the military life there, but this man married to a German wife was not deeply anti-German; he felt that Germany was adolescent. Lawrence in these years rarely uttered a pro-British sentiment about the war.

Viola Meynell, a young poet who was the daughter of the Catholic writers Wilfrid and Alice Meynell, offered the Lawrences a house in which they lived from late January until the end of July 1915. This was at Greatham, in Sussex, where Wilfrid Meynell had bought a small circle of old cottages and given them to his daughters for homes, in order to create a little family colony. One of the daughters, Madeline, was married to a brother of E.V. Lucas, the popular essayist. Lawrence looked upon Percy Lucas with a somewhat jaundiced eye, seeing him as "a loafer who lived off the bounty of his father-in-law and let himself be controlled by women." He drew a portrait of Lucas in an acid little story, *England, My England,* which became the title of a 1922 collection of tales.

While at Greatham Lawrence met several other important new friends, Lady Ottoline Morrell, member of an aristocratic family from the region in which Lawrence grew up, now married to a commoner, Philip Morrell, a Liberal Member of Parliament and others. Lady Ottoline collected authors and artists at her homes in Bloomsbury and Garsington, Oxfordshire. One of these was Bertrand Russell, whom she brought to Greatham to meet Lawrence. He and Russell agreed that the war was a monstrosity, and for a while a strong sympathy existed between the two men. But Lawrence was working out his anti- intellectual theories about the power of "blood-knowledge," and such ideas ultimately caused Russell to shrink from him. Russell says in *Portraits From Memory* (1956), "it was only gradually that we discovered that we differed from each other more than we differed from the Kaiser." At the time however, Russell thought so highly of Lawrence's opinions that he thought of killing himself after some harsh criticism from Lawrence. In early 1916 he broke off the friendship, and years after Lawrence's death wrote an essay about him with a pen dipped in vinegar.

The Rainbow

Lawrence completed *The Rainbow* at Greatham. Edward Garnett had not approved of it, and Duckworth, the publishers for whom Garnett worked, did not bring out the book. It appeared under the auspices of Methuen in September, while the Lawrences were living in the Vale of Health, at Hampstead. Two years earlier the critics had generally accepted *Sons and Lovers*, that story of a young man's love affairs in the colliery country and his inability to break away from his mother; but now they fell upon *The Rainbow*, the story of a Midlands farm family and one of its members, Ursula Brangwen, whose search for identity took her through some erotic experiences that shocked the Victorian readers. In November a police-court magistrate declared the book obscene, fined the publisher, and ordered the destruction of all existing available copies of the book. Philip Morrell courageously brought the matter up twice in Parliament, questioning the legality of the proceedings, but he was smoothly muffled by the Home Secretary, Sir John Simon who, some 20 years later, appeased rather than muffled the Nazis.

The Rainbow was, and still is, an avant-garde novel. There is good reason to suspect, as Richard Aldington and others have pointed out, that the suppression was as much on account of the war as of obscenity. The British forces were not doing well on the Western Front in 1915, and recruiting lagged; in Lawrence's book, Ursula makes fun of the uniform of her lover, Skrebensky, who fights in the Boer War.

In writing *The Rainbow,* Lawrence broke new ground. It begins traditionally enough, somewhat in the manner of *Sons and Lovers,* with overtones of Hardy, but after a time it becomes an entirely different production, particularly in its representation of states of consciousness. At the beginning, *The Rainbow* is the chronicle of a farming family the Brangwens in the Midlands; it is a story of the soil, told at times in almost Biblical rhythms. But the pace, the tone, the angle of vision, the philosophical values of the book, are all changed by the time the narrative focuses on a third generation member of the family, Ursula, one of the first "modern" women in fiction. Lawrence described Ursula's love affair with Anton Skrebensky in a candidly physical way that shocked the reviewers of 1915, and he also attempted to convey impressions of the consciousness during sexual ecstasy. At the end of the book, the girl sees the rainbow arching over the earth and envisages it as the promise of a new life: pettiness will be swept away before grandeur.

Women in Love

Lawrence had intended to go to America after the publication of *The Rainbow*, and he and Frieda had obtained passports; but the troubles over the novel delayed him. At the end of 1915, poor and embittered, they moved to the coast of Cornwall, where for nearly two years they lived in a cottage at Zennor. The stony fields and the black nights over the sea matched Lawrence's mood. He took parts left over from 'The Sisters' and shaped them into *Women in Love*, continuing the story of Ursula. He added caricatures of some of his new friends, including Lady Ottoline, who appears as the rather monstrous Hermione Roddice, slave to her will. For two of the characters,

Gerald Crich and Ursula's sister, Gudrun Brangwen, Lawrence borrowed characteristics from Murry and Katherine Mansfield.

The action of *Women in Love* takes place some years after that of *The Rainbow*. Ursula is at last to find a measure of fulfilment in Rupert Birkin, a somewhat Lawrence-like figure who is an inspector of schools. But first Birkin has to escape from the toils of Hermione and her will. This is, perhaps unconsciously, a reflection of Lawrence's will-driven mother, and of Jessie Chambers. Almost perversely, Lawrence often seemed drawn to women of this type, of which Mabel Dodge Luhan, in New Mexico, was a later example. But he caricatured the type most fully in the character of Hermione, who eventually loses Birkin to Ursula. Meanwhile, the young mine-owner Gerald Crich has taken up with Gudrun Brangwen, who like her sister has become a teacher. The two couples—there is a strange bond between Gerald and Birkin, most apparent in their incense wrestling scene—go together to the Continent; Birkin marries Ursula, but Gerald and Gudrun forego the legal ceremony.

Lawrence meanwhile seems to have realized some kind of blood-brothership with a local farmer, as described in *Kangaroo* (1923). The long section 'The Nightmare' of *Kangaroo* reports some of Lawrence's wartime experiences in Cornwall. From this, his letters, and the memoirs of some of his friends, the tormenting events of the period can be partly reconstructed. The singular-looking, red-bearded man was an object of suspicion to most of the Cornish people: he spoke out boldly against the war, he loathed the new Lloyd George government, and he had a German wife. Later the police harassed the Lawrences.

In late 1917, the American poet H.D. lent the Lawrences her room in Mecklenburgh Square while her husband, Richard Aldington, was away on the Western Front. In London they met H.D.'s American friend, Dorothy Yorke, whom Lawrence was to portray as Josephine Ford in *Aaron's Rod*. By the end of the year, the Lawrences had moved to a mountainside cottage which his sister Ada had rented for them in the Derbyshire highlands.

They stayed there until after the war, occasionally visited by Dorothy Yorke or going to see friends in Berkshire, stopping off in London on the way. Lawrence was called up several times for physical examination for military service, but was rejected because of his weak chest. In *Kangaroo* he describes about this.

During these years Lawrence published very little, and his principal writing activity was his essays on American authors, published in 1923 as *Studies in Classic American Literature*. Towards the end of the war, Lawrence thought with longing of America, but also of the South Pacific, about which Herman Melville had written. In those last unhappy years he was to spend in England, Lawrence yearned for lands of gleaming sunshine.

Soon after Frieda arrived in Italy, she and Lawrence went briefly to Rome and then to a farm in the mountains above Caserta. Since this was too cold they moved on to Capri, arriving in time for Christmas. Lawrence remembered those icy mountains, however, and used them for the ending of his novel *The Lost Girl* (1920). On Capri, the Lawrences met the popular novelist Compton Mackenzie, who treated them cordially, though Lawrence wrote of him satirically in his letters at the time and later portrayed him in an uncomplimentary way in two later short stories "The Man Who Loved Islands" and "Two Blue Birds."

In 1920, Lawrence's new American publisher, Thomas Seltzer, finally brought out *Women in Love.* A court action against the novel failed. Compton Mackenzie's English publisher, Martin Seeker, launched the book in London in 1921. Lady Ottoline Morrell, who knew years before of the portrait of herself in the book, had long been estranged from the Lawrences. The composer Philip Heseltine, who appeared as Halliday in the story, bluffed Seeker out of fifty pounds for damages. Beyond all these considerations, *Women in Love,* with its profound exploration of human relationships, its many-sided portrait of a region, and its magnificent prose, is regarded as Lawrence's best novel.

At the time of his return to the Mediterranean, then, Lawrence was reestablished as a novelist; and, under the touch of southern sunlight he began to write prodigiously, producing poems, travel books, and fiction in abundance, as well as essays such as those of his two volumes *Psychoanalysis and the Unconscious* (1921) and *Fantasia of the Unconscious* (1922). In these books he attacked Freud. Even work he had left unfinished was completed at this time, including the novel *The Lost Girl* (1920), which Lawrence had begun before the war, intending to call it 'The Insurrection of Miss Houghton.' It was this book above all that reestablished Lawrence as a publishable writer, for it won the James Tait Black Memorial Prize of Edinburgh University, the only official honour he was to be given during his lifetime; like Joyce and Proust he was ignored by the Nobel Prize committee.

The first period of Lawrence's career as an author ended when he completed *Sons and Lovers* in Italy in 1912. All his earlier work had been concerned with the Midlands except *The Trespasser*, which swung between the south London suburbs and the Isle of Wight. En route to Italy in 1912, Lawrence wrote a few sketches of Germany, but his new life really began when he and Frieda crossed the Alps. In that last draft of *Sons and Lovers* he was casting off the shackles of the past, and he began work on the books that were to become *The Rainbow* and *Women in Love*.

Similarly, at the end of 1919 and in the autumn of 1925, a return to Italy meant a new stimulus to his writing and, in each instance, the beginning of a new literary period. In 1925 he had exhausted his North American material after he left New Mexico. In the year after he came back to Italy, he began writing the novel of his last phase, *Lady Chatterley's Lover,* and those last years of his life were spent on the Mediterranean coast of France. But this was a dying Lawrence— by contrast, the man who went south in November 1919 was a man making a new beginning after the war years in England. Indeed, Lawrence's discoveries and rediscoveries of the bright South are somewhat comparable to the experience of Van Gogh.

At the beginning of March 1920, the Lawrences moved to Taormina, Sicily, where they lived for two years amid olive groves and lemon trees at an old villa called Fontana Vecchia.

Aaron's Rod

During his two years' residence at Taormina (in 1920-21), Lawrence made several trips to the European mainland, to Venice, to the Austrian Alps, and to visit Frieda's mother at Baden-Baden. A journey to one of the Mediterranean islands resulted in his brightly coloured travelogue *Sea and Sardinia* (1921). At Taormina he wrote many of the poems of *Birds, Beasts and Flowers*, including "Snake," which describes his encounter at a water-trough with "one of the lords of life." In 1921 he finished *Aaron's Rod*. Set in England and Italy, it was the first of his 'leadership' novels, revealing his interest in one of the acute problems of the modern world.

Revisiting Capri during his stay at Taormina, Lawrence met an American couple who were to remain his staunch friends for the rest of his life: Earl and Achsah Brewster, who had a young daughter Harwood. Lawrence met the Brewsters, who were painters, after someone thought that Mrs Brewster's portrait of St Francis looked like Lawrence and brought him to see it. The Brewsters, who had expected to meet a ravaged and tormented man, were delighted to find him bright and full of life and laughter. They invited him to visit them in Ceylon, where they were going, and to bring his wife, then with her mother in Germany.

Ceylon

In February 1922, the Lawrences sailed for Ceylon, where they stayed a month with the Brewsters in their bungalow in the hills above the Kandy Lake. Early Brewster went each morning to study Pali at a Buddhist monastery; Lawrence, who had earlier expressed an interest in Buddhism, refused to accompany him. The afternoons were ferociously hot, and Lawrence became ill, but in the evenings he would join the Brewsters and Frieda in singing old ballads and acting charades. Here he wrote a notable poem, "Elephant," which described the ceremonial procession for the Prince of Wales. Lawrence a few years later put the Brewsters into a satirical little story called "Things," about wandering Americans who study "Indian thought" and collect bric-a-brac all over the world.

Australia

Early in May in 1922 the Lawrences arrived in Western Australia, where they met the nurse, Mollie Skinner, whose novel about that region Lawrence was later to revise; it appeared in 1924 as *The Boy in the Bush,* by D. H. Lawrence and M. L. Skinner. In late May Lawrence and Frieda passed through Sydney and moved into a cottage on the coast at Thirroul, New South Wales, where they stayed for nearly three months. Here Lawrence wrote *Kangaroo*, the second of his 'leadership' novels. On 10 August the Lawrences at last sailed for the United States, for San Francisco, on a ship that touched at Papeete, Tahiti, as well as at Katherine Mansfield's native Wellington, New Zealand.

New Mexico and Mabel Dodge Sterne

Lawrence and Frieda were going to America in 1922 because they had been invited to Taos, New Mexico, by Mrs Mabel Dodge Sterne (Mrs Luhan), a wealthy hunter of celebrities who felt that Lawrence could express in verse and prose the wonder she felt in New Mexico.

When at last they arrived at Lamy, the railway station near Santa Fe, Mrs Sterne and Tony, her Indian husband were there to greet them. It was 10 September 1922, the eve of Lawrence's thirty-seventh birthday. The ample Frieda and the frail, red-bearded Lawrence descended from the train to meet the square little woman and her massive, braided Indian. "Frieda", Mrs Sterne recorded in one of her moments of grotesque candour, "immediately saw Tony and me sexually." Mrs Sterne meanwhile felt her womb rouse "to reach out and take Lawrence." The Indian drove them across the rocky desert to Santa Fe. It was too late to go on to Taos, so the Lawrences stayed in Santa Fe that night, in the little house of Witter Bynner, the poet, who disliked Lawrence on sight. Nearly thirty years later, with Lawrence long dead, Bynner wrote one of the less friendly memoirs of him, *Journey With Genius.*

In saying that New Mexico was the greatest experience from the outside world he had ever had, Lawrence was not referring to people; unluckily, his new life could not be spent uninterruptedly with scenery. On that first morning in New Mexico Mrs Sterne took them all over to Taos, where she put the Lawrences into an adobe house. They went to supper at Mrs Sterne's hacienda that was stuffed with the paraphernalia she had accumulated in Europe the kind which Lawrence would later make fun of in his story "Things." In the dim, sunken dining-room, candles flickered amid bronzes, but the setting, only inspired Lawrence to comment "It's like one or those nasty little temples in India!"

Soon the hostess' frontier sophistication began to wear Lawrence: "Too much Mabel Sterne and suppers and motor drives and people dropping in." Before Lawrence had time to catch his breath, Mrs Sterne hustled him away with Tony, to see Indian dances at the Apache reservation. Lawrence liked these dances.

While he and Tony were gone, Frieda eagerly unrolled the family secrets before Mrs Sterne. The two women contrived an intimacy that enraged Lawrence. But he proposed that he and Mrs Sterne work together on a book about her life. Frieda kept intruding with a vigorous broom, sweeping the floor fiercely and singing stridently. She succeeded in sweeping away the plans for collaboration. Ten years later, Mrs Sterne would tell her frenzied side of the story in *Lorenzo in Taos,* which has aptly been called "Lorenzo in Chaos."

At the beginning of December the Lawrences withdrew to a five room log cabin at Del Monte ranch in the Sangre de Cristo range above Taos. They annoyed Mrs Sterne by bringing with them two Danish painters from the Taos art colony. Mrs Sterne had pointedly snubbed these men, Knud Merrild and Kai Gotzsche, who could now, when she came up for a visit, run off chuckling to hide among the trees with Lawrence.

It was a savage winter, the mountains snow heavy and the pines and spruces ice-packed; far below, a crooked line in the valley marked the Rio Grande. Lawrence had for a pet the dog named Bibbles—little Walt-Whitmanesque bitch—about which he wrote a poem. In Lamy Lawrence and Frieda stayed, as on later occasions, at the Hotel Monte Carlo, to be called the San Remo in *The Plumed Serpent*: "rough, but it's kindly and human." The Lawrences went to see the pyramids at Teotihuacan, and visited other places in the vicinity before they finally moved on to Jalisco state. They rented a house in Chapala which was used for Kate's living quarters in *The Plumed Serpent.*

USA

In July Lawrence and Frieda went to New York by way of New Orleans and Washington, and for a month stayed in a cottage at Union Hill, Dover, New Jersey. Lawrence made several trips to New York City to see his American publisher, Thomas Seltzer. The people in Union Hill recall Lawrence, and remember that Thomas Edison was frequently in the vicinity, trying to develop a synthetic rubber from a plot of milkweed which he had under cultivation near Lawrence's cottage. Local residents believe that the two men met and exchanged ideas.

Frieda at this time wanted to return to Europe and Lawrence did not. She went alone, in August, to Baden-Baden and London. It was the first real separation, a definite split, in the Lawrences' married life. Murry, who had founded *The Adelphi* in order to give Lawrence a forum, wanted him to come to England and take over the magazine; but Lawrence held back. He went to Los Angeles and, in September, travelled down the west coast of Mexico with Kai Gotzsche, who wrote to his friend Knud Merrild that he thought Lawrence was from time to time insane. Lawrence meanwhile was rewriting, and considerably changing, Mollie Skinner's Australian novel, *The House of Ellis*, into *The Boy in the Bush*. After staying a month at Guadalajara, Jalisco, Lawrence in mid-November went to Mexico City and a few days later sailed from Vera Cruz for England. Frieda had cabled him imperatively to join her, and he had written from Guadalajara, "I'll come back and say how do you do! to it all. I am glad if you have a good time with your flat and your children'-and he had added coldly, 'When I come we'll make a regular arrangement for you to have an income if you wish."

Lawrence hated the place when he saw it again. Murry recalled that he looked at London "with a greenish pallor"; he might justifiably have been green-eyed if he had known that Frieda had proposed to Murry that they become lovers. Out of loyalty to Lawrence, Murry refused, in what he later wrote of as the 'great renunciation' of his life. Nearly seven years later, in Vence, the little town in France where Lawrence had died shortly before, Murry and Frieda at last became lovers, and he noted, "With her, and for the first time in my life, I knew what fulfilment in love really meant. "But in 1923 he could only tell Frieda, 'No, my darling, I mustn't let Lorenzo down—I can't."

Lawrence revisited his native Midlands and found the sooty industrialism depressing. He and Frieda had made peace and went to Baden-Baden together for two weeks in February 1924. The next month they returned to the United States, bringing with them the lone recruit Lawrence had been able to enlist for the ideal colony he wanted to found in the New Mexican mountains, the utopia he called Rananim from one of his friend Koteliansky's Hebrew songs. In London Lawrence had tried to persuade Murry and others to join him in creating a pantisocracy in the Rockies, but in an alcoholic 'Last Supper' scene at the Cafe Royal, all but one had refused. The single colonist was a painter, the Honourable Dorothy Brett, daughter of Viscount Esher and a friend of Lady Ottoline Morrell. Dorothy Brett was later (1933) to write one of the genuinely good memoirs of Lawrence: *Lawrence and Brett, A Friendship*.

Kiowa

In March 1924 Brett and the Lawrences arrived at Taos, and in early May moved up into the Sangre de Cristo mountains to a small ranch Mabel Dodge (now Mrs Luhan) had given to Frieda, the ranch that was eventually called Kiowa. Lawrence had not enjoyed his stay in Taos. Mrs Luhan resented Dorothy Brett; who had an ear trumpet called Toby, which Mrs Luhan felt was a 'spy'. And two young house guests-a would be writer named Clarence Thompson and a man who was later to be a distinguished student of Indian anthropology, Jaime de Angulo—became embroiled in the Lawrences' affairs. Lawrence and Frieda were glad to be up on the mountain; Brett took a house nearby. But no Rananim developed.

In October, accompanied by Dorothy Brett, the Lawrences went to Mexico City. In November they settled in a little house in Oaxaca, with their friend staying at a hotel. But she went back to Taos the following January, after Frieda announced thunderously that she didn't want anymore of 'the Brett' and her curate-and-spinster relationship with Lawrence.

In February 1925 Lawrence finished *The Plumed Serpent*. After this he fell into a terrible illness, which a doctor in Mexico City said was tuberculosis. Lawrence for the remaining five years of his life never referred to his disease except as trouble with his 'broncs'. In early April he was back at Kiowa ranch, recuperating in the mountain sunlight. In September he left America for the last time, and at the end of the month he and Frieda arrived in England. After visiting London and crossing to Baden-Baden, they settled for the winter on the Italian Riviera, at Spotorno, near Genoa. There they rented the Villa Bernarda from an Italian army officer, a dark, vivacious little man, Angelo Ravagli, who twenty years after Lawrence's death was to marry Frieda. While at the Villa Bernarda, Frieda was visited by her two now grown daughters, Barbara and Elsa. Lawrence at one point went by himself to Capri for a while.

Early in May 1926, the Lawrences moved to the house that was to be the most famous of all they had lived in, the Villa Mirenda, outside Florence, which they rented for two years. There was one more visit to England, which Lawrence still disliked, and he and Frieda returned from time to time to Baden-Baden and visited other parts of the continent. Frieda complained to friends at this time that her intermittently ill husband was now impotent.

Villa Mirendra (Italy)

At the Villa Mirenda Lawrence wrote his last novel *Lady Chatterley's Lover,* which he arranged to have privately printed and circulated. The book was suppressed in England and the United States and later the courts in those countries declared that it was not obscene and permitted it to be published unexpurgated. While he was working on the novel, Lawrence knew that he would be reviled for having written so candidly of love, but he had a message for the modern world, which he felt had become over intellectualized and, through industrialism, inhumanly mechanized. He felt that modern men and women had broken 'the true pact between the body and soul. *Lady Chatterley's Lover* was a serious attempt to bring them back into a balanced relationship.

This, then, despite its reputation as a notable example of erotica, is essentially a philosophical book. Indeed, it is one of Lawrence's four major novels. The two most important—and this is a widely accepted critical estimate—are *The Rainbow* and *Women in Love*, with *Sons and Lovers* and *Lady Chatterley's Lover* at a somewhat lower level of excellence. These novels are novels of ideas. In them, Lawrence reached the peak of his imaginative writing; they represent the most harmonious balance between what he was trying to say and the way in which he said it.

The three 'leadership' novels—*Aaron's Rod, Kangaroo*, and *The Plumed Serpent*—are less effective in achieving such a balance. They are, however, magnificently written, and present luminous pictures of Italy, Australia, and Mexico. But *Aaron's Rod* is hardly a story; it is a succession of pictures of the modern world, ranging from England to Italy, with Aaron finally being magnetized by Lilly. In *Kangaroo*, the Lawrence-like man Richard Somers lives for a time on the Australian coast with his German-born wife Harriet, and meets the Sydney lawyer Ben Cooley, who has a physical resemblance to a kangaroo, from which he takes his nickname—a rather totemic figure. Somers, disgusted with Europe is for a while drawn to Kangaroo's secret political organization, the "Diggers." But Somers rejects both the fascists and socialists, and decides to stand by his own sacred individuality. Lawrence, antagonistic to democracy, never seems to have realised that only a democracy makes such an attitude possible. In *The Plumed Serpent* Lawrence went back on the principles of individualism expressed in *Kangaroo* and let his central character become part of a mystic movement, with political overtones, in Mexico.

This central character was not, this time, a Lawrence-like man but rather a Frieda like woman, Kate Leslie, who out of weariness with Europe goes to Mexico City. There she meets a somewhat Lawrence-like figure Cipriano (emblematic name), General Viedma. He introduces Kate to his friend and associate, the mystic demagogue Don Ramon Carrasco, who is attempting to revive the religion of the ancient god Quetzalcoatl. The revolution of Ramon and Cipriano is successful, but hardly convinces the reader, since it omits all politico-economic considerations and exists almost entirely in terms of primitive, hypnotic religion.

H. T. Moore and Warren Roberts observes, "Lawrence's prose, often slapdash but always glowing with life, takes the reader physically into Mexico. And, as Kate sits there, silently appears an old man with one egg held up mysteriously, like some symbol and this is exactly right, on the surface a venerable merchant holding up part of his wares for display, yet underneath he is like a mystic messenger from beyond, from what Lawrence elsewhere called 'the fatal Greater Day of the Indians,' as contrasted with 'the fussy, busy, lesser day of the white people.' Lawrence conveyed these ideas better in short stories, however, than in *The Plumed Serpent.* There is, for example, the unfinished fragment "The Flying Fish," from which the few words quoted above are taken, and the purely symbolic story 'The Woman Who Rode Away.' He was also more effective in expressing his ideas in travel sketches interspersed with reflection, such as those in *Mornings in Mexico.*"

Lady Chatterley's Lover

But in *Lady Chatterley's Lover* Lawrence was once again able, as in *The Rainbow* and *Women in Love* to convey ideas in terms of a novel. He wrote three drafts of this book before turning it over to Orioli for the Florentine printing of 1928. The book is so well known that it hardly needs a summary, only an indication of what Lawrence was trying to accomplish in it. An important point to note is that, even before Sir Clifford Chatterley was, sexually incapacitated by a wound received in the First World War, he had not taken "the sex thing" very seriously in his month of marriage to Constance preceding his departure for the Western Front. Yet Connie, whose father calls her "a bonny Scotch trout", is a normal young woman who wants fulfilment. After Clifford comes home-perhaps a bit too symbolically mechanized by his wheelchair Connie has a love affair with the clever playwright Michaelis; but he is too intellectualized for Connie, and at the same time his sex is dog-like; he is one of those men whom Connie thinks of as trotting, sniffing, and copulating. Mellors, on the contrary, is a man who has learned the sacredness of love. But he is also aware of the shame that many modern people feel about performing the act of love-the act which Mellors, in his efforts to burn such shame out of Connie, bluntly gives a four letter name which throbbed on the page when the first readers of *Lady Chatterley* saw it there in 1928; it was then a secret expression, belonging to the gutter. Now that the battles of the 1950s and 60s have been won, that word and many others formerly forbidden appear frequently in novels. They are usually employed in a manner Lawrence would have considered obscene, as readers of his essays on pornography will discover.

Such words had appeared earlier in serious modern literature, in James Joyce's *Ulysses*, which first came out in in 1922 and at once became an item for tourists from English-speaking countries to take out of Paris and smuggle into their homelands. But after an American legal decision of 1933, *Ulysses* could be published lawfully and was no longer a contraband trophy. *Ulysses* was declared to be not obscene because it reflected life. But the intention of *Lady Chatterley* is beyond argument. Lawrence disliked Flaubert and Tolstoy, in their different ways, almost as much as he disliked Joyce, and often said so. Tolstoy's *Anna Karenina* had betrayed the marriage agreement, and so had Flaubert's *Emma Bovary:* both these authors sent their heroines to death by suicide. Lawrence on the contrary led Connie Chatterley towards life. In the spring of 1927, while still working on the book, Lawrence made a tour with Earl Brewster of the Etruscan tombs and ruined cities along the western (Maremma) coast of central Italy. Lawrence wrote a series of essays *Etruscan Places,* 1932 in which he expressed his admiration for a 'blood-knowledge' culture which the brutal and machine-like Romans had destroyed.

Aldous Huxley and his wife Maria were occasional visitors at Villa Mirenda, and the Lawrences liked them, even if Lawrence cared little for Huxley's clever novels. Huxley was in Lawrence's view over-intellectualized (as Lawrence himself of course was, and this is one reason he fought against the condition in others); but Huxley paid him serious, open-minded attention when they argued about science, which to Lawrence had become one of the great menaces of the world.

Switzerland

In January 1928, while at Les Diablerets, Switzerland, Lawrence received a visit of homage from an articulate member of the young generation, Rolf Gardiner, whose ambition (later realized) was to revive ancient English customs and ceremonials. Another visitor, whom the Lawrences later stayed with in Bavaria, was the German physician and playwright, Max Mohr.

In June 1928, the Lawrences left Villa Mirenda forever, and went to Switzerland with the Brewsters, spending the last part of the summer in a chalet at Gsteig bei Gstaad, not yet a famous resort. Lawrence was intermittently very ill, but the attempt to arrange for subscribers to receive their smuggled copies of *Lady Chatterley* in different parts of the world gave him surges of energy. Yet he was also capable at this time of detachment; just before going to Gsteig he wrote, at Chexbres-sur-Vevey, his charming little essay on *Insouciance*, later collected in *Assorted Articles* (1930). In it he expressed a wish that a little English woman at his hotel would not care so much about everything. And Lawrence's last notable work of fiction emphasizes such a withdrawal. This book was *The Escaped Cock* (1929; also known as *The Man Who Died)*. The story takes place in a colony of the Roman world, and concerns a prophet who has been crucified and who, after his resurrection, gives up his prophesying, to find fulfilment in love with a virgin priestess of Isis.

Lawrence painted at Gsteig: when Maria Huxley had brought some canvases to the Villa Mirenda he had taken up that activity again, this time not copying, as in his youth, but painting landscapes and portraits, often mingling religion with eroticism.

By mid November, Lawrence and Frieda had settled for the winter at a hotel in Bandol, on the French coast; by mid March they were at Paris. There they met the exciting Harry and Caresse Crosby, new American friends whose Black Sun Press first published *The Escaped Cock* and other work by Lawrence. In April he and Frieda went to Spain, where they stayed until mid June.

Lawrence's Paintings

Lawrence then travelled to visit Orioli in Florence, while Frieda went to see the exhibition of her husband's pictures at the Warren Gallery in London. The richly coloured paintings attracted the scorn of some of the critics and the attention of Scotland Yard. Policemen removed thirteen of the pictures. A police magistrate threatened to have them burned, but let Frieda's solicitor take them upon assurance that they would not be exhibited again in England. The book of coloured reproductions, *The Paintings of D.H. Lawrence*, was suppressed, but a new and different version of it appeared in 1964, published openly in Britain and America.

Lawrence's pictures took second place to his writing, yet when he learned that the Condon magistrate might order them to be burned, he wrote to tell Dorothy Warren that he did not under any circumstances, or for any cause want his paintings destroyed. He was willing to do his bit to help the cause of English liberty, but "to admit that my pictures should be burned, in order to change an English law, would be to admit that sacrifice of life to circumstance which I most strongly disbelieve in." He would not be a martyr.

H.T. Moore and Warren Roberts comment, "Perhaps his best painting is one of those now in Texas: *Boccacio Story*. This canvas has a living quality, with Lawrence's rich colouring; and it presents a dramatic human picture (the gardener, sexually exposed, lying asleep, and the startled nuns discovering him): the positions of the gardener's legs and arms form balanced angles, the nuns appear in juxtaposition to two white dogs on the opposite side of the picture, and the furrows of earth running in somewhat different directions in the centre and background of the painting give it a rhythmic quality. This is heightened by the rows of delicately coloured, plumy trees in the background. There is an almost equally fine effect in 'Red Willow Trees' in the Karavas collection: three naked men in the foreground bathe in a stream that winds among hills and vermilion willow trees, with a slope full of umbrella pines beyond. Again the composition has balance and wonderful colour. Many of the paintings, however, are fairly crude— Lawrence was particularly bad at drawing arms— but most of them strike the attention forcibly, and the colouring is often as rich as in Lawrence's poetry and prose."

Late Work

Lawrence, infuriated by the seizure of the pictures and the bowdlerization of his book of poems, *Pansies* (1929), became desperately ill in Florence. In July Frieda brought him to Baden-Baden for a rest, and in September they returned to Bandol, where they rented the Villa Beau Soleil. En route they had stopped in Bavaria, where Lawrence wrote one of his greatest poems, "Bavarian Gentians":

> let me guide myself with the blue, forked torch of this flower down the darker and darker stairs, where blue is darkened on blueness.

Lawrence knew that he was near death, which he had held off for so long, to the astonishment of doctors. He allowed one to examine him in Bavaria because the man was also a poet— Hans Carossa— who was amazed that Lawrence could go on living.

Meanwhile, in England, Lawrence's pamphlet 'Pornography and Obscenity' was having a brisk sale. It was soon to be followed by a little book of his finest essays, *A Propos of Lady Chatterley's Lover* (1930). Lawrence on his sunlit coast wrote another remarkable poem, "The Ship of Death:"

> build your ship of death. Oh build it!
> for you will need it
> For the voyage of oblivion awaits you.

And he wrote one more prose piece long enough to be made into a book: *Apocalypse* (1931), his last religious utterance. The essay grew out of his interest in the Book of Revelation, stimulated by the English artist and mystic Frederick Carter.

By 6 February Lawrence was for the first time ill enough to move to a sanatorium. His London friend, the painter Mark Gettler, recommended the specialist, Dr Andrew Morland, who in turn recommended the sanatorium the Ad Astra at Vence, in the hills above Nice. Frieda lived at a nearby hotel. Lawrence's visitors included the Aga Khan, H. G. Wells and the Huxleys; the American sculptor Jo Davidson made a bust of him. Now he was burning away in his illness.

On 1 March Lawrence left the sanatorium for the Villa Robermond, now the Villa Aurella, in Vence. A doctor came to give him a morphine injection. Frieda remembered it was painful. On the night of 2 March 1930, at ten o'clock, Lawrence died. He was buried in the local cemetery until, in 1935, when Angelo Ravagli went to Vence and had his remains cremated. He brought the ashes to America, where they rest in a tomb at Kiowa ranch. Frieda is now buried in front of the tomb, which looks down the mountainside to the Rio Grande; it has become a place to which literary pilgrimages are made.

Lawrence, a controversial figure for most of his life, became the cause of even greater contention soon he died. Many of the obituary notices were downright vicious. A particularly nasty one appeared in *The New Yorker*, written by Genet (Janet Flanner), who reported that Lawrence "had a fancy for removing his clothes and climbing mulberry trees" only one of the many *canards* about Lawrence. T.S. Eliot, Clive Bell and J.C. Squire were among others who wrote denigratingly of Lawrence. Lawrence was, however, staunchly defended in the press by such old friends as Catherine Carswell. Lady Ottoline Morrell, who had forgiven Lawrence for portraying her as Hermione spoke up for him in a public letter signed by her initials. Murry was anonymous in his defence of Lawrence. E.M. Forster, under his own name, wrote of him with generosity and appreciation.

2

D.H. Lawrence's Major Novels

Lawrence is a great English novelist. His major novels are *Sons and Lovers* (1913), *The Rainbow* (1915), *Women in Love* (1920), and *Lady Chatterley's Lover* (1928). A critical analysis of the same is as follows.

Sons and Lovers (1913)

The first of D.H. Lawrence's major novels *Sons and Lovers* is based on Lawrence's own early life in the Midlands' coal-mining village of Eastwood (Nottinghamshire), on his relationships with his mother and with his father who was a mineworker, and on those who were his early women friends Jessie Chambers (Miriam), Louie Burrows and Frieda Weekly (Clara Dawes).

The composition of his autobiographical novel therefore coincided with a period of multiple crises in his life. Frank Kermode writes, "Lawrence's *Sons and Lovers* is probably still the best known of the novels and it would be wrong to cavil at this, for it is certainly a great achievement." Keith Sagar in his work The Art of D.H. Lawrence thinks that *Sons and Lovers* is known for its immediacy and realism. This novel is better than his earlier work *The White Peacock*. Sagar seems to admire Lawrence for the improvement in form as well.

The plot of the novel is almost autobiographical. Eastwood is called Bestwood in the novel; the character who corresponds to Lawrence himself is Paul Morel. Morel will have a relationship with his mother as Lawrence had it. Then Miriam is Jessie Chamber's Lawrence's lover and Clara, reflects Lawrence's wife Frieda with whom he eloped.

Mr. Paul is also Lawrence's father. The story is this: The storyline of the novel is this: Walter Morel, his wife Gertrude and their children live in "The Bottoms," the housing complex for coal miners built by the firm of Carston, Waite and Co. on the site of "Hell Row." It is down the hill from the village of Bestwood.

There is what we can call a lot of misery and squalor. Mrs. Morel, aged 31, married eight years with two children now and one on the way, feels that she is an outsider in this community. She has come down from the village of Bestwood. It is three weeks since they moved in and she does not know any of the other women there.

Her son William, aged seven, has gone to the fair while her daughter Annie aged five, remains at home, complaining that she should go too.

At half-past twelve William rushes in asking for a quick dinner so that he can catch the merry-go-round at half-past one. But in middle of his meal of batter-pudding and jam, William hears the music from the fair, and rushes out. His mother reminds him to take his pudding and two-pence.

William shows his mother all the sights of the fair.

She feels that her home is fixed and stable but that her life is dreary and hopeless and will be until the children grow up.

Mrs. Morel comes of a proud, Dissenting middle-class family with memories of ancestors who fought against Charles I. She inherits the uncompromising tradition of English Dissent, and though her family has been impoverished, she has an inherent aristocratic temperament derived from her family tradition of high standards. The father Walter Morel, a miner, is a contrast to his wife, both on his background (he is the grandson of a French refugee and an English barmaid) and in his easygoing, pleasure-loving, spontaneous temperament. The massage is an unhappy one: Mrs. Morel's strictness and truthfulness are outraged by her husband's slackness and deceitfulness. In the war between them, the children take the side of the mother.

Later in the evening her husband returns very pleased with himself and somewhat drunk. He has a gingerbread for her and a coconut for the children. Mrs. Morel comes from a solid burger family. Her father, George Coppard, was an engineer with a proud spirit, and her mother was a woman of small build who was gentle and kind. Mrs. Morel remembers how she was favoured by many men at her father's dockyard, and she remembers being assistant to an old mistress at a private school. But most of all she remembers John Field, whose Bible she still keeps.

When she was 23 she met Morel, who was then 27, a warm and humorous man. The two were opposites in nearly every respect. She was stern, aloof and high-minded, while he was full of a "sensuous flame of life." Yet he represented a world she did not know, and this charmed her. He was enchanted with her beauty and refinement.

The wedding took place next Christmas, and gradually the relationship deteriorated. Morel signed a pledge to drink and they moved into what she thought was his own house. But as she wearied of love-talk, she was upset to realize that he was incapable of understanding her and that he was not satisfied to be in her company alone. She was relieved when he returned to doing small jobs around the house. Then in the seventh month of marriage she found bills in the pocket of his wedding coat. She was stunned to discover not only that they had not been settled, but also that he had not enough money in his account to cover them.

The next day Gertrude went indignantly to her mother-in-law's, and the elder woman revealed how she remorselessly cheated her own son and how she owned the house that the Morels lived in, charging them a rent that was much high. Gertrude's opinion about her husband crystallized at that point.

In October Mrs. Morel's nearest neighbor told her that her husband had been a dancing master in the Miners' Arms club room for over five years, with some notoriety attached to him. Another neighbor implied that Morel drank, and then was surprised to find that Mrs. Morel did not know it.

After their first child William was born, Morel was good to his wife, but soon he became jealous of Gertrude's attentions to their young son.

Mr. Morel did not work properly in the office. Often he disrespected his seniors. So he got poor pays. He was to give 30 shillings a week to his wife for family expenditure. But he gave her less, squandering his money on drinks.

When the novel opens Morel is working badly, and Gertrude, who is trying to save some money for her confinement, resents his carousing. On Tuesday, Morel is in fine spirits. He whistles and works happily, then spruces himself up to go out with his friend Jerry Purdy. Gertrude hates Purdy, not only because of his control over her husband, but also because of the hatred he engendered in his own wife before her untimely death of consumption.

Jerry arrives to announce that they are walking the ten miles to Nottingham. The men go from tavern to tavern along the way so that Morel must take an hour's nap before entering the city. There they dine with Jerry's sister and go to the Punch Bowl for pigeon racing and skittles, which gain Morel half a crown in winnings. They catch the train for home at seven-thirty.

Mrs. Morel looks after the children. Both William and Annie are playing. She puts them to bed at 7 o'clock. Morel returns home. He is drunk. Mrs. Morel picks up a quarrel with him to have drunk. He bolts her in a room.

The setting for the novel is full of contrasts. "The bottoms" is not only in a valley, but it contains the bottom level of the human in the lives of the coal miners and their families in contrast in the middle-class life up the hill at Bestwood, where Gertrude is from. Because of the coal the landscape at The Bottoms is full of pits and railroad lines, yet all around is farmland and lush country vegetation. What impresses Gertrude most is the degrading life within the mining community.

The Bottom aptly recalls us the Bottom of the poor blacks in Toni Morrison's novel *Sula*.

In the pattern of symbols in this chapter, the "nasty alley of ash pits" is dominant, standing for the nastiness of real life in the coal miners' dwellings. The name Morel, very close to the word moral, is also common name of mushroom, implying the lowliness of the family that earns its living in the black underground.

Morel's morning routine begins at five o'clock or earlier. He does not awaken his wife to cook for him, but makes his own breakfast. Gertrude feels relieved during this time, for it is a period of peace for her.

Then he leaves for his work.

Shortly Mrs. Morel is pregnant with her third child and she delivers it. Mrs. Bower and Mrs. Kirk, the friendly neighbors help her.

Morel arrives in a bad mood. Mrs. Bower tells him the news of his son (Paul's birth), and he grunts in reply. She pours him a drink and serves him his dinner.

Mr. Heaton, the young Congregational minister, visits Mrs Morel every day. He has lost his first baby and his wife and now depends on his friendship with Gertrude. The new boy is his godson. He occasionally stays to tea, holding the baby while Mrs. Morel makes preparations.

One evening after the parson's visit, Mrs. Morel takes Annie and the baby out because she wants to avoid a fight with Morel, who had kicked William. She goes to the cricket ground to sit under the alders.

When the red sun cuts the horizon's rim, she lifts the child to the vision and he lifts his little fist. She names him at that moment: Paul. Mrs. Morel goes home to find the house empty; but her husband is home by ten o'clock. The day ends peacefully.

The following Wednesday he is broken and deeply in debt. He steals a sixpence from his wife's purse. She discovers that the sixpence is missing when she goes to greengrocer. After searching for it, she knows Morel has taken it and, since this has happened twice before, she decides to confront him with his theft. He denies taking the money and then makes a show of leaving home with his belongings wrapped in a large, blue-checked handkerchief.

The strongest scene in the second chapter 'The Birth of Paul, and Another Battle,' is the angry confrontation during which Mrs. Morel is badly hurt by her drunken husband.

Morel gradually gets better, but he wants his wife's attentions to continue even though he is not suffering. A long peace ensues, but it arises from her new freedom from him, not from a new love for him. In reality Mrs. Morel is casting him off and turning to the children.

Mrs. Morel gets another child called Arthur. The new son likes his father. Mrs. Morel is happy.

William and Paul are in stark contrast to each other. William is strong and big, while Paul is delicate, quiet and prone to follow after his mother. Paul's sensitivity causes his father to rage. In real life, Lawrence did not love his father adequately and he regretted for this.

Mrs. Morel is a gutsy lady. She is social. She joins the so called Women's Guild where women could raise their voice against man's whisky and cigar politics.

Gertrude gets William a position with the Co-op, much to the annoyance of Morel, who wants him to go down into the mines. William goes to night school for shorthand and becomes a good bookkeeper. Then he teaches in the night school. He also is a prize-winning runner.

When he is 19 years old, William leaves the Co-op for a much higher job in Nottingham. Mrs. Morel hopes William can help the other children along.

Then he gets a job in London at a high salary. He writes his mother about it, but his going away hurts her.

Where the first chapters deal with short intervals of time and flashbacks, the third chapter 'The Casting off of Morel – the Taking on of William,' takes on a long interval that includes of conception and birth of Arthur and the teenage progress of William's studies, jobs and awards. Through hard work Mrs. Morel has seen to it that her children have education, and

William provides her with an income that increases astonishingly with time.

The family moves from the Bottoms to a house on the brow of the hill, looking out over the valley. An old ash tree is in front of the house, and the west wind, blowing through it, makes it shriek.

Paul watches the evening sights until the last colliers straggle home. Then he goes to the kitchen to console his mother about his father's absence.

Morel is only happy when he works with his hands around the house. He can even interact with his family then and he sighs happily. Paul and Annie like to help him make fuses, with which he will blast down the coal in the pit. He delights Arthur with tales of Taffy.

Paul is taken with bronchitis and stays home from school on his mother's orders. We should know that Lawrence was affected by tuberculosis later.

The children enjoy hunting for mushrooms or picking blackberries since the family's poverty requires their resourcefulness.

William and Paul are rivals for their mother's love, and when William goes to Nottingham, Paul becomes his mother's companion.

In the winter evenings the children play together after dark. They inevitably end up fighting. After one such fight Paul sees a giant red moon, which reminds him of a passage in the Bible, and he makes haste to be friends again with the enemy, Billy Pillins.

The three children go to the train station to meet William while Mr. and Mrs. Morel nervously wait at home. The train comes late. He has presents, purchased at a special stop at Sethley Bridge. William finally gets home to greet his parents and shares the gifts with them. The family enjoys the season, and everyone feels sad at William's departure.

The fifth chapter is called 'Paul Launches into Life.' A year after William goes to London, during the time after Paul has finished school but not yet gone to work, Morel suffers a compound fracture of the leg and is hospitalized. The pit-lad announces the catastrophe to Mrs. Morel, who laments her husband's clumsiness. Mrs Morel prepares herself and packs the necessary things for her husband's hospital stay, all the time afraid that this time he has really ruined them.

The next day while Annie and Arthur are at school Mrs. Morel tells Paul her inmost thoughts while he paints. We should know that Lawrence was a painter too.

Paul has no other ambition than to work for a reasonable wage and, when his father should die, to live a happy and peaceful life with his mother.

One day Paul joins a clerk Thomas Jordan's Surgical Appliances in Nottingham. Mrs. Morel is pleased of this.

The next morning Paul finds out how much the train ticket will be, and his mother expresses her disappointment as William could not send home money to help just now. In fact, she is somewhat bitter than William is making a lot of money and, in spite of his promises, sends nothing home anymore. She is rankled that William spends so much money on his girlfriend.

By now William is seeing a lot of "Gipsy" whose real name is Louisa Lily Denys Western.

Paul works with Mrs. Pappleworth. He picks up mail from Melling. Then he works with many girls like Fanny and others. Finally he catches the 8:20 train for home. His mother is happy.

Paul settles in his routine. For companionship Paul prefers the girls to the men who seem narrow and boring. Poly says she will cook his lunch, and soon Paul eats with the girls in a circle around him, listening to his every word. He feels he belongs to Polly. He draws Connie at her spinning wheel. He jokes with Louie and prompts the condescending Emma to show him how she works. This kind of scenes dipped in sex are common in the novel. Kate Millett, the famous feminist in his article related to Lawrence's *Sons and Lovers* writes this: "Paul is indeed enviable in his rocklike self-sufficiency, basking in the reverence of the bevy of women who surround him, all eager to serve and stroke — all disposable when their time comes. Meredith's *Egoist* is a comic exposure; Lawrence's is a heroic romance. When Paul first ventures forth into the larger male world, it is again the women who prepare the way for his victories. In a few days he is a favourite of all the 'girls' at Jordan's Surgical Appliances. 'The girls all liked to hear him talk.' They often gathered in a little circle while he sat on a bench and held forth to them, laughing" (p. 153). We are told that "they all liked him and he adored them" Only of the ironies of this chapter is in its title, 'Paul Launches into Life.' For in one sense Mrs. Morel is launching into life for the second time, the first being through William Paul. But is life equivalent to work? Paul does not essentially change by going to work for Jordan's, and he returns each night to his home. Symbolically he adds a workspace to a life he carries on much the same always. Both he and his mother have the best of both worlds, of work and of each other. Paul begins a new role with respect to his mother since William has gravitated away from her to his new girl; as he himself realizes, he is now the man in his mother's life.

Arthur grows up to be a vital, graceful boy who is entirely self-centred. He is irritable to his mother, whom he loves, and an enemy of his father, whom he had loved earlier but now has grown to hate. Morel himself degenerates, and seems to take delight in disgusting his family. Aurthur becomes so irritable that when he wins a scholarship to the Grammar School in Nottingham, his mother decides to let him live in town during the week and come home only on weekends. Annie is still a junior teacher, but will soon earn enough to pay her own way. Now Mrs. Morel draws close in spirit to Paul.

William has become engaged to the Gyp girl Western. He brings her home. This time he does not bring any presents to the family. His sweetheart is much shoddy and she displeases everyone. She sits like a princess among peasants. When Mrs. Morel advises William not to marry her, he says he is helpless. She tells him of her own bad marriage.

Paul has done well at Jordan's, but his health has suffered. So one Monday in May Mrs. Morel suggests that they visit the Leivers' new farm. The son and mother continue on to Willey Farm in the resplendent landscape. A heron floats overhead.

Paul stops to pick flowers for his mother, who is very happy. Keith Sagar writes, "Flower themes are woven into the whole novel so skillfully that only cumulatively does one recognize their symbolism." Finally they come on the farm house where a 14-year-old girl disappears in the doorway and Mrs. Leivers welcomes them in her home. While the women talk, Paul goes out to survey the land. There Miriam, the young girl, speaks with him, shyly and somewhat distantly.

The mother and son will have tea with the Leivers. Paul plays with Miriam sometime.

The next Tuesday morning a telegram from London announces that William is ill. Morel rushes to London and finds William unattended and almost unconscious on his bed. The doctor diagnoses a peculiar kind of pneumonia. In spite of her prayers and efforts, Mrs. Morel cannot revive her son and at two o'clock in the morning, he dies.

On Saturday night Paul sees his father and mother on their return from London. Mrs. Morel is in a state of shock and barely recognizes Paul. Paul and his father arrange the chairs to support the coffin, which arrives at ten o'clock carried by six bearers. Mrs. Morel is lost in grief.

William is buried on Monday in the little cemetery on the hillside. Mrs. Morel now wishes she were the one to die. She will not communicate with Paul, who tries to break through her grief. On December 23 Paul brings home his five shillings and falls very ill. Mrs. Morel turns from her grief to tend him, afraid that he will die. In his delirium she calls out to him, ending her silence, and he rallies. His aunt later claims that Paul's illness saved his mother. Paul is in bed for seven weeks, and Mrs. Morel roots her affection in him.

Part I ends with the death of William. This is psychologically the only event that could free Mrs. Morel so that she might turn her attention to Paul. Ironically the bridge between Part I and Part II is the meeting of Paul and Miriam.

Part II begins with the chapter 'Clara.' If the part first is dominated by Miriam, Part II is dominated by Clara. However, Mrs Morel predominates the whole novel.

Paul is now friends with the two youngest boys at Willey Farm. Edgar, the oldest, holds himself aloof and Miriam stays away to protect her romantic image of herself. She sees herself as a princess turned into a swine girl. She is deeply religious, and wants to make up for her humble surroundings by learning everything she can. Although she thinks men are brutal and sensitive, she feels that Paul is different. When he is very ill, she thinks then she can love him because she is for a moment stronger than he.

She and Paul develop love out of "their common feeling for something in Nature."

But it is Miriam who lingers longest over his sketches, captivated by the life he injects into the natural world. Once when she tries to extort a profession of love from her five-year-old brother Hubert, Paul hates her for her extreme emotion. Paul, used to his mother's cool reserve, is shocked by the naked emotions of this girl.

When Paul returns to Jordan's, his hours are better. On Wednesday afternoons he goes to art school, which is provided by Miss Jordan. One evening in the summer Paul and Miriam walk home from the library.

Mrs. Morel is angry when Paul arrives home. She does not like Miriam and feels as if she is the sort of girl who will suck the very life out of her son. Paul is caught between the pleasant memory of Miriam and his mother's obvious wrath. He protests that he and Miriam only like to talk, but she fears Miriam's depth and Paul's susceptibility.

What we notice gradually is Mrs Morel's possession of Paul. This is much autobiographical. Lawrence once wrote to Edward Garnett that: "It follows this idea: a woman of character and refinement goes into the lower class, and has no satisfaction in her own life. She has had a passion for her husband, so the children are born of passion, and have heaps of vitality. But as her sons grow up, she selects them as lovers—first the eldest, then the second. These sons are urged into life by their reciprocal love of their mother—urged on and on."

Later Paul and Miriam make picnic to Hemlock Stone, and Wingfield Manor, where they love each other. The unnatural intensity, the clenched will of Miriam, relates her unmistakably to Hermione Roddice of *Women in Love*, even in its physical manifestation, a heaviness, almost a clumsiness in her movement.

When Paul is 20 years old his family can afford their first vacation away from home, and they take a cottage at Mablethorpe. At supper the evening before they are to leave, Paul reads a poem about the place by Jen Ingelow to Miriam with the whole family listening, the women jealously trying to be foremost in Paul's esteem.

From the start of the book Lawarence emphasizes the religious nature of Mrs. Morel, but her rational morality is quite different from the deep and emotional faith of Miriam. Miriam's religion goes beyond the church into nature, with which she has a rich communion that is in some ways related to her growing love for Paul.

Miriam's lusty nature and sense of possessiveness recalls us Thomas Hardy's character Arabella Donn in his novel *Jude the Obscure.* It may be noted that Lawrence followed Hardy in many ways. Hardy's character Arabella possesses Jude and forces him for marriage and wastes his life.

Lawrence's use of symbols here extends the range of earlier symbols. The moon, once a symbol of Mrs. Morel's alienation from her husband and union with nature, becomes a symbol of the pain of young love for Paul and Miriam. The umbrella, symbol of William's love for his mother, is damaged by Geoffrey and pronounced broken by Paul, who knows its significance for his mother. The idyllic setting of Willey Farm is now seen as a breeding place where Miriam's inhibition about her own sexuality stem in part from her shunning the more graphic aspects of farm sexuality.

Arthur is now working in the electrical plant at Minton Pit. One night he does not come home, and Paul and his mother discuss his lack of common sense. The next morning a letter arrives from Derby—in it Arthur explains that he has gone with Jack Bredon and enlisted in the army.

In the autumn exhibition of students' work in the Castles, Paul has two works that win first-prize awards. Mrs. Morel is as proud of his artistic achievements as she was of William's sporting trophies.

One day Paul unexpectedly meets Miriam in town. With her is Clara Dawes, who has become separated from her husband, Baxter Dawes, who hates Paul. In fact, Daws is Paul's senior in the office. Only Mr. Pappleworth's mediation keeps the two from fighting. Dawes, Paul thinks, has taken Louie Travers, a sister-in-law, as his mistress. The next Saturday evening Paul and Miriam discuss Clara. Paul sees in Clara an admirable fierceness, and his admiration of her makes Miriam brood.

Paul takes Pappleworth's place as spiral overseer and looks forward to a substantial raise at year-end. Friday is the night that Miriam comes to Paul for her French lesson. They love to be together in spite of their discords.

As in many other chapters, the title of this one 'Strife in Love,' has many implications. It refers not only to the strife in the love between Paul and his mother. There are also echoes of the continuing strife between Baxter and Clara Dawes. Finally there is the strife caused by Arthur's unfortunate decision at the outset.

The Sunday after Easter Paul goes to Willey Farm for tea. Paul shows Mrs. Leivers and Miriam some thrush's eggs, carefully finishing them out of the nest and replacing them. After tea Paul and Miriam sit again in the hay. Paul tries to read, then shoos away Bill the dog. He says that he has no right to come to Miriam as he does unless they intend to marry.

Paul and his mother go to Lincoln, and Paul notices that his mother is growing old. Over tea Paul tells his mother about Clara. Mrs. Morel is not hostile to the idea of Clara, even though she is seven years older than Paul. We need to know that Lawrence loved and married Frieda, a Professor's wife and Frieda was seven years senior to Lawrence. In *Sons and Lovers* Clara does not marry Paul though she remains his mistress for some years. A similar situation occurs with Sue Bridhead in Hardy's aforesaid novel *Jude the Obscure*. There Sue, Jude's cousin could not marry him. She marries a teacher. Then Jude by force marries Arabela. But then Jude and Sue understand each other and live together. They get three children.

In Lawrence's novel Clara is Mrs Morel's double. Both like each other. Mrs Morel likes Clara because she is not too possessive of her son as Miriam.

A week later Annie marries Leonard of Birmingham, Arthur marries Beatrice. Mrs. Morel, however, cannot bring back Arthur from the army.

One evening Paul and Miriam work together in the hay and walk together in moonlight. The next day Clara monopolizes Paul as she joins the boys in a game of jumping over hay. Miriam is tortured by their attraction to each other, and she sees that Paul will choose the lower side of himself over the higher. Paul chafes against Miriam's continued hold over his ideal self, and when she is 21 he writes that she is a holy nun and he has given her what a mystic monk would give to a mystic nun. This cuts Miriam to the soul. Yet in spite of his need to find elsewhere what Miriam could not give him, Paul knows that Miriam possesses him utterly. Miriam is also convinced of this.

As the title of the chapter 'Defeat of Miriam,' implies, Miriam seems to be defeated repeatedly in this chapter, by Mrs. Morel and then by Clara Dawes. Yet throughout this stage of her relationship with Paul she becomes increasingly convinced that in some very fundamental sense Paul belongs to her totally.

Now 23 years old Paul wins a first prize and sells a picture for 20 guineas. His mother is very proud of him, and he wants to share the money with her. Morel is also proud of his son. He says that William would have done well too if he had not died.

Paul is invited to dine at Mr. Jordan's.

Now Paul is finished trying to find God outside himself and depends on finding God inside himself. He looks to life and discusses class and personal worth with his mother. She wants him to move up in class and to marry a lady. Yet Paul remains bound to Miriam and unconsciously drawn to Clara. His mother urges him to consider happiness, but Paul wants fullness of life. Mrs. Morel fears that in this way he will slowly kill himself, and she blames Miriam.

Morel is held responsible for his own collapse. Keith Sagar says, "He had denied the God in him." It is true that the father is later, in *The Lost Girl,* for example, to receive his apotheosis. But it does not follow that Mrs Morel must be in the tradition of destructive women. Her role in *Sons and Lovers* is nearer to that of Lydia Lensky (it is no coincidence that Lydia was Mrs Lawrence's name) in The Rainbow. There is a destructive element in her relations with both husband and sons; but the overriding impression is of a normality and strength of character which serves as a standard against which the other women in the novel are judged and found wanting."

Through Clara, Paul becomes acquainted with the advanced social thinkers of Nottingham. He visits Clara's home in Bluebell hill and meets Mrs. Radford, Clara's mother. Clara and Mrs. Radford are making lace in the kitchen. Mrs. Radford seems glad to have a man around.

At dinner time he walks with her. One day he discovers that she married at 22, was married for five years and left her husband three years ago. Clara woodenly says that in a way she has been asleep, that her husband never could get through to her, and that she left him because he was unfaithful to her. Over tea she takes off her wedding ring and spins it like a golden globe on the table. Paul sees their relationship as friendship only. He fee that if he should ever marry, it would be to Miriam. He even tells Clara this. Miriam knows the attraction Clara has, but she is convinced that the higher side of Paul will triumph over baser.

At Willey Farm Paul tells Miriam that as a young man of 24 he should be ready to marry. He tells her that they both know that they cannot face physical intimacy with each other, though they are intimate spiritually. Finally they kiss, and although she protests Paul should posses her, she shies from him. When he leaves her he sees her as a kind of disembodied spirit. She fights against herself to bring her mind accept him as her physical lover, but cannot.

Paul wants impersonal love, but Miriam wants only intensely personal intimacy. She does not accept what he wants from her, and he cannot tolerate what she forces upon him.

Paul becomes successful as an artist and is ambitious for himself and his mother. He criticizes her gently for not managing Minnie the servant girl well. They take a vacation to the Isle of Wight, and Mrs. Morel finds it difficult to keep up his peace. Paul is often reminded of her age and her tendency to become ill. Paul's affections now fix upon Clara. He is intimate enough with her to touch her. Then that Saturday evening after work they walk in the park, where he kisses her on the face. Finally they walk beside the swollen Trent and Clara asks why Paul has left Miriam. He says that he does not want to get married. The consummation with Clara is wonderfully done. The significance of the experience is conveyed largely in the symbolism of the Trent in flood.

At Clifton village, they have tea. They look so happy and vital that the landlady is gladdened by them, and she gives them three dahlias as a present when they leave.

Miriam is surprised to hear that Clara is coming to tea to meet Mrs. Morel. She asks to come too, and Paul assents. On Sunday Paul meets Clara at Keston. She is beautifully dressed and wears a hat with silk roses. He picks hips for her lapel along the roadside. They pass the coal pits, and Paul rhapsodizes about coal mining. Entering the house, Clara meets and shows her pictures of the family, then returns to the kitchen. Clara and Mrs. Morel strike up a conversation about Nottingham.

Paul is shaped by four major factors in this chapter 'Passion.' His mother is growing old and ill. Miriam has been rejected temporarily while he seeks another kind of love experience than she is capable of giving him. Clara is taken on as the person who can give him experience of passion, which Paul now sees as essential to his development as a person. Paul is also becoming convinced that he can make a living with his art.

Women's rights at the time of the novel were just beginning to boil up into acts of violence and demonstrations. Clara is in the suffrage movement, and she tries out many of the movement's ideas. She dresses daringly and faces criticism at home and a blemished reputation outside for her brazenness. She attends meetings and lectures.

One evening after the theater Paul meets Baxter Dawes in the Puch Bow. Dawes is down and out, having been estranged from his mistress as well as his wife. Paul feels intimately close to Dawes because of Clara. Because he is his superior at Jordan's, Paul offers Dawes a drink. Dawes refuses and then berates Paul's observations on war by alluding to the theater, and to Clara's being with Paul there. Dawes jeers that Paul took a whore to the theater, and Paul throws half a glass of beer in his face. The doorman escorts Dawes out of the tavern. Then the barmaid and a friend of Paul's warn Paul that Dawes will be out for him. Mr. Jenkinson goes with Paul when he leaves.

One morning several days later Paul collides with Dawes on the stairs at Jordan's. Although Paul tries to hide in his work, Dawes overhears Paul speaking to Clara on the voice tube. He threatens Paul, and Thomas Jordan threatens to fire him. Then Dawes shoves the little Mr. Jordan down the steps to Franny's room and departs. Afterwards Mr. Jordan dismisses him and summons him for assault. At the trial Paul confesses that the whole thing began when he took Dawes' wife to the theater, and the case is dismissed, much to Mr. Jordan's dismay. Clara is angry that her name has been used in court, but she gets over it.

Mrs. Morel hears the whole story and warns Paul that the end of it may be dangerous. Paul tells her that his love for Clara, like her love for him, is not very deep, and he wonders why he cannot be held by love. He says he would not like to marry Clara. In fact, he cannot give himself in marriage to any woman while his mother is alive.

In spring they go to a cottage near Theddlethorpe and live as man and wife. Nottingham knows about their affair, but accepts it because they are discrete. At the seashore, the two rediscover each other. One morning Clara and he go for a swim on the Lincolnshire coast, and as she runs towards the water Paul wonders how a thing so small compared to nature's grand scheme can absorb him as she does.

The scene recalls us Hardy's Sue Bridehead who finally refuses to stay with Jude. The loss of his children turns Jude against religion; Sue, however, sees the tragedy as a sign from heaven that she must repent and conform to tradition. Jude proposes marriage but she declares that she is still Phillotson's wife and she goes back to him. Lawrence himself has written on Hardy's novel. Lawrence found Sue 'the production of the long selection by man of the woman in whom the female is subordinated and who therefore only seems to exist to be betrayed by their men. Paul now asks whether Clara will ever marry him, and she replies that she cannot divorce Baxter Dawes. It is not that she feels she belongs to him, but that she feels he belongs to her.

Clara is fulfilled both by being married to Dawes and by having Paul's passion. She gains assurance through Paul, and knows they must finally separate. She knows that even if she marries Paul, he will drift off.

Not to speak of, one night Dawes confronts Paul and beats him severely. Paul is shocked of this. Now he avoids both Clara and Miriam. Unfortunately his mother is ill at the time.

Morel comes for a visit on Saturday and awkwardly greets his ailing wife. Mrs. Morel stays in Sheffield for two months, then wants to go home. She is driven home through the August sunshine. She seems lively and alert. At home neighbours and friends have turned out to see her. Arthur carries her indoors, and she expresses her joy to be home. She sees her sunflowers in the backyard garden and is delighted.

The name of Baxter Dawes in the title of this chapter is significant, for through his appearance Paul and Clara realize they cannot marry. Because Dawes separates the two and for all. Paul becomes free again. That way he can attend to his mother in her illness with no other attachments as meaningful as the one to her.

Dr. Ansell tells Paul that Dawes is in the fever hospital, and Paul offers to see him. Dawes has been sulking, but he does not refuse to see Paul. Murderous hatred has formed a bond between the men.

Now Mrs. Morel's health worsens and she dies. The family buries her beside William's coffin. Paul mourns uncontrollably.

Paul is now like a man without a foundation and he looks for someone to understand him.

The 'Release' of the title of the fourteenth chapter is fraught with meaning. The great release, surely, is the death of Mrs. Morel. Paul is also released from Clara, and thus Baxter Dawes is released from his lonely exile from humanity. With release comes freedom, but also a sense of drifting. Paul is no longer bound, so he has no idea of where to look for solidity. The contrast between Paul and Dawes is revealed through the visits Paul makes to the ill man. Paul paves the way for the reunion between Clara and Bexter.

The graveside symbol that tells most about the Morel family is the corner of William's coffin that is visible in the open grave ready for Mrs. Morel. The two are buried side by side, leveled by death. William was his mother's first love, and she meets him again before Paul. The reminder also serves to point out the fact that both are killed by those they love the most.

Now Clara disappears with Dawes to Sheffield and Morel returns to his daily round. The family home breaks up, Paul going to live in Nottingham. Paul's last satisfactory painting is done on the day of his mother's death. He walks as if in an unreal world, except in the thick blackness of night.

Paul meets Miriam after dinner before the fire Miriam seems old to him, stiff and wooden. Paul says he has broken with Clara. Then Miriam suggests that they be married. She says she might prevent him from wasting away. Paul protests that she wants to possess him to extinction, and to her rising bitterness, he says he will go abroad. He decides then not to follow her into the infinite darkness, but sets himself resolutely toward the city lights.

In the final illumination, the images of vegetation (wheat), flesh (speck of flesh), fire (tiny spark), and the stars (sun and stars) come together and draw the interwoven strands of many symbols to a single point. Throughout the book these images have been used in many ways, as in a tapestry against the black background of night, and here they provide the stuff of the life affirming moment. Stripped of all props and supports, Paul chooses for life.

Lawrence's *Sons and Lovers* is a psychological novel. The book was early regarded as a vivid presentation of the working of the Oedipus complex. However, Lawrence was not acquainted with Sigmund Freud's theories when he started work on the novel in 1910, but had come into contact with them before completing it in 1912.

The novel is about early Lawrence. Jessie Chambers whom he depicts unfairly in the role of Miriam wrote her *D.H. Lawrence: A Personal Record* in 1935.

The Rainbow (1913)

Lawrence wrote *The Rainbow* in 1913. First he called it *The Sister,* and then *The Wedding Ring.* Then he found it too bulky and divided it into sequels *The Rainbow* and *Women in Love.* Methuen published the novel, and faced the court enquiry under the Obscene Publications Act of 1857. The London magistrate Sir John Dickinson ordered the destruction of all the 1014 copies of the novel. Lawrence's efforts to protest against this failed.

Lawrence's novel received a harsh criticism. Lawrence's novel received a mixed response and harsh criticism. Lawrence wrote to literary agent Pinker: "I should like to know what Henry James and Bennet say of the book. I know Henry James would hate it. But I should like to know.... I think it would be a really good thing to get the public protest from the authors—Bennet, etc. John Drinkwater came in just now—he is anxious to do something. Very many people are in a rage over the occurance. Will you organize a public protest, do you think?—it would be best." Robert Lynd in *Daily News* wrote, "Lawrence's reputation must suffer from the publication of such a book as this." James Douglas attacked Lawrence saying that a book should be more beautiful than reality. John Galsworthy added: "Frankly—I think *The Rainbow* is aethetically detestable. Its perfervid futuristic style revolts me. Its reiterations bore me to death."

There were also good reviews about it, though they were rare then. An unsigned reviewer in *Standard* wrote this that *The Rainbow*, a book dealing with the history of three generations of a Nottinghamshire family, is by far the most difficult task Lawrence has yet attempted. Catherine Carswell's review was fair enough. She wrote, "This is a book so very rich both in emotional beauty and in the distilled essence of profoundly passionate and individual thinking about human life, that one longs to lavish on it one's whole-hearted praise." However, modern criticism for the novel is quite fair. Marvin Mudrick writes, "True enough there is, beside it, no family-chronicle novel in English that deserves mention; and anything that will certify the respectability of *The Rainbow* is to be prized." Lawrence's letters to Garnett speak of his art and religion. He writes, "My great religion is a belief in the blood, the flesh, as being wiser than the intellect. We can go wrong in our minds. But what our blood feels and believes and says, is always true."

The novel is set in Lawrence's own background, the English Midlands. The subject is three generations of the Brangwen family extending from the middle of the ninenteenth century to the early years of the twentieth century.

The Rainbow opens with a general survey of the Brangwen family. Of farming stock, they have lived for generations at Marsh Farm, near the village of Cossethay on the border between Derbyshire and Nottinghamshire, beside the slow-running Erewash river. Two miles away, the church-tower of neighbouring Ilkeston dominates the landscape. Whilst not wealthy, the Brangwens have enough to make them independent. They cultivate the rich farmlands and the menfolk are identified with their lot, they live fully in the activities which wrest their livelihood from the earth.

The Brangwen women, however, tend to look outwards to society, and to emulate their social superiors. Less satisfied than their men, they aspire to something above and beyond them and in yearning towards these aspirations, they become more satisfied. Tom, the protagonist of the first generation has this about his mother. Lawrence writes:

"She stood to see the far-off world of cities and governments and the active scope of man, the magic land to her, where secrets were made known and desires fulfilled. She faced outwards to where men moved dominant and creative, having turned their back on the pulsing heat of creation, and with this behind them, were set out to discover what was beyond to enlarge their own scope and range and freedom....She strained her eyes to see what man had done in fighting outwards to knowledge, she strained to hear how he uttered himself in his conquest, her deepest desire hung on the battle that she heard, far off, being waged on the edge of the unknown. She also wanted to know, and to be of the fighting host" (pp. 2-3).

Keith Sagar observes, "This is the question that dominates the structure of the novel. Each generation takes up the struggle afresh. Each has a different starting-point and fifferent conscious objective."

During the 1840s the Indsutrial Revolution begins to impinge upon the life of Brangwens, Collieries spring up around them and a canal is constructed across their fields; the railway runs along the valley bringing the possibility of easier communication between industrial and rural life. The Brangwen of this period has six children and it is with the life of Tom, the youngest, that the story is concerned. His mother's favourite, he is sent to the local Grammar School, but learning is a burden to him; when Tom is seventeen his father dies after an accident and the youth is left to run the farm. Six years later his mother dies and when his sister Effie gets married he is alone at Marsh Farm.

When a Polish woman, Lydia Lensky, widow of a doctor, come to Cossethay as housekeeper to the vicar, Tom realizes that she, with her foreign ways and remoteness from the everyday life of the village, has a strong attraction for him. She is older than Tom and has a four-year-old daughter Anna. It should be known that Lawrence himself married a Frieda, seven years older than him, and Frieda was a German. When Lawrence married her, Frieda had three children whom she left behind to her ex-husband. Tom decides that he must marry her. On a cold March evening, dressed in his best clothes and with a bunch of daffodils, he goes up to the vicarage to propose. After a brief hesitation, Lydia accepts and their agreement to marry is followed by an ecstatic and wordless embrace before Tom leaves for Marsh Farm again.

The daughter of an aristocratic Polish landowner, Lydia had married a young doctor, Paul Lensky, an active patriot and revolutionary. They had two children, both of whom died from diphtheria before their parents were forced to flee to London as refugees. There, Lensky worked tirelessly for his cause, but soon after his third child, Anna, was born, he died, leaving Lydia unprovided for in a foreign land. She went to Yorkshire as nurse to an aged rector; on his death she went to Cossethay and her fortune became linked with that of Tom Brangwen.

Like Tom Lydia too feels a strange attraction between them, yet when she has accepted him and is ready to offer herself wholly to him, he is bound by inhibitions which stifle her soul. The wedding takes place and Lydia is a difficult one, for it is only rarely that they are fully attuned to each other.

Later Lydia becomes pregnant and Tom gets attached to Anna. Anna grows stronger year by year. She goes everywhere with him, round the farm, driving in the little horse-carriage to the town and finally every week to the market. Tom wants to make her into a lady.

Tom's elder brother Alfred illicitly connected with a genteel widow living in the village of Wirksworth and Tom, out of curiosity, go to visit her one day. Tom is profoundly impressed by the gentility and superiority of the woman and by the cultured air of her drawing-room with its many books and its piano. Once again he yearns for something beyond the limitations of his own life and at home Lydia recognizes his dissatisfaction. When she reproaches him with it he is at first astonished, but this episode ends in a tender reconciliation in which new and deep understanding of each other comes to the couple.

This is the first realization of the rainbow symbol. But it is presented as the creation of an environment in which the two get satisfied. Lawrence writes:

"It was the entry into another circle of existence, it was the baptism to another life, it was the complete confirmation. Their feet trod strange ground of knowledge; their footsteps were lit-up in discovery. Wherever they walked, it was well, the world re-echoed round them in discovery. They went gladly and forgetful. Everything was lost and everything was found. The new world was discovered, it remained only to be explored. They had passed through the doorway into the further space, where movement was so big, that it contained bonds and constraints and labours, and still was complete liberty. She was the doorway to him, he to her.... They did not think of each other—why should they? Only when she touched him, he knew her instantly, that she was with him, near him, that she was the gateway and the way out, that he was beyond, and that he was traveling in her through the beyond. Whither?—What does it matter?" (p. 91).

Now Lawrence begins to speak of the second generation Branwens. Lawrence is concerned with several generations of the Brangwen family and here, through the replacement in Anna's affections of Tom by Will, he is showing the inevitable cycle of history in which the older generation is unwillingly compelled to give way to the younger. By the end of this chapter 'Wedding at the Marsh' the main focus of interest has shifted from Tom and Lydia to Anna and Will.

At the age of nine Anna is sent to school, first to the village school in Cossethay and later to a school for young ladies in Nottingham. At neither school does she make any real friends and she comes to the conclusion that education is pointless. The first person outside her own family group to make any real impression on her is an old Polish friend of her mother, Baron Skrebensky, now vicar of a country parish in Yorkshire. She admires most of his aristocratic bearing and freedom of spirit because they chime with her desire to be a lady.

Then when she is 18, her cousin Will Brangwen, son of Tom's brother Alfred, comes to work as junior draughtsman in a lace factory in Ilkeston. When he is invited to Marsh Farm, Ana is excited at his arrival. Gradually the two fall in love with each other, though at first neither knows how to express it.

Will's hobby is wood-carving and he makes Anna a present of a butter-stamper. Soon after, he begins a carving depicting the Creation of Eve for a church panel, inspired to carve the Eve by his love for Anna. A strange night-harvesting episode, in which Will and Anna set up the sheaves in shocks, results in their deciding to get married.

Tom facilitates Anna's marriage with his cousin Will.

The wedding day arrives at last and all the Brangwen family gathers for the celebration. Anna, beautiful and elegant, is escorted to the church by her father and, after the marriage service is over, the whole party goes first to Will and Anna's little cottage to drink to the newly married couple; then they go to Marsh Farm where the wedding meal has been prepared. Then there is carols and an old Christmas play. Finally the evening draws to a close.

Here Tom's old uncertainties and longing are seen again as Anna's marriage recalls to him his own with Lydia. By the end of the chapter five 'Wedding at the Marsh' however, the centre of interest has shifted completely. It is with Anna and Will that the power of youth, life and emotion now lies.

During the honeymoon period Will and Anna are at first engrossed in each other, staying in bed half the day and taking little notice of the outside world. Their bed is a hub for the wheeled universe. At the still centre they lie "complete and beyond the touch of time or change." Lawrence writes:

> "They found themselves there, and they lay still, in each other's arms: for their moment they were at the heart of eternity, whilest time roared far off, for ever far off, towards the rim. Then gradually they were passed away from the supreme centre, down the noise and the friction. But their hearts had burned and were tempered by the inner reality, they were unalterably glad" (p. 141).

This period of ecstasy makes Will feel disturbed at the defiance of natural order, but he comes to accept it. Then Anna moves into the world again by giving a tea-party; this angers Will and a feeling of tension arises between the two.

Anna has no faith in the established religion, but Will has it. He is, moreover, attached to the church. So both quarrel over their faith and church matters. Anna is suspicious and jealous of her husband's religious spirit, and since he himself cannot relate it to a way of life, she succeeds in destroying it. In doing so, she unintentionally transforms him from an original artist into a mere craftsman in the William Morris style. Still they are united in a passionate nighttime sensuality but have no daylight union.

Then Anna becomes pregnant. She informs Will about it, just making him quite happy. There is a strange scene in which Anna tries to assert herself by dancing naked in her bedroom at a late stage in her pregnancy; this infuriates Will. With the birth of the baby, Ursula, both Anna and Will relax into a brief period of peace.

The next chapter 'The Cathedral' begins with a flashback to a time before the birth of Ursula when Anna and Will go on a visit to Baron Skrebensky and his second wife. The older couple are both magnetic and elusive. Will finds, as his father-in-law found before him, that the Baroness teases and tempts him, openly flaunting her sexuality, but at the same time repulsing him, making clear her superiority. Anna is intrigued by the Baron who, though old and wizened, has a fiery quality inside him which attracts her. During this visit the Baron's infant son is introduced to the reader; later he is to figure largely in the life of Ursula.

From Baron Skrebensky's house Anna and Will make a visit to Lincoln Cathedral. The cathedral moves each of them in a different way. Will is moved by a deep spiritual reverence for the beauty, mystery and rich life of the building; Anna, on the other hand, is willing to be attracted only by the human quality of the stone carvings and reads her own drama into the little stone faces. With calculated meanness she takes away Will's joy in the perfection and wholeness of the cathedral itself.

What we notice is Will is a mystic, while Anna is earthly. She is a Lawrentian woman.

One day Anna delivers Ursula, facilitating a strong bond between Will and Ann. As Ursula grows, a strong bond develops between her and her father. When a second child, Gudrun is born, Will devotes himself to the older girl and she goes everywhere with him. He makes baby-furniture for her and wooden dolls, helps to bath her and often takes her into the church whilst he practises the organ.

The year passes and two more girls are born to Anna. Now Will, like his father before him, begins to get restless. He goes out on his own, not caring for his family responsibilities. One Saturday night he goes to the Empire Theatre in Nottingham to see a variety show. There he flirts with two girls. Anna senses this, and both mingle into each other. A fifth child, a boy, is born, and gradually Will grows into a responsible member of the community. He organizes a woodwork class for the village boys and takes his place in the village life.

The close bond between Will and Ursula recalls that between Tom and Anna during Anna's childhood. There is a darkness in Will's character, however, that was never evident in that of Tom. Little Ursula is at the opposite pole bringing light to set against his darkness.

Meanwhile Tom and Lydia continue to live at Marsh Farm with their sons, Tom and Fred. Tom, the son is short, dark, attractive, full of energy and intelligence. He is sent to London to study engineering and there he does well in his studies and prospers. Fred is fair and blue-eyed. He looks after the farm now onwards.

One spring morning when Ursula is about eight years old. Tom drives to the Saturday market in Nottingham, telling his wife and son that he might be home later that night. By evening rains is falling heavily and Fred is restless and depressed; nevertheless, he and his mother and Tilly the serving-woman all finally go to bed and the farm is left in darkness.

Tom Brangwen, having spent the evening drinking at the Angel Inn in Nottingham, sets off for her home in torrential rain; he is just sober enough to find his way to Cossethay and the farm, but there he finds several inches of water already cover the ground and the stable and outhouse are awash. Puzzled by the increasing volume of water he sets off to find where it is all coming from but, half-drunk, he stumbles and falls and, unable to rise, he is carried away by the flood of water.

The first cycle of the Brangwens's history ends with Tom's death, but continuity is preserved through Ursula's visits to her grandmother and her dim understanding of her Polish heritage.

Ursual, now growing up, finds herself increasingly in charge of the younger children and the representative of the Brangwen family. It is irksome to her that she is unable to have any privacy and that she is never considered as an individual.

Anna settles for the ring of physical considerations having had fleeting glimpses of the rainbow in the hazy distance. Lawrence writes:

"She was straining her eyes to something beyond. And from her Pisgah mount, which she had attained, what could she see? A faint, gleaming horizon, a long way off, and a rainbow like an archway, a shadow-door with faintly coloured coping above it. Must she be moving thither? Dawn and sunset were the feet of the rainbow that spanned the day, and she saw the hope, the promise" (p. 192).

This indicates the active end of the second generation Brangwens.

When she is 12, Ursula is sent to Nottingham Grammar School and for a while escapes the burden of home. When at home, she enjoys the times of peace, although the Christian church and the Bible revolt her. As she grows into adolescence, Ursula is less and less willing to accept the mystic spirituality of the biblical stories. With the realisation of her selfhood she feels that her religion must be able to help her live her life. So she rejects the idealism of Christianity and turns again to a life of the imagination, becoming in her dreams rich, great, or heroic by turns.

At this time, with her soul open for some new influence, Anton Skrebensky, son of her grandmother's old friend, the Baron, comes into her life. His parents are now dead and he has joined the army; he comes with Ursula's uncle Tom to stay at Marsh Farm. The two young people are attracted to each other and he becomes a constant visitor to the cottage. He takes to the neighbouring Derby and they visit the fair together; that evening they kiss for the first time. Then his leave ends and he returns to his army unit. They exchange a few post-cards and she makes a cake for his birthday. When her uncle Fred decides to marry a local schoolteacher great celebrations are planned and Skrebensky is invited to the wedding.

Ursula falls in love with Anton. They spend their time together. He returns once more to his regiment; soon after, the war is declared against the Boers. Anton is sent to South Africa but come to the Marsh for a day before he leaves. Yet the two seem to have lost contact and they part without warmth at the station.

As the first generation had taken the rhythm of its life from the seasons, the natural cycles of birth, death and fruition, pagan, with only the first glimmer of spiritual aspiration, so the second generation lives within the rhythms of the Church year, and Ursula's young life gladly responds to this cycle, each week turning about the precious Sunday, and each year on Christmas and Easter.

The focus of the story has now shifted completely to Ursula, yet there are constant reminders of the cycle of family history repeating itself; she and Anton walk under the ash-trees on Cossethay hill "where her grandfather had walked with his daffodils to make his proposal, and where her mother had gone with her young husband." Ursula shares her father's mystic beliefs and inherits her mother's doubts; though the book reflects change, it also maintains continuity, particularly in the symbol of the rainbow which, once of significance to Anna, is now a vital part of Ursula's thought.

Ursula is now almost at the end of her school career and she works at her studies unwillingly but firmly because she believes that through her academic work she may achieve a measure of independence. It is here she is forced by her colleague Winifred Inger for lesbian affair. This revolts her.

Later Ursula's uncle Tom falls in love with Winifred Inger and the two marry, freeing Ursula from the clutches of Inger.

Her schooldays now over, Ursula lives at home and helps with the household chores, but the disorder of the domestic life and the unruliness of the younger children anger and distress her. She begins to hate her mother's way of life. Meanwhile, Will Brangwen turns again to his wood-carving, then to painting and to the making of jewellery, always seeking a satisfaction that he is unable to find in his own work.

Ursula joins a school as teacher in Ilkeston. The school is chaotic: its headmaster bullying, and students very nasty. She yet controls them at the expense of her own belief in freedom and love because she has to subjugate the children in order to live with them. Here she befriends Maggie Schoolfield, a teacher.

This is a very bitter chapter in which Lawrence expresses all his own grievances about teaching and about education. He appears to have little faith in the possibility of liberalising education, which in those days was conducted in a rigid and cruel disciplinarian fashion.

Then Will finds a post as Art and Handwork Instructor for the county of Nottingham. The Brangwens move from Cossethey to Beldover. Now Ursula joins a college. Gudrun attends the art school in Nottingham. Ursula performs well at the college, and passes her intermediate arts exam. A little later she finds the study of Latin, French, Anglo-Saxon, quite boring. She suddenly hears of Anton's arrival. He is on leave before going to India and proposes to come to Nottingham. She is delighted to meet him again and immediately feels a strong physical bond with him. Her studies become insignificant to her, and she lives in and through her sensual passion for Skrebensky. In the Easter vacation they go away together, pretending they are married, first to London and then to Paris. On their way back to England they visit Rouen and there the seeds of their separation are sown. Ursula returns to college, and left alone in London. Skrebensky writes to her pressing her to marry him; after a while she acquiesces almost without realizing it. They become engaged and the wedding is arranged. Yet they have little in common except their physical lust for each other; her ideas make him angry and afraid, and she feels shut in by him and wants freedom.

When the time for her examination arrives she goes to London to take them; after her practical examination they go out to a dinner at hotel on the river near Richmond. There he tries to fix the time for their wedding, but she tells him that she does not wish to marry him. To her dismay, he bursts into tears and she has to comfort him; this results in the breach being patched up, but Ursula knows that he has nothing to offer her except physical passion.

Keith Sagar observes, "Ursula is the first 'free soul' in the English novel. The structure of the novel must change to accommodate her desperate search for bearings." Like Ellie in Shaw's Heartbreak House, Ursula is looking for "life with a blessing," which is what the rainbow specifically symbolizes in the novel.

She fails her degree, but this does not incline her more towards marriage, because the thought of Skrebensky and India begins to offend her soul. They are both invited to a large house party in Lincolnshire and there she tests him by trying to gain complete satisfaction from their intimacy. The result is that he is left completely drained and they feel dead towards each other. Soon after, she leaves, not intending to see him again. For a while he is frantic, suffering anguish and dread; then he decides that he must marry to save himself from the horror of the separation. He proposes to his colonel's daughter, is accepted, the marriage is quickly arranged and he goes out with his new wife to India.

Here the hollowness of Skrebensky is fully evident; not only is he unable to satisfy Ursula but also he is afraid of the emptiness of his own life; he makes a hasty and loveless marriage in order to save face and to fill the gap left by Ursula.

After she leaves Skrebensky, Ursula returns home, drained and empty. Her family is angry when she tells them that she has broken her engagement. Then she realizes that she is pregnant with Skrebensky's child; part of her responds joyfully to the knowledge. She writes to Skrebensky begging his forgiveness, telling him of her pregnancy and offering to go to India.

As the days drag on Ursula receives no answer to her letter. A revulsion begins to set in and she is overcome by profound apathy. On an October afternoon of torrential rain she slips out of the house to walk in the county. Suddenly some horses surround her. They gather on a log bridge which she has to pass over and as she moves towards it they move onwards and wait her again. Suddenly they gallop, making a wide circle round her; with them behind her the way seems to be clear; she goes on, making for a gate in the field, when again the horses gallop towards her, this time veering slightly to pass her on the path. They gather again and Ursula, by now terrified, plans to climb a tree and drop down on the other side of the hedge; this she does as the horse gallops towards her again.

Eventually she arrives home, wet through and utterly distraught. She goes to bed and develops a delirious illness which is some sort of nervous breakdown. During her illness she loses the child, but she had already decided not to unite her life with that of Skebensky. When she receives a cable from him which tells her of his marriage it merely makes her despise him.

Convalescent, her mind strives to find a purpose in life, to seek "the creation of the living God." The mining community around her seems to be dead and life completely corrupt. Then she looks out of the window one day and sees a rainbow beginning to form. She seizes for herself God's promise and at last hopes to returns to her faith in the future.

This last chapter is heavy with symbolic meaning. Ursula has to go through the crisis of suffering and physical destruction before she can emerge into new life. Only when she has overcome the physical strength and sexuality represented by the horses is she able to find spiritual hope.

Ursula's end, and her waiting in hope reminds us Paul's similar condition at the end of *Sons and Lovers*.

Keith Sagar thinks *The Rainbow* is Lawrence's Isaiah, a reaffirmation of Noah's covenant from generation to generation. When Lawrence chose to call his novel *The Rainbow* he was endowing it with a rich train of associations, for the rainbow is an evocative image, exciting wonder, a sense of mystery and an apprehension of beauty. Legend has lent to it a mythical and magical significance with stories of the Land at the End of the Rainbow and tales of bags of gold buried where the rainbow touches the earth. Above all, however, it is the sign of God's promise to Man that life will continue, that "seedtime and harvest...shall not cease." It is a symbol of hope that there will be a future, however destructive the past may have been.

The Rainbow is generally considered one of Lawrence's major achievements, but it is by no means a perfect novel. It is, in fact, a curiously uneven novel, beautiful, evocative, poetic prose being interspersed with purple passages and often with tiresomely repetitive words and phrases.

The nineteenth century vision had certainly perished in the hands of Galsworthy, Bennett and Wells. Lawrence breaks out simultaneously from the nineteenth century aesthetic and metaphysic to new shapes and new patterns of perception, thought and feeling. Like, James Joyce and Virginia Woolf, Lawrence stands supreme as a modern novelist.

Women in Love (1920)

In the autumn of 1916, Lawrence wrote excitedly to friends about the newly-completed *Women in Love:* "it is a terrible...and wonderful novel"; "I know it is true...The world of my novel is big and fearless—yes, I love it..."; "the book frightens me: it is so end of the world. But it is, it must be, the beginning of a new world too"; 'it is the book of my free soul.' These and other passages from letters express his sense of having stretched his own talents and challenged the world. According to Michael Bell, "It has been recognized that *Women in Love* relates to *The Rainbow* in a more complex fashion than being simply the second half of an originally integral conception. *Women in Love* became a different kind of book."

J. Middleton Murry, Lawrence's friend observes, "*Women in Love* is five hundred pages of passionate vehemence, wave after wave of turgid, exasperated writing impelled towards some distant and invisible end."

Ursula Brangwen, at 26, and her sister Gudrn, at 25, are unmarried and living at home, teaching at a grammar school. Gudrun, who has been an art student in London, observes that marriage is the next step. Both are nervous of the subject. They set out to see a relative's wedding taking place at Willey Green near their Midland mining town of Beldover.

Smartly dressed they appear out of place on their walk; Gudrun hates the way the mines spoil the countryside. At the wedding, Gudrun is attracted by the bride's brother, Gerlad Crich, the son of the colliery-owner. Handsome and successful, he looks an upright English gentleman. Ursula wonders about Rupert Birkin, whom she knows slightly as a school-inspector. Slight and pale and unconventional, he hides his awkwardness; she is irritated and charmed by him. She watches, too, the striking, aristocratic figure of Hermione Roddice, a remarkable woman and an intellectual. Beneath her imposing public figure Hermione feels valnerable; she depends on her relationship with Birkin and dreads losing him.

There is a cheer from the crowd when the bridegroom arrives late and chases after the bride. The girl's father, Will Brangwen, a school handicraft instructor, plays the wedding march. When the guests leave the church Hermione possessively seeks out Birkin.

The Criches' home, "a sort of manor farm," is in the country but within sight of smoke from the mines. Gerald is host after the wedding because his father is ill. Birkin and the eccentric Mrs. Crich talk about people. She speaks enigmatically about her children.

During lunch the talk becomes general and theoretical. Hermione and Birkin are opposed to "a spirit of emulation" in society; Gerald thinks it a spur to productivity and progress. After the meal Birkin and Gerald discuss the bride's conduct in racing with the groom at the church. Birkin defends spontaneous individuality. There is a tension between the two men.

Birkin visits Ursula at school. Ursula begins to feel the excitement of love and Birkin looks at her with a new pleasure. Hermione now intrudes, having spotted Birkin's car. They discuss the reproduction of flowers, and Hermione (who admires the small wood-carvings that Gudrun specializes in) invites the sisters to stay at Breadalby, her father's country-house.

Birkin is furious with Hermione when (misinterpreting his own views) she suggests that education develops consciousness at the expense of spontaneity. Her claim to value animal instincts, he tells her, is only a form of intellectualism. He accuses her of a lust for power. Birkin tells Ursula that sensuality is all he values now as a key to living.

The next Saturday Ursula and Gudrun walk to Willey Water, the lake at Shortlands. As they reach the boathouse Gerald dives and they watch him swimming. Gudrun envies him, and envies men their freedom to do as they please. This leads to discussion of Gerald's improvements at the mines and the accident in which he killed his brother.

Birkin and Gerald meet on a railway platform, waiting for the London train, and travel together. An article in Gerald's newspaper argues that the county will soon be ruined unless new values can be found. Birkin does not believe that people are willing to break up existing society to create a new world. Industrialised England has become dreary and inert with materialism. Gerald lives for his work, he says, and for making things go. Birkin's ambition is private: his ideal is an ultimate marriage.

At the Pompadour Gerald finds Birkin drinking with a girl called Minetee. Birkin tells her about Gerald's career as a solider, explorer and (now) mine-manager. Gerald feels an awful, enjoyable power over her, a lust mixed with cruelty; she seems to him a victim. They are joined by a dark, slim young man with a high-pitched voice, called Halliday. His attitude to Minette, who has been his mistress, is peevish. She is pregnant and considers having a child beastly. There is a raffish jaded immorality about Halliday and his friends. The party moves on by taxi to Halliday's home, where an Arab servant is treated contemptuously. Gerald's attention is caught by a wood-carving from the Pacific, showing a woman in labour, suggesting the extreme of physical sensation, beyond the limits of mental consciousness. He wonders if the piece is obscene. Soon afterwards everyone goes to bed.

Gerald wakes beside Minette who is still asleep; her defencelessness excites him once more. He joins Halliday and Maxim Libidnikov who are sitting naked by the fire. Halliday praises nudism. Gerald thinks it undignified, but he enjoys feeling free for once from respectability.

Gerald stays for several days. Finally he quarrels with Halliday and is on the point of punching him. He leaves, regretting only that he has not paid Minette. Gerald reflects that he is a whole man, the others Birkin included-half-men. Minette will marry Halliday because a half-man is what she wants.

Early in the summer Ursula and Gudrun visit Hermione at Breadalby, a fine old house in the Derbyshire countryside. The other guests include Birkin and Gerald; Sir Joshua Mattheson, a sociologist; Sir Alexander Roddice, Hermione's brother and a Member of Parliament; an Italian countess; and a German girl. Ursula feels unhappy at the clever but shallow conversation in this upper-class, cultured, cosmopolitan company.

The bond between Hermione and Birkin is under strain. Hermione belittles him. During a discussion of education, they quarrel when Hermione talks about the freedom she finds in knowing things-especially in her knowledge of the stars. Knowledge is like bottling up freedom, Birkin asserts.

Birkin regrets her roughness and goes penitently to her room. Hermione is overwhelmed by a wish to break him down and strikes at his head with a heavy paperweight; he fends off her second blow with a book. Hermione sleeps after this. Birkin stunned, goes out into the county where he rolls naked among flowers and branches, tired of people and uniting himself with nature.

The house-party is dominated by these developments between the two strongest personalities. Other relationships are advanced which include an improvised ballet and a morning swim. Gerald is increasingly attracted by Gudrun, although he regards her as a social inferior, and Birkin is drawn to Ursula.

Ursula's dislike of Hermione grows. Gerald and Birkin have adjacent rooms; they discuss the Brangwen sisters and the people they met in London.

Going home from school, the sisters watch Gerald forcing his terrified Arab mare to stand at the railway crossing while a goods-train roars by. Ursula is horrified. Gudrun is shocked but excited. Two workers watch the girls pass by in their brilliant clothes. One tells the other he would give a week's pay for five minutes with Gudrun.

One morning the sisters are sketching by Willey when Hermione and Gerald come up in a boat. Hermione greets Gudrun and insists on seeing her sketch-book. Gerald recalls Gudrun's words by the railway.

Ursula wanders to the bank of a stream and meets Birkin working on a punt by a mill-pond. He takes her over to a small island. He is pleased by the thought of an uncontaminated world, empty of people; but Ursula knows that humanity has a long way still to go.

In the mill-house Hermione, asserting herself, measures the floors and compels Birkin to accept an expensive Persian camel-hair rug, though he does not want to take it. Over a picnic they talk about will-power, which Hermione claims is the secret of her success: Gerald, she says, was right to impose his will on his horse.

Birkin sends Ursula a note inviting the sisters to tea; Ursula decides to go alone. When she arrives, Birkin tells that they must pledge themselves for ever, as friends at least.

They watch the antics of two cats, Birkin's tom chivying a stray female. Ursula is angered by Birkin's defence of male superiority; his cat is like Gerald with his mare, she says. They continue to discuss Birkin's theory of balance between the sexes. Ursula tells him about her first love-affair with an officer Skrebensky (treated in *The Rainbow*). He thinks her reckless and exciting. She asks him to say the words 'my love' and-simply, for once-he does.

Mr. Crich gives a lake-party every year; this time the Brangwen sisters attend it. The girls are happy. Ursula sings in German. When Birkin and Gerald join them, Gudrun is dancing before a herd of bullocks. Birkin dances for Ursula. Gudrun races at the bullocks, alarming Gerald: the cattle can be deadly. A few moments later Birkin tells Ursula that he loves her.

Birkin reflects on love and death, modern reality, dissolution, and the end of the world. When darkness falls they kindle decorated lanterns: Ursula depicts a moon and a sea-bed with crabs; Gudrun's flowers and a cuttle-fish with a cold gaze which frightens her. Gerald and Gudrun kiss and set off in the canoe, watching the fireworks and lanterns on the lake.

Suddenly there is shouting. Gerald's sister Diana has fallen over-board; a young doctor has gone in after her. Gerald, recalled to practical duties, goes to the rescue—in vain. Both Diana and the doctor die.

Ursula, profoundly depressed, broods about death. Suicide is repulsive but death has a romantic attraction: it seems pure.

Birkin arrives as the Brangwen children, Billy and Dora, are going to bed. Ursula sees his gentleness with Billy, kissing him goodnight; but she tells him he looks offensively ill: he ought to look after himself.

On his sick-bed Birkin contemplates the prospect of marriage and domesticity, without enthusiasm. He is dissatisfied with everything except the idea of freedom. Women are possessive. They want to be dominant, like the ancient goddess, Great mother of all things. The thought of woman as a maternal tyrant horrifies him. A man and a woman should not be broken fragments of a whole; a man should have his pure freedom, a woman hers.

Gerald visits him; he is still fond of Birkin and is now protective towards him, but cannot take him seriously as a man. He talks about Gudrun and about his family's reaction to Diana's death. Winifred, his younger sister, needs a teacher-perhaps Gudrun. They talk about education. Gerald hated school but is reluctant to question English methods. Birkin proposes a blood-brotherhood of eternal friendship. Gerald is uncertain about this. We need to know that, like Shelley, Lawrence wanted to build a pantisocracy in New Mexico.

Ursula forgets Birkin for a time and resumes her old interests and friendship. Gudrun is planning to go abroad. They visit a Mrs. Kirk who was once Gerald's nurse.

At Shortlands Mrs. Crich is dying. He has always tried to serve both God and his own workers-infuriating his wife by his charity. She has submitted to him but remained apart in spirit, like a "moping dishevlelled hawk." Mr. Crich has given his love to Winifred, a sensitive, strange child, now about thirteen. He is hoping that Gudrun will agree to leave her school post and come to look after her.

Birkin goes to the South of France to recover from his illness. Ursula feels unhappy and lost. On the evening of his return she finds him throwing stones at the moon's reflection in the mill-pond, and cursing the ancient goddess, Mother of all Things, whom he associates with it. But soon, although Birkin is determined not to make love, they are nestling together, kissing.

Next day Birkin thinks he may have been wrong. Perhaps he talks too much. He continues to meditate. An African statuette at Halliday's. delightfully elegant, comes to mind: it represents thousands of years of a purely sensual culture. Suddenly there is a way out of this labyrinth of thoughts and fancies. He believes in a personal integrity beyond all emotions—including love and desire—which combines independence with obligations to others. He must ask Ursula to marry him.

Urusla is out when he arrives. He tells her father that he means to propose.

Ursula discusses marriage with Gudrun; they are still close but conscious of differences. Ursula is protective towards men, Gudrun is fearful of them. Ursula decides that she will accept Birkin only if he is prepared to love her absolutely.

Birkin is angry with Ursula. He goes to Gerald at Shortlands and finds him, uncharacteristically, bored; they discuss cures for boredom; Birkin suggests work, love and fighting.

After a London exhibition of her wood-carvings Gudrun is welcomed back to Shortlands. Winifred gives her flowers. Mrs. Crich has promised to provide an artists' studio at the house. He likes Gudrun to sit with him; she keeps him in touch with live.

Next day is a half-day for Ursula. Birkin calls at her school and asks her out for a drive in the afternoon. In the car he gives her three rings.

They drive to Southwell and have tea near the Minster, forgetting Hermione. She thinks him like one of the sons of God in the Bible who loved the daughters of men. Birkin wants to wander the world with her. They write letters of resignation from their jobs, and, truly united, spend a night together in Sherwood Forest. They wake laughing and thrilled by something more than love: a sense of the night and of mystery.

Gerald is frightened by his father's approaching death. His mother urges him to look after himself. Walking to Gudrun's home, he tells her that he cares for nothing but her. He kisses her, under a bridge where the miners take their sweethearts; she enjoys reflecting that he is the miners' master.

The old Mr. Crich dies. After days of loneliness Gerald visits his father's grave and then steals into Gudrun's room, with clay from the grave still on his boots. Leaving in the dawn he is comforted and happy, but Gudrun feels old and is glad to be rid of him. Their night together has not been such a union as that of Ursula and Birkin in the forest.

The Brangwens are to move house. Ursula puts off deciding on a day for the wedding.

Gerald speaks to Birkin about his own hopes of marrying Gudrun. Birkin is unenthusiastic. He dislikes the world all in couples. He believes in something broader: a perfect friendship between two men in addition to marriage. Gerald declines this offer. The 25th chapter ends with an explanation of Gerald's position. He is approaching marriage without sincerely committing himself to Gudrun.

Ursula and Birkin buy an antique chair in a sale at the market. Birkin praises the early nineteenth century when such craftsmanship was still possible, but Ursula is annoyed by his love of the past. The girl is pregnant; the couple are obliged to make a home—no chance for them of foreign travel. The young man looks 'rat-like' to Ursula, a product of modern urban life at its worst. But Birkin insists that the world in future will belong to such ordinary folk; exceptional people like the Brikins will have to live among them as well as they can.

Birkin and Ursula marry now. The Brangwen family has moved. The sisters go to the house to fetch Ursula's things. Contemplating the bare rooms, Gudrun senses that a normal, settled marriage would be intolerable.

Christmas approaches. Gerald and Gudrun are to meet the Birkins in Austria. On the way they spend an evening at the Pompadour. Minette is there and makes it clear that she has been Gerald's mistress.

The Birkins, exulting in their departure from England, make the long boat and train journey to Austria, arriving at their Innsbruck hotel by sledge over the snow. Mr. and Mrs. Crich are already there. At dinner they talk about how conventional the English are. Birkin is glad to be abroad. They go on next day to a hostel in the mountains. Gudrun is sensitive to the isolation; she feels lost when Gerald makes love to her. They meet the other guests. Gerald dances with a Professor's daughter. Gerald excels at winter sports. Indoors, Gudrun gets to know Loerke—whom Gerald and Birkin detest—pleased by his stories of early poverty and by his aesthetic idea. Art, he believes, is separate from life; she agrees. He shows her a picture of a statuette he once made in green bronze, representing Lady Godiva, naked on a great horse. Gudrun takes Loerke's side.

Ursula wants to leave; the snow pains her. Gudrun presents her with coloured stockings; but they are growing apart. Ursula has accepted Birkin's ideals; her sister cannot go beyond love because she has never reached it. Gerald confesses that he can hardly bear his passion for Gudrun, and Birkin offers his friendship in support. Desperate and bewildered by Gudrun's behaviour, Gerald replies sceptically. The Birkins go south to Italy.

The conflict between Gerald and Gudrun now frightens them both. His love seems to her like a frost. She forces him to say that he cannot love her, then that he does. She humiliates him, admitting to Loerke, in his presence, that they are not married. The curious, perverse flirtation which she develops with the sculptor leads to the catastrophe. She and Gerald make arrangements to part, and she goes with Leorke. Gerald meets them, knocks Loerke down, almost strangles Gudrun, and goes off alone into the snow to his death.

Lawrence's novel *Women in Love* is a classic attack on stark materialism, based on industrial revolution in England. S. J. Miko observes, "This brings us back to the use of 'dialectic' to refer to the structure of *Women in Love*. There are at least two basic ways in which the term may be applied: it can refer simply to the argument which goes on between Ursula and Birkin, an argument which develops through both intellectual and emotional oppositions, sometimes violent, but finally achieveing a kind of resolution. It can also refer to the thematic opposition between intellectuality and sensuality which we have been noticing."

Lawrence believed that ugliness was the tragedy of England: industrial progress had brought ugliness into towns, house, schools, and furniture; into marriage, work and all human affairs. Materialism was like a disease. "Nag, nag, nag" about politics and money, he complained, was all the modern English were fit for. On one occasion he called *Women in Love* "purely destructive," and although it is not that, it is an attack on materialism and on the utilitarian outlook of twentieth century industrialism. Ugliness was made worse by the war. The nineteenth century's confidence in progress and order was dwindling fast among intellectuals.

Nonetheless, Lawrence was enthusiastic about novel-writing, and about what might be done to start a new world. According to myth, the phoenix, his emblem, died in fire and was born again. In spite of its pessimism, *Women in Love* reflects the exuberance of a confident artist. It offers a vision of personal freedom in marriage and friendship. Birkin's view of marriage is a plea for emancipation, for men and women; it leads to his dislike of possession (Hermione has tried to possess him). A responsible freedom (not the licence of Halliday and his circle) is the only way, Birkin and Lawrence assert, to resist the dreary nagging of the modern world.

Sexual impulse is only a part of Lawrence's recognition of the complex experience of men and women in love. Birkin is bashful in courting Ursula (in Chapter 14); Gerald relishes power over Minette (in Chapter 6); a shared pleasure in violence unites Gerald and Gudrun; and Ursula vacillates between hatred and love of Birkin before their marriage. The aggressive and fearful undercurrents of human nature; discussed during these years by Freud, are explicit in *Women in Love*.

Lawrence was not a Freudian, though he thought Freud interesting, and was perhaps influenced by Freud in rejecting "the old stable *ego* of the character" (in traditional fiction).

A new conception of integrity in character required experiment with technique. Lawrence rejected plot and contrivance in favour of organic structure: a novel was to be shaped by its own inner nature. When *Women in Love* first appeared some critics thought it formless. "A book which is not a copy of other books has its own construction" he wrote; what an imitator might consider faults he would call characteristics. J. I. M. Stewart has pointed out in *Eight Modern Writers* the extent to which the novel is conventional: it uses a country-house party to assemble its characters; a story of two sisters and their young men is likely to remind us of Jane Austen's *Pride* and *Prejudice* (1813) and George Eliot's *Middlemarch* (1871-2); taking the main characters abroad for the final chapters is an old device. *Women in Love* is effective in many ways that are equally traditional: in its landscapes of the Midland countryside spoiled by the mines; in its minor characters, like Gerald's old nurse, or Winifred with her pets; and in its picturing of English society in transition.

Lady Chatterley's Lover (1928)

Lawrence's last great novel *Lady Chatterley's Lover* found a mixed response as *The Rainbow*. An unsigned reviewer wrote,

"There has been brought to our notice within the last few weeks a book which we have no hesitation in describing as the most evil outpouring that has ever besmirched the literature of our country. The book is Lawrence's *Lady Chatterley's Lover*. Unfortunately for literature as for himself, Lawrence has a diseased mind. He is obsessed with sex. We are not aware that he has written any book during his career that has not over-emphasized this side of life."

J. Middleton Murry who was a friend of Lawrence wrote in the *Adelphi*, "One thing is certain. No one who reads *Lady Chatterley's Lover* to the end with the responsiveness without which the book is not merely obscene but nonsense as well will be troubled by its obscenity." Still the expurgated version that was brought in the US contained the best of Lawrence and it moved the readers one day.

Mrs Lawrence wrote of the book's fate to the publisher thus: "It is a relief to know that you are bringing out the only authorized edition of *Lady Chatterley's Lover* in the United Sates, after all the expuraged pirated editions. Lawrence considered it his greatest work, and I feel that even in this revised form it has all the beauty of the original edition, and that it suggests to the greatest possible extent the original strength and vigour."

In *Lady Chatterley's Lover* Lawrence is determined to face the problem of creating a resurrection story which is literally phallic, with a real man as the phallus-bearer. This man is a freed man. The germs for this story were seen in his earlier work *The Man Who Loved Island.*

The simple story of the novel is this: Constance (Connie) Chatterley is married to Sir Clifford, a wealthy and cultured mine-owner in Derbyshire. A war wound has left him paralyzed and impotent, and he increasingly devotes all his energy to the management of his mines and to himself. Constance grows restless within the confines of their marriage. She has a brief and superficial affair with Michaelis, a young playwright, then enters into a passionate relationship with Sir Clifford's gamekeeper, Oliver Mellors. He is an ex-officer who rose from the ranks, a forthright, individualistic man uncontaminated by industrial society. Connie becomes pregnant and attempts to conceal the father's identity from her husband. She later confesses and asks him for a divorce. Sir Clifford considers Mellors his social inferior, therefore not worthy, and refuses to release her. The lovers depart and, though separated, wait hopefully for a time when the obstacles between them will have been surmounted and they can be united. The novel was denied full publication in England for over 30 years because of its sexual explicitness.

An expurgated version, released in 1932, contained none of Lawrence's detailed descriptions of the sexual act and eliminated all four-letter words. The unexpurgated text became freely available in 1960 after Penguin Books survived a prosecution under the Obscene Publications Act in 1959. Defence witnesses at the trial included E. M. Forster, Hellen Gardner, and Richard Hoggart, and the verdict marked a major victory against literary censorship. Lawrence's two earlier versions of the novel have been published independently as *The First Lady Chatterley* (1944) and *John Thomas and Lady Jane* (1972).

In the autumn of 1925 Lawrence's own withdrawal from Europe ended. New Mexico had given him the renewal he had sought. Keith Sagar observes, "The phallic symbol takes over many of the associations of the earlier rainbow symbol, and through this, a sense of relatedness to the greater purpose of creation." Lawrence wrote: "It will be a phallic rather than a sexual regeneration. For the phallus is only the great old symbol of godly vitality in a man, and of immediate contact. It will also be a renewal of marriage: the true phallic marriage. And, still further it will be marriage set again in relationship to the rhythmic cosmos." In *Sons and Lovers*, Lawrence had interpreted sexual experience more conventionally, as a loss of innocence and paradise. In this novel, the lovers flee from the little, unreal life-denying day of humanity as in the painting *Return to Paradise* in a rather forlorn attempt to regain the innocence, wonder and faith which sexual experience is now seen to generate.

Lawrence then mentions an unexpurgated edition of *Lady Chatterley's Lover*, "this tender and phallic novel, far too good for the public"; its central aims is the restoration of phallic consciousness', something really deeper than cerebral sex-consciousness, in fact "the root of poetry, lived or sung".

The first version of the novel *The First Lady Chatterley* was written from October 1926 to early March 1927. Frieda's jumbled account suggests that Lawrence's main artistic aim was to relate the questions of class against class, and soul against body. Typically, Lawrence solved his problems as they arose, and the result was a novel of moderate length instead of the long short story which he originally intended. Published as *The First Lady Chatterley*, it is in most respects rather dull, with few poetic overtones. Characteristically Lawrence soon set to work on its improvement and expansion, finishing this second version in the summer of 1927. So "improper" was it, he decided to follow Norman Douglas's practice, and have it printed privately in Florence, at two guineas a copy. With this in view he began a final revision, introducing important changes, and completing the work very rapidly by the opening of 1928; the title he had in mind was *Tenderness*.

The second version *John Thomas and Lady Jane* contains much that is new, and is half as long again as the first; the introduction and the main action (before Lady Chatterley's departure for the Continent) are expanded to more than double their previous length. Lawrence's principal aim was to give the story greater probability and imaginative cogency. It is much more detailed, introduces more characters for the Wragby Christmas season, evokes more successfully the emptiness of Lady Chatterley's life, and suggests a greater reality in the love that gives new life to her and the gamekeeper Parkin. The theme is reinforced in lyrical passages which fuse human revitalization and joy with natural growth. Contrastingly, more emphasis is placed on industrial blight: "Out of the orgy of ugliness and of dismalness and of dreariness, would there, could there ever unfold a flower, a life with beauty in it?" The heroine Connie finds the modern civilization as impotent. Her husband's crippleness symbolizes this in part. The third version shows incidental pruning and much reorganization.

The principal changes in the opening of the story result from the introduction of new characters. The first of these, Tommy Dukes, speaks for Lawrence, and presents the "democracy of touch" theme; we have never had "proper human contact", he says, agreeing with Connie that a civilization will come, when life flows and nobody cares "terribly about money, or owning things, or bossing other people". Nevertheless, Dukes is Lawrence's shock-tactician; in his bold intellectualism on the subject of sex he prepares the way for both the story and an unconventional feature in its expression. He believes ill "having a good heart, a chirpy penis, a lively intelligence, and the courage to say 'shit!' in front of a lady". Michaelis, a newcomer in *Lady Chatterley's Lover*, is introduced" largely for satirical reasons, but he is given an important part in the preliminary story, ultimately to make Connie realize the "great nothingness of life" before sh ; meets the gamekeeper Mellors.

In accordance with Lawrence's continued aim to increase the probability of his story, Mellors is very different from the Oliver Parkin of the first two versions. He is less churlish, less politically extreme, and far better educated. He had been an army officer in India, can speak well when he wishes, and has a natural distinction. The vernacular returns readily when he is moved: "Ma lass!... I love thee an' th' touch on thee. Dunna argue wi' me! Dunna! Dunna! Dunna! Let's be together." Not one of the gamekeepers has known real love. The second Parkin suffers from the traumatic experience he had with Bertha Coutts when he was a boy. Mellors's misfortune was to fall in love with cultural and spiritual types, clearly based on Miriam and Helen Corke. All three are repelled by their marital experience.

The endings of the three novels vary considerably. The first Parkin becomes secretary of a Communist branch in Sheffield. Some amusing working-class family scenes underline the question of class division and the extent to which people are one in their feelings. Lawrence's view is that we are united by "the stream of desire"; it is that which "makes a nation a nation". Yet, though their love is intended to signify a move in this direction, Connie's desire to escape "the whole leprous contamination" of Wragby, and marry Parkin—"Anything, to be in contact with life. And if she could possibly be in contact with the working people, well and good"—is hardly a convincing note on which to end.

The second variant, a meeting of the lovers in Hucknall Church and a walk in the woods towards Felley Mill, could have been used more judiciously to give imaginative expression to Lawrence's idea of an eventual return to the "lusty" days of old England, when some "curious blood-connexion held the classes together". In *Lady Chatterley's Lover* the Sheffield scenes are omitted, but the emphasis on the 'democracy of touch' is maintained. Connie tells Mellors that he has the courage of tenderness which will make the future; he believes that it makes men really men and not so 'monkeyish', and that it is especially necessary for the English to "get into touch with one another".

Duncan Forbes agrees to pose as Connie's lover in order to procure her divorce, but Clifford's resistance makes her tell the truth. His collapse into a state of infantile dependence on Mrs Bolton leads to repulsive physical intimacies, and Lawrence's causal relationship of these with a fierce awakening of steely energy and business acumen in industry reinforces the theme of the necessity for a new life-flow to restore sanity and happiness to western civilization. In a long concluding letter, coloured by illusions to the Etruscan way of life which recall Lawrence's 'Autobiographical Fragment,' Mellors insists that the industrial problem will not be solved by money ("getting and spending", in Wordsworth's phrase) but by training the people to live, and live handsomely; they should "be alive and frisky, and acknowledge the great god Pan."

F.B. Pinion observes, "Unfortunately Lawrence's sense of humour deserted him when he was fired by zeal as a priest of love or prophet of doom. One can hardly take exception to his intentions in *Lady Chatterley's Lover*: it is in the execution that he shows want of judgment, and in one way or another this is true of each version of the story."

In *Lady Chatttirley's Lover* Lawrence gives greater emphasis to the social aspect of Connie's sexual disillusionment. Her girlish experience in Germany (based to some extent on Frieda's), stimulated by thrilling 'soul-enlightening discussions' on 'the sex thing', had proved 'a bit of an anti-climax by comparison with the higher and more wonderful visions of woman's freedom. Her husband's sexual incapacitation as a result of terrible war injuries gives ample probability to her love-affair with Michaelis, but it is her complete disenchantment with him and the society which he and Clifford represent which makes her realize the genuineness of the passion that springs up between her and Mellors.

But for symbolical repercussions, Clifford's impotence and dependence on mechanical transport might be regarded as superfluous. He has never been interested in physical fulfilment.

Clifford hopes that Connie can subordinate it; at worst, if lack of sex is disintegrating, that she will 'go out and have a love-affair'. Keith Sagar affirms, "Clifford's sterility is germane to her class. Nothing creative is to be expected from his class."

Individual fulfilment comes from a true relationship in love. Its realization leads to new life-values, and hence to social and industrial regeneration. Such is the faith which inspires *The Rainhow* and *Women in Love*. With a minor qualification, it is the subject of *Lady Chatterley's Lover*, Lawrence combining tenderness with sensual fulfilment as the basis of his 'democracy of touch'. No rainbow of promise appears; the *dies irae* is imminent "if things go on as they are," but nothing can destroy Mellors' faith that the crocus will continue to bloom. The novel is primarily an allegorical statement of Lawrence's faith in the emergence of a new life and society.

Past and present, a contrast between 'Merrie England' ('Shakespeare's England') and the death of spontaneity in the present, reaches its crescendo in the very centre of the story. Its prelusive notes occur in the wood beyond the park, "a remnant of the great forest where Robin Hood hunted." For Clifford it is "really the heart of England," and he declares his intention to keep it intact. As he does so, Connie hears the eleven o'clock hooter of Stacks Gate colliery, but he is "too used to the sound to notice". They are a reminder of an alien element; Clifford's chair is another. The war has made him an impotent cripple; he wishes to have a son to ensure that this part of England will be preserved. He is mentally alert, but Connie knows that he has suffered the "bruise" of a shock which is steady paralysing his "affective self."

The dying movement to Lawrence's theme is the drive Connie takes in central England, "the England of Robin Hood, where the miners [prowl] with the dismalness of suppressed sporting instincts" when they are not at work. Dismal, blackened Tevershall is "the utter negation" of natural beauty and gladness, "the utter death of the human intuitive faculty". In it she sees a new "under-world" race, overconscious on the politico-economic side but dead on the spontaneous and intuitive. She feels that "with such creatures for the industrial masses" there can be no hope.

Significantly the next action is Connie's visit to the keeper's hut, where she sees brown chickens "running lustily". The first dandelions are "making suns"; everywhere leaves and flowers are opening. "Everywhere: the bud-knots and the leap of life!" In this way Lawrence repeatedly links the revival of nature with his theme of human recovery.

Connie is very happy to meet Mellors. She loves him instantly as he represents life. In this state of physical ecstasy, she has to listen to Clifford reading Racine and stressing the need of "classic control", while wishing he could be with his technical books, or his pit-manager, or his radio. Connie's sexual experiences have been such that she still has much to learn. It is after her drive in the Midlands that Mellors's haste upsets her psychologically, so that she finds intercourse physically ridiculous, and resents his use of dialect. Immediately she is sorry, ceases to resist, and reaches a consummation which evokes the finest prose-poetry in all three versions of the novel. She is "born: a woman"; she is "still a little afraid", but her hands move down his back, and the touch of him is like "the sons of god with the daughters of men". She wonders at the unspeakable beauty of his warm living body where it had previously repelled her, and she even enjoys essaying the dialect herself.

It is part of Lawrence's allegory that, under the influence of Mrs Bolton, Clifford becomes more interested in capturing "the bitch-goddess" by "brute means of industrial production." Clifford, in short, is completely opposed to the "democracy of touch" principle which is the basis of Mellors' faith in a future civilization. Mellors is Lawrence's mouthpiece.

Marion Wynne Davies observes, "Whether the implications of *Lady Chatterley's Lover* are always presented clearly and completely in the novel may be questioned when one reads Lawrence's afterthoughts in 'Apropos of *Lady Chatterley's Lover*'. *Niaiseries* notwithstanding, he undeniably succeeded in his principal aim: to make men and women "think sex, fully, completely, honestly, and cleanly". Sanity and wholeness of life can come only "when our sexual act and our sexual thought are in harmony, and the one does not interfere with the other. The tragic age and 'the ruins' with which the novel opens refer not just to the calamity of recent war but to the 'dead' and 'meaningless' bodies which three thousand years of idealism have strewn across the stage of life. The question at stake is 'love among the ruins' of the modern world; it is the one which occupies Birkin's mind as he enters London and describes his feelings as 'real death.'" Nearly all modern sex, he write in 'Apropos' is "a pure matter of nerves, cold and bloodless"; it may produce 'a sort of ecstasy and a heightening of consciousness' for a time but, "like the effect of alcohol or drugs", it is "a process of impoverishment". Sex which comes naturally from "warm blood-desire" (and Lawrence links this with the rhythm of the days, the seasons, and the universe) is life-giving, and it is the deepest of communions when consummation for man and woman is reached simultaneously. "Most folk live their lives through and they never know it", Mellors says. Rather fearful at first, Connie glories in having realized "her sensual self, naked and unashamed". "There was nothing left to disguise or be ashamed of. She shared her ultimate nakedness with a man, another being." This indicates the kind of liberating effect which the book generates. The "forked flame" which love has created in Connie and Mellors is the "cloven flame" of *The Plumed Serpent*. It implies an equilibrium or equality in marriage, and a oneness of spirit which separation cannot extinguish. For Ramon its house is "the tent of the Holy Ghost"; for Mellors, it is Pentecost.

3

D.H. Lawrence's Minor Novels

Lawrence has written many novels and yet all of them are not his great works His minor novels are *The White Peacock* (1911), *The Trespasser* (1912), *The Lost Girl* (1920), *Aaron's Rod* (1922), *Kangaroo* (1924), *The Boy in the Bush* (with M. L. Skinner, 1924), *The Plumed Serpent* (1926) and *Mr Noon* (1984)

The White Peacock (1911)

Lawrence's earliest surviving writing of any substance are handful of poems, the play called *Collier's Friday Night,* some stories, including an early version of 'The Ordour of Chrysanthemums,' and his first novel, *The White Peacock*. This last work was begun in 1906 and after multiple revisions, finished in 1910. Borrowing the plan to describe the developing relationship between two couples from George Eliot, the great novelist of the Midlands, produced what he called "a florid prose poem." The milieu is cultivated middle class; the pits and colliers of the region are almost entirely omitted. This is so understandable, given the youth and the aspirations of the author, that the pretentiousness and falsity of much of the book must be called innocent. Frank Kermode writes, "For all that, *The White Peacock* is often very impressive, not only in the delicacies of natural description, but in the quiet presence of themes and images that later grew dynamic." The vicious circle Lawrence was to try so hard to break the spoiling of women by men, and their consequent spoiling of their sons, who, etiolated by their mothers is already in his first book. The narrator, Cyril, is a cruel caricature of a refined young Lawrence, who cannot quite bear to think of women as sexual beings. The strong George Saxton declines, like Lawrence's father, into drunkenness.

The story of George is an ineffective tragedy. It should have been something stronger. George Saxton is a young farmer, handsome, able-bodied, and, outside his own work, wholesomely commonplace. But he has for neighbours a cultured family of higher social status who are on friendly terms with the Saxtons. Letty, his daughter, is a full-fledged flirt, fascinating and conscienceless. She turns George's head, and makes violent love to him. Even after she has married a rich husband, and he has declined on his humble cousin Meg, she does not leave him alone, but dangles her charms before his eyes and disturbs an honest life with a vision of what was never meant for him.

Cyril, the narrator of the story, has a strong liking for George, but unfortunately he takes an interest in the farmer's welfare. From Omar Khayyam George has to go on to George Moore. Aurbrey Beardsley and Arthur Melville are spread before his eyes. Letty talks French at him and even Latin. They talk Strauss and Debussy at him while he and Meg are keeping a public-house. No wonder he takes to drink, and that we leave him doubtfully recovering from delirium. There are other symptoms of ruin. They have stuffed his foolish head with foreign ideas, and he thinks that if all had gone well he would have been a poet or something, like Burns. Poor George! Letty, the white peacock, was bad for him. Still worse was the literary and unhumorous Cyril, who sees ordinary English rustics through the morbid eyes of Tchekov or Maupassant.

But the tale displays aimlessness. A good deal of the conversation is quite banal, despite its suggestions of advanced culture; for when such names as Ibsen, Gorki, Schopenhauer, Maupassant, Clausen, Debussy, and others startle the stillness of the woodland, as they frequently do, we have a feeling that it is not the characters but the author who is uttering them. And the reader is annoyed by the insubstantiality of Cyril Beardsall, in whose mouth the whole story is put. He appears to have poetic thoughts, to sketch from nature, and to work in the fields; but for much of the book he is a wraithlike person who appears to be present without being seen.

Violet Hunt said "The novel, by a new writer, is really an important contribution to literature, and we hope that it will meet with some of the attention it deserves."

Lawrence's characters simply do not know that class exists. His scene is laid in a district in the Midlands, partly agricultural, partly mining, and his characters are the sons and daughters partly of miners and partly of quite small farmers. In this remarkable world of his there appears to be no 'country' at all, no great families, no squires, hardly even a person. And these sons and these daughters of small farmers would do credit to any Hampstead gathering of blue stockings. So *The White Peacock* sounds like a proletarian novel.

As a story, *The White Peacock* is the tale of several families bicentrally revolving round two young men who are full of free passions. The one of them goes up the material scale of life; the other descends it, towards passionate ruin, drink and tragedy.

The Trespasser (1912)

D.H. Lawrence has given us in *The Trespasser* a remarkable study of a tragic theme, enveloping it, however, in an ironical rather than in a tragical atmosphere.

The theme of *The Trespasser* is simple— the passion of the married man Siegmund for enigmatic girl Helena, its fruition in a few days of union, and then an enforced separation, followed by Siegmund's obsession on suicidal despair and death.

From the opening chapter we are stuck by the author's skill in catching shades of social atmosphere. Siegmund, whose vocation is that of violinist in a London theatre, is bound fast in the squalid cares of a suburban lower-middle-class environment. He has married, young and penniless, with Beatrice, now a disappointed, embittered woman who is dragged down by the weight of family worries, and the threadbare poverty of struggle to maintain the gentilities she was formerly accustomed to. In his soul Seigmund is free, but he has the sensuous, sensitive nature of the poet, who lives for his imaginative visions, while crushed outwardly by the hostile pressure of unyielding facts.

The story opens with Siegmund's escape from his household, for a seven days of happiness with Helena, on a long-projected holiday in the Isle of Wight by the sea. Siegmund has the poet's capacity of enjoying things; he sees and responds instinctively to the forces and appearances of life. Helena's is a more egoistic nature. The picture of her relation with her lover suggests deep reservations, as of a woman who cannot lose sense of her own identity even in the supreme intimacy of love. Perhaps this is the secret of the tragedy that now swiftly develops.

With unobtrusive art Mr. Lawrence scatters hints about Siegmund's unstrung nerves, of his brain sick with overwrought tension, of his morbid susceptibility to gloomy ideas, when most full of joy he is accessible to sudden revulsions of disgust at life's blankness. As the hour of enforced separation draws near he is assailed by an accelerating horror. His physical collapse, with a sun-stoke hinted, is manifest in his speech and bearing. He drags himself across London at night to his suburban home, where he is greeted by his wife and children with frigid, insulting silence. Siegmund hangs himself, and here again the description of the finding of the body by his wife is poetic realism of a Dostöevskian order.

One critic called the novel a morbid tale of seven days in the life of Siegmund MacNair, a violinist. *The Trespasser* combines some of the exquisite imaginative writing in modern fiction with nakedness of physical detail that is almost morbid in its ugliness.

Siegmund's wife rises on the stepping-stone of the tragedy, which she has only allowed to affect her to the extent of making her an interesting object of pity, to prosperity as a popular mistress of a boarding-house. Helena, after a year's poignant anguish, allows herself to be given rest and warmth by Cecil Byrne. Siegmund is sacrificed to his women-folk, and especially to Helena, who is revealed in the twice repeated allegory.

Helena is a neurotic Wagnerite. There are more hints of the future, as when Helena is described as "belonging to that class of 'dreaming women' with whom passions exhaust itself at the mouth."

The fact is that *The Trespasser*, like *The White Peacock* before it, deals in an extremely sincere and interesting way, be it said-with abnormal persons.

The whole crisis of civilization, even the war, Lawrence came to think, stemmed from it; sexual candour, natural sexual activity and the full marital relationship, would be restored only with great effort, and after an apocalyptic upheaval. In so far as there are early traces of this doctrine in *The Trespasser* the book has its importance. The suicide of Siegmund-his 'trespass,' to use a favourite French pun of Lawrence's-lays the death of a natural man at the door of the refined Helena; and there is something about the design of the book.

The Last Girl (1920)

Alvina, a pianist at the show, falls in love with Cicio, an Italian member of the troupe. Cicio is superficially a rather low Neapolitan *ragazzo*, but underneath there is a Lawrentian male, black-eyed, dominant, blood-consciousness. Alvina joins the troupe and after many adventures marries Cicio; they go off to their Italian mountain solitude, where she is left when Cicio goes to war.

This last part of the book owes much to Lawrence's elopement, and has some of that travelogue quality which Lawrence also allowed into *Aaron's Rod*. It indicates his total rejection of an England.

The story is the story of Alvina Houghton, the daughter of a draper in Woodhouse, a mining town in the Midlands. It is built up of solid fabric. If you want a truthful description of a draper's shop, evident knowledge of his stock, and a faithful and keen yet not satiric or sentimental description of James Houghton, Mrs. Houghton, Miss Frost, and Miss Pinnegar, here you have it. Alvina seemed the most likely instrument to transmit Mr. Lawrence's electric shock through the calicos, prints, and miners' shirts by which she stood surrounded. Again, "She was returning to Woodhouse virgin as she had left it. In a measure she felt herself beaten. Why? Who knows...Fate had been too strong for her and her desires. Fate which was not an external association of forces, but which was integral in her own nature." Such phrases taken in conjunction with the fact that Alvina, having refused her first suitor, wilted and pined, and becoming a midwife mysteriously revived in the atmosphere of the Islington-road.

Mr. Lawrence's own grasp of the central theme of his story, of the peculiar attraction which held Alvina and Cicio together, despite an amount of ecstatic hatred that would have sufficed to separate a hundred ordinary lovers for ever, may possibly be profound; but he does not convey it to us. He writes of his characters as though they were animals circling round each other; and on this sub-human plane no human destinies can be decided.

Katherine Mansfield (1888-1923), short-story writer and the wife of J.M. Murry and also a close friend of the Lawrences adds this about *The Lost Girl:* "Lawrence denies his humanity He denies the powers of the imagination. He denies life-I mean *human* life. His hero and heroine are non-human. They are animals on the prowl. They do not feel: they scarcely speak." The heroine, Alvina, is the daughter of James Houghton, a Midland draper, whose soaring ambitions and refined and elegant tastes are out of place in the small industrial, vulgar-minded town of Woodbridge, ('Woodhouse'), which "hated any approach to originality or real taste." All James's schemes for imposing his 'robes et modes' on Woodbridge fall flat, all his later fantastic speculations bring him to grief. His falling business and invalid wife are only sustained by the devotion of two women-the self-sacrificing Miss Frost, the governess, and the practical manageress, Miss Pinnegar. With subtle art Mr. Lawrence exhibits and brands the grubby, ugly industrialism and stodgy, unimaginative bourgeois mediocrity of Woodbridge society through the medium of James's commercial folly and Alvina's unorthodox passion for the wandering Italian, Cicio. Alvina has already sent two suitors about their business, and the sketch of her hesitating aversion for the second, the flat, pale, dry school teacher, Albert Witham, whose persistent gallantry "that completely missed the individual in the woman" finely illustrates Mr. Lawrence's uncanny skill in analyzing the love instincts.

Mr. May and Madame are the important characters in the novel. Alvina at one stage liked to marry Alexander Graham, but her mother disliked him. Then she liked Albert Witham, a teacher, and later his brother Arthur, but they seemed vulgar. Then she disliked Dr. Mitchell.

The picture is an extremely brilliant one, done with a dexterous lightness of touch that is irresistible. And the aesthetic charm deepens when Alviana, now married to Cicio, is transported to the latter's narrative village, Pescocalascio, in the Alban mountains. The study in the last fifty pages of the wild, savage beauty of this primitive environment and of its pagan-minded hill peasantry is done with a poet's insight into the elemental forces of incorrigible nature.

More vital are Lawrence's predilections in making his heroine choose Cicio, a rather repellent creature at first, whose mandoline-serenading suggests the howling of an amorous cat. Whether Lawrence intended this effect or not, he draws Cicio according to his Italian formula; he is a sensualist, one of the regressive type, his mind subservient to his senses, cat-like, tiger-like. Lawrence could not bear sex-jokes, and it is significant that Cicio starts the joke that changes Alvina's name to "Allaye." Such is his fascination that she prefers him eventually to material comforts and conformity. His appeal makes her powerless, and sexually he 'assassinates' her.

As a criticism of Midland culture and mentality it invites comparison with Mr. Arnold Bennett's pictures of the *Five Towns*.

All that matters at the end of the war is that they are together. The novel ends rather exquisitely on a single note of uncertainty, but there can be no doubt that Alvina has found herself, and that her faith in life is sure.

The Lost Girl is unilinear in construction, with no complication of plot. It is diversified by the introduction of a variety of minor characters and scenes.

By and large, however, the novel assumes three phases, of which the first and the last are real and form a strong contrast in shade and tone, while the middle remains transitory and colourful, a curious compound of the real, the exotically bizarre, and the bogus.

The idea of the Natcha-Kee-Troupe (probably an Indian concept) may have come from Dickens's *Hard Times* or from George Morre's *A Mummer's Wife* as F.B. Pinion guesses in which the heroine deserts a family of drapers business to marry an actor whose company she joins.

Anxious to write a perfect selling novel, after the banning of *The Rainbow* and the delay in the publication of *Women in Love,* Lawrence had subdued the sex element, and thought of a story "passable from Mudie's point of view." One page was rewritten. Sales were disappointing but, ironically, thanks, no doubt to Rachel Annand Taylor, the novel was awarded the 1921 James Tait Black Memorial Prize.

Aaron's Rod (1922)

Lawrence's friend J. Middleton Murry thinks that to read *Aaron's Rod* is like to drink of a fountain of life. According to him, "Mr. Lawrence is like the little girl. When he is good, he is very, very good; and when he is bad, he is horrid. Now we feel that he will never be horrid again, but go on from strength to strength, until the pre-destined day when he puts before the world a masterpiece. For Mr. Lawrence is now, indisputably, a great creative force in English literature. We have always believed he was that potentially; even when we have crusaded against him, we have merely been paying tribute to his power. No other living writer could drive us to a frenzy of hostility as he had done; no other fills us with such delight."

Aaron's Rod is an important English novel after the World War I. According to reviewers, it is more significant than James Joyce's *Ulysses. Ulysses* is sterile, and *Aaron's Rod* is full of the sap of life. The novel makes a phase in Lawrence's creative life. *Aaron's Rod* shows that Lawrence has gained the one thing he lacked: serenity.

Lawrence's began *Aaron's Rod*, at the end of 1917, finished it in September 1919, revised it in 1921, and published it in the following year. The lack of impetus in *Aaron's Rod* has often been discussed; Lawrence put it aside several times, and in its present form it owes a good deal to the Italian journey he was at last able to make in late 1919. The first conception belonged to the war period, the black days of 1917 and 1918. Lawrence wanted to leave the country for Italy or for the U.S.

Lawrence's principle of leadership, on which he had been meditating for some time, gets its first fictive expression in *Aaron's Rod*. The book is rooted in the war, but contemplates a post-war Europe cheapened and debilitated-still at the end of an epoch rather than a beginning. Everything is tainted, from sexual relations down to food and drink. If the servants are dead so are their masters. The world is like a shell-shocked soldier, unhurt but wounded somewhere 'deeper than the brain.'

The story concerns Aaron Sisson, a miner who walks out on his wife and children one Christmas Eve and becomes a flautist in the Convent Garden orchestra; and Rawdon Lilly, a born leader, a separate man who serves without humility, and dominates without arrogance. Lilly, like Birkin in *Women in Love*, is often made to seem ridiculous; even the narrator calls him "poor Lilly." Yet Lilly has power, and the text establishes it. "Freak and outsider as he was," Aaron reflects at the end, "Lilly knew."

Aaron himself is perhaps another aspect of Lawrence. He leaves his wife "because I'm damned if I want to go on being a lover, to her or anybody"; he is less opinionated than Lilly, but equally certain that the need for male separateness is not consistent with the love of woman. His flute enables him to survive alone, and is commended as a flexible, unmechanical, monodic instrument, as well as the emblem of male creativity. Lilly fights it out with his wife, Aaron simply and admirably departs. His wife had supposed herself "as woman, and particularly as mother...the first great source of life and being, and also of culture. The man was but the instrument and finisher...It is the substantial and professed belief of the whole white world." At this point the book, using Aaron's marriage as a text, begins to preach at us: the men of the white world accept these claims, "conspire to agree that all is productive, all that is fine and sensitive and noble, is woman. Aaron, however, has a spirit which will not worship a woman. So he breaks into clean upright separateness, understanding that a man must not be given to a woman; when there is love consummation it must resemble Whitman's 'Dalliance of Eagles,' each bird borne on its own wings at the moment of ecstasy." But given the age, the end of the long-drawn-out Christian epoch, Aaron is better without a woman. The novel is known for Lawrence's paradox of plot. On the one hand, Lawrence tells us about woman as a mother cult, and on the other hand, his double, that is Aaron distances away from woman for happiness in life. Feminists attacked Lawrence for all this.

Lilly's disgust at the married state—"égoisme à deux!... two in one-stuck together like jujube lozenges in little boxes"—is reflected in his struggles with his own wife; as a woman, confident of her superior role, she resists his natural authority over her. This resistance to authority has corrupted the world. The higher human types—Aztecs, Red Indians—disappear; the lower types—"Chinese, Japs and Orientals," flea-bitten Asiatics, Africans cringing but bullies in the mass—these are the world now, when "man's spirit has gone out of" it. Lilly's own salvation lies in strife.

Given the tone of *Aaron's Rod*, it is not surprising that the writings on the metaphysic which are contemporary with it are even harsher and more drastic in their recommendations. As early as 1915 Lawrence was telling Russell about the need for revolution, citing English sexual conduct as evidence, but also urging the abolition of private property, and contemplating action on behalf of the cause he and Russell, briefly, took up. But he told Russell he must drop his democracy. "There must be an aristocracy of people who have wisdom, and there must be a ruler." This belief grew if anything stronger while its concomitant-the need for the British to see that all hope lay in "the adventure into the unexplored, the woman"—was much qualified. The doctrinal works of the *Aaron's Rod* period are very speculative, but attend to practical and political problems, for the most part providing extremely undemocratic, anti-liberation solutions.

The first of the two related themes is personal: how to attain in marriage that individuality and uniqueness which for Lawrence is man's most precious goal in life. The radiance has gone; the blue ball of illusion which Aaron had cherished from childhood is smashed. Love has been soured by the demands of a possessive, querulous wife. He has developed a hard, resistant core, but can no longer escape reality in whisky, woman, or music.

Aaron sends what money he can to support his wife and children, but, after returning and finding that she still wants "to win his self-betrayal out of him," he leaves London for northern Italy, regarding his action as "a natural event." One evening his thoughts return to her, the iron pressure of her persistent will, and her assumption that woman in her maternal role is "the centre of creation" and man a mere "adjunct." She was certain there was nothing greater for him than "to be perfectly enveloped in her all-beneficent love;" it was "written in eternal letters, on the iron tablet of her will," that he must yield to her.

Aaron and Lilly come from the same district, the same class, and have an almost uncanny understanding of one another. They represent Lawrence's views; the difference is that Lilly has arrived, and Aaron is learning by painful degree. Both agree with Josphine Ford that men are simply afraid to be alone. Lilly is learning to possess his soul in patience and peace, and hopes that his wife Tanny will have her Nirvana too; "then there we are, together and apart at the same time, and free of each other, and eternally inseparable." Only after his flute is smashed by the bomb does Aaron escape form "*the cul de sac* in which he had been running for so long." He had been untrue to himself more than once, yielding to "the quicksands of woman or the stinking bog of society." His flute-playing symbolizes his readiness to escape, to evade self-responsibility.

The image of Astarte at the end suggests that all Aaron's mistakes have been made in love, with his wife at Beldover, Josephine Ford in London, and the *marchesa* in Florence. The community of miners, children, and wives in the early part of the dream, with the absurd figure of a man stuffed like a Bologna sausage for consumption by his fellows, refers to Aaron's life and work at Beldover, and more particularly to his loss of individuality within his miners' union.

F.B. Pinion observes, "The second of the two related themes which gives an abstract coherence to this artistically unsatisfactory novel is political. As secretary of his union, Aaron had come to the conclusion that organized benevolence is 'all righteous bullying, like poison-gas.' For him all forms of a good-will are the same, whether from the spokesman at the miners' meeting, the landlady of the Royal Oak, or his own wife. Lawrence associates love and dependence with Socialism, and it is significant that two prominent members of the Bohemian group, Jim Bricknell, who aches for love, and Josephine Ford, who seduces Aaron, both want a bloody revolution."

Instead of crying out for love, there must be obedience to an incalculable power-urge. Men must submit to the greater soul in a man; and women, to the positive power— soul in man. Such is the Lilly-Lawrence message. Aaron wishes to know to whom his soul must submit, and the answer is "Your soul will tell you." However unacceptable Lawrence's views, he holds fast to his central principle: the absolute freedom of the individual to make his own choice.

Lawrence expresses various things incidentally. Lilly and Aaron agree that men should cease groveling in married life, and stand up and stick together, since manhood is more important in human welfare than home and children.

Kangaroo (1924)

The whole of *Kangaroo*, except the last chapter (which was written at Taos), was completed in seven weeks, after the Lawrences had settled in a furnished bungalow by the Pacific, south of Sydney.

Early in 1922, the Lawrences went east, stopping briefly in Ceylon on the way to Australia. Between April and August, when they left for New Mexico, they lived rootlessly in a country Lawrence found interesting, though in the end lacking the possibility of a new life. In June and July he wrote

Kangaroo, adding a final chapter on arrival in New Mexico. Hastily written and often very flat, *Kangaroo* is nobody's choice for Lawrence's masterpiece, but it has a special interest. His Australian admirer Katherine Susannah Prichard protested against its acceptance as "an authentic picture of Australia"; Lawrence, by his own admission, knew very little about it, 'felt blind to it,' as Somers says in the book, and was especially ignorant about its democratic politics.

Somers and his wife are Europeans; William James, the Cornishman, is but half assimilated. But Jack, the young ex-soldier, is wholly Australian-easy, tranquil, indifferent, yet with a dark fire in him that blazes out into instinctive, reckless action. His wife Victoria is instinctive in a more wistful way. Willie Struthers, the Labour leader, is seen twice at crucial instants and often heard of; and then, dominating the action of the book, there is his rival Mr. Cooley, nicknamed "Kangaroo," the leader of the Diggers; a strange mixture of culture and will, intellect and a deep essential tenderness, whose love of his fellowmen consumes him as a victim in the end.

Here Somers is partly Lawrence himself. An unsigned Reviewer in *Times Literary Supplement* said, "Mr. Lawrence can be as unscrupulous as Balzac, but he is much wittier; and then he knows when he digresses. Kangaroo is perhaps the weak spot in the book; both in the inner man and in his outer likeness to the national animal he is something of a chimera, though a generous one. But the tense climax of his end and the whole Australian scene fit close to the design. And for that scope and design one may feel gratitude; it shows once more that a novel need not be a mere love-story, but can blend a deep interest of thought with astonishing vividness in externals."

Lawrence did not like Australia. He called it a substandard civilization. According to him, life in Australia is old type. Even he speaks of the white race in the East. Lawrence admired the gulf between the native servants and the whites in India; he made Somers shrink from his friend Caldecott when he hugged him; and as much as the vacancy of Australian freedom he hated Australia's messy equality and proletarian manners.

Lawrence wrote, "They are ten times more foreign to me…than Italian scoundrels, or even Indians living in almost exactly what I was used to as a boy"(p. vii).

And the fantasy of Lawrence, the leader of men, on which *Aaron's Rod* came to its uncertain close, is critically explored in *Kangaroo*.

First Somers must dominate his wife; and Kangaroo records the ensuing marital conflict. Somers cannot have an easy permissive Australian love-marriage; he wants monogamy and mastery. "You can't have two masters in one ship," he says; Harriet "was to submit to the mystic man and male in him." He quite understands why Harriet contemptuously refuses to do so; he is not yet worthy, has not yet opened "the doors of his soul and let in a dark Lord and Master for himself." He knows he is still cursed with mother-love, whether his real mother's in dreams, or Harriet's.

In this condition he cannot act, cannot yield to the male temptations of political action. He certainly cannot identify his own apocalypse or utopia with that of socialism, and hesitates to identify his authoritarianism with that of the Digger movement, led by Kangaroo. This is the oddest and perhaps the most profound issue in the book. Kangaroo is a strange doppelganger for Lawrence—a viserotonic Jew, very loving, who is finally shot.

And Somers accepts the Kangaroo position that men need a father rather than a suffering saviour, though an obsession with Law (as represented by woman) is, on another view, exactly what is wrong with the Jews. He will even accept Kangaroo as a kind of god, and contemplate a union between them: kangaroo and tiger rather than lion and unicorn, the fat and the thin, the outgoing and the isolate, solar plexus and sacral ganglia divided between two persons. But although Kangaroo is a son of man, he loves not woman but man; Harriet turns against him, and Somers rejects him.

So Somers rejects Kangaroo's love, can even watch him die without admitting that he loves him.

Somers left Australia, that "vast continent…devoid of speech" so horrible in its machine civilization, because it emphasized his impotence. It was as hateful as the old Europe, still existing "under the withered, repulsive weight of the Hand of the Lord, that old Jew." Only the bush was satisfyingly manless, unfriendly, beautiful. Somers-Lawrence must depart, to continue the search for some place where he could reconcile his apocalypticism with his scepticism.

The main subject is a continuation of *Aaron's Rod*. From Europe, Italy in particular, Lawrence brought all his anxious political pre-occupations. In Australia he was evidence of trade unionism and social indifference; but most of the political background of the novel, including the anti-Digger organization, was gathered from the columns of *The Sydney Bulletin*. The story of Kangaroo and his death as a result of riot is Lawrentian fantasy.

The Boy in the Bush (1924)

Lawrence visited Australia and wrote his leadership novel *Kangaroo* (1924). He befriended an Australian nurse Miss. Mollie Skinner who had already written a novel. Then the two thought of collaboration over its revision. Lawrence rewrote it as creatively as he could. Lawrence found in *The Boy* another congenial double, realizing his own passional hopes in the virgin bush, commending blood-knowledge.

Lawrence's Kangaroo proved beneficial as certain parts of that novel are really worth reading. Likewise, his *The Boy in the Bush* written in partnership with M. L. Skinner, is again interesting.

The story is this: Jack Grant, afterwards to be the Boy in the Bush, has been sent to Australia to make his way because certain high-spirited pranks at school, and afterwards, have got him into ill-odour and convinced his parents that Antipodes is the best place for him.

The facts of his career show him to be a handsome, self-willed young scapegrace, with a physical attractiveness to woman of which he is determined to make the most and which he justifies by identifying it with the law and lord of his being. Mr. Lawrence, more didactic in this novel than ever before.

"Forward to the animals!" then, appears to be Mr. Lawrence's slogan. At one point it looked as though the whole of his hero's troubles would have been solved by his becoming a naturalized Turk. He wanted two or more wives and he wanted unquestioning obedience. "You won't oppose me when there's anything I want to do, will you?" He almost plaintively demands of Monica, who, already the mistress of two men, might be expected to be complaisant to a third. "What's the good of keeping your virginity!" later he urges Mary. "It's really mine.... You will come with me to the North West and be my other wife." Mary declines, and charges Jack with want of feeling in thus pressing his suit. "I don't care about feelings," he characteristically replies. "They're what people have because, they feel ought to have them. But I know my own real feeling. I don't care about your feelings." Following this rebuff Mr. Lawrence gives a page of Jack's indignant musings. "Why, Mary ought to go down on her knees before the honour, if I want to take her." But this mood passes too, and like Whitman, he sighs for the companionship and outlook of animals. "Vision is no good. It is no good seeing any more. And words are no good. It is useless to talk. We must communicate with the arrows of sightless, wordless knowledge, as Jack communicated with his horse, by a pressure of the thigh and knees."

L.P. Hartley writes in *Spectator* in 1924 that, "But the greater part of *The Boy in the Bush* is articulated clearly enough, and what do Mr. Lawrence and Miss Skinner mean by it? In none of his earlier novels has Mr. Lawrence come out into the open as he has in this."

John Edwin Muir observes, "Mr. Lawrence's most obviously striking quality as a writer is a kind of splendour, not of the spirit, nor of the mind, but of the senses and the instincts."

On the whole the book is disappointing. Hasty, ragged, over-emphatic writing spoils the beauty of the details, and the imposed, rigid philosophical system crushes out the substance.

The Plumed Serpent (1926)

Charles Marriott writes "All through Mr. Lawrence's later fiction *Kangaroo, The Ladybird, St. Mawr,* and now this novel of contemporary Mexico, we have the odd feeling that he is looking behind him for something that is really ahead. That the complete unity which he, through his principal characters, desires may have existed at an earlier stage of man's development." Katherine Anne Porter adds, "This book is a confession of faith, of mystical philosophy of D.H. Lawrence, Mexico, the Indians, the cult of the Aztec god Quetzalcoatl—the Plumed Serpent—all these are pretexts, symbols made to the measure of his preoccupations. It seems only incidentally a novel, in spite of the perfection of its form; it is a record of a pilgrimage that was, that must have been, a devastating experience."

This is one of the three leadership novels. As the last leadership novel *The Plumed Serpent* could not be a success, though Lawrence said that it was his best.

Frank Kermode adds this, "Few have agreed with Lawrence's own opinion—in any case quickly given up—that *The Plumed Serpent* was his best novel. It did what a novel could do, without totally collapsing, to feed his metaphysical fury and his fantasies of world decadence restored by sexual reformation and leadership. Narrative is pushed almost to the limit of self-absorbed prophetic sermonising; it survives, but by comparison with the work of the great period it is inelastic and deficient in its own kind of life."

Mr. Noon (1984)

This is an autobiographical novel – more or less a sequel to *Sons and Lovers* – about a Nottinghamshire school teacher who like Lawrence himself in 1912, travels to Europe and falls in love with a German aristocrat who is then unfaithful to him. The first part of the novel appeared as a short story in 1934; the second and larger part was never published and the manuscript disappeared for many years. *Mr. Noon* was first published in its entirety in hardback in 1984, and was widely hailed as a major literary event. David Lodge says, "It crackles with energy. It is a reckless, risky book that makes much of our own contemporary fiction seem over-anxious to please and impress. Its belated appearance is cause for gratitude and celebration." According to Antony Burgess, "Brilliantly comic, pathetic and very sharp in its observation of provincial mores before the First World War... *Mr Noon* is, with all its faults – most of them willed, perverse and very Lawrentian–quite entrancing."

Mr. Noon Part I evoked a mixed response in 1934. Most reviewers had strong and contradictory views about it: several thought it very good, others that it should have remained unpublished. Those reviewers who were using the American edition concluded that the fragment dated from the pre-war period.

The contemporary reviews were mixed. The reviewer in *The Times* suggested that *Mr. Noon* "must really be read rather as a curiosity" and quoted the last few paragraphs as an example of "its odd button-holing, interjectory style". Pruette commented on Lawrence's "providing his own Greek chorus of what is meant for sardonic comment, but is actually nothing but rather vulgar and unamusing carping." Dilys Powell in the *London Mercury* noted that part I "has none of the signs of Lawrence's maturity except a certain truculence in mood and patches of a cynical devil-may-care manner." But the lighter tone appealed to other reviewers as realistic. The scene and the talk is as exactly reproduced as in a Bennett novel, and produces an effect of realism. Currie Cabot in the *Saturday Review of Literature* was complimentary about its "deft satire" and noted that *Mr Noon* "reveals a Lawrence who might have been, if he had so chosen, a dryly humorous, inimitable observer of surfaces of those flaws and trivialities of human nature which are the stuff of which 'characters' are composed."

Lindeth Vasey writes, "The reviewer in *The Times Literary Supplement* did note *Mr Noon*'s relationship with *The Lost Girl* in date and one character; he felt it belonged to a time when Lawrence 'seemed deliberately striving for a wider popularity.' If *Mr Noon* had been published immediately after *Lost Girl*, reviewers could have been expected to notice the similarities in tone and setting, and they would probably have reacted to the later novel as they had done to the earlier: The Lost Girl received mediocre reviews in England, with some reviewers criticising it as a throwback to early writing, while those who liked it did not think it was the author at his best. Only a few had been extremely enthusiastic, mostly in the USA."

4

D.H. Lawrence's Short Novels and Short Stories

Lawrence wrote many books of short novels and short stories. As in the case of Joseph Conrad, he expanded a short story into a short novel, sometimes.

Lawrence's Short Novels

Lawrence's short novels are *The Fox* (1919), *The Captain's Doll* (1921), *The Ladybird* (1922), *St Mawr* (1925), *The Princess, The Virgin and the Gipsy,* and *The Man Who Died* (*The Escaped Cock*, 1927).

Monroe Engel in his article on Lawrence's short novels writes that "Lawrence's stories have a richness and intricacy—purposeful, and also nearly accidental virtues—that summary cannot suggest. What should be suggested is the achievement not only to form—which often appears to be lacking in the long novels of the same period—but of something very close to formula. There is a bold repetition—often with increasing evidence of intention—of certain elements, principally: the objective and fluent style; analogy—generally animal analogy; disordered relationships; the opposition of traditional love and a new kind of relationship between the sexes, dramatized by a contest between these forces for a neutral beloved; the use of magic; and the visionary ending, associated with the emergent theme of resurrection, and given final importance in *The Man who Died*. Altogether, these short novels constitute an extraordinary body of imaginatively realized thesis fiction."

As Lawrence wrote to Edward Garnett he experienced all this in his fiction. Like Joyce and Woolf he got away from "the old stable age of the character" and made his characters fall into "some other rhythmic form." The extremity of Lawrence's views required highly formal expression to be in any way acceptable, and the artifice of these short novels is nearly as formal as ballet or ritual dance. These stories would not have made Mr. Lawrence's reputation, but they sustain it.

D.H. Lawrence is one of the few best modernist English writers. He is a multifarious personality, a prolific writer. We may study him fruitfully as a novelist, short story writer, poet and critic. In a way, he is a psychological thinker. Lawrence as a modern writer stands alongside Henry James, Joseph Conrad, James Joyce, Virginia Woolf and E.M. Forster.

Lawrence is a major novelist with *Sons and Lovers*, *The Rainbow, Women in Love, Lady Chatterley's Lovers, The Aaron's Rod, Kangaroo* and *The Plumed Serpent.* His minor novels for example *The White Peacock. The Trespasser* and *The Lost Girl* can be neglected. Yet his minor novels or novella sometimes the lengthened short stories include *St Mawr. The Man Who Died, The Fox* and others. Monroe Engel observes, "Lawrence's short novels are a special and sustained achievement belonging roughly to the last decade of his life." It is of course not clear at precisely what point the long short story becomes the short novel, but with *The Fox* (1918-19: revised and lengthened in 1921), not only does Lawrence writer a story that is appreciably longer than his earlier stories (about three times the length of "The Prussian Officer," for example), but he establishes certain themes—and, more peculiarly, certain patterns and devices for vivifying these themes—that become generic for his longer stories.

A study of Lawrence's minor fiction is what follows now.

The Fox (1918-19)

The Fox is a kind of a comedy. Two girls star in the story. They have some fowls and cattle, and a fox carries the fowls in the dark. There is some disorder in the narration. Here the fox represents an escape in the girl's life.

The Fox, sounds commonplace enough in outline. Two young women who have been land girls during the war run a farm together. One night a young soldier calls by chance at the farm. He stays and finally courts the younger of the two women. Her partner is furiously jealous and tries to dissuade her from marrying him. To his despair, she almost succeeds in doing so. He returns to the farm, and half accidentally, half purposely, in felling a tree for them, he manages to kill the obstacle who stands between him and the woman he longs for. Actually the story is very strange; it moves, as does real life or as does the best sort of lyrical poetry, upon two or three planes or consciousness at once: the result is an extreme richness and intricacy of texture.

The two girl-farmers in *The Fox* are intensely real, closely and humorously studied, and so is the willful, laconic boy who breaks in on them. Again there is a touch of fantasy in the fox's spell, which merges, however, in a sense of the oneness between man and nature. The atmosphere round the farm is drawn close with a physical tenseness—the attraction is inexplicable, painful, almost terrible, and brings a tragedy.

The Captain's Doll (1921)

This is a story about beauty. Again, the meaningful working of the story depends on an overt analogy—between Captain Hepburn and the doll portrait that Hannele makes of him, but doesn't make him into. For this time the analogy is a kind of anti-analogy—the doll is what Captain Hepburn must not become: "any *woman*, today," the Captain says, "no matter how much she loves her man—she could start any minute and make a doll of him. And the doll would be her hero; and her hero would be no more than her doll."

Again, as in *The Fox*, the story starts with disordered relationships, and the action concerns the choice a neutral person, Hannele, must make between conventional love and a new kind of relationship.

The Captain's Doll is an original and unexpected stroke of Mr. Lawrence's writings. And he keeps the eye of a poet; wonderful, among all his scenes and settings, is the mountain walk here, and the glacier.

The Captain's Doll, the scene of which is Cologne during the British occupation, is done in the comic spirit—for all that it contains a violent death. Countess Hannele and Captain Hepburn have been lovers, but her conscious regard for him is expressed in a doll. After the death of his wife he asks Hannele to marry him, to honour and obey but not to love. "All this about love," he said, "is very confusing and very complicated."

The Ladybird (1921-22)

Penguin published Lawrence's collection of novella called *The Ladybird* in 1921. The book had three stories. *The Ladybird, The Fox* and *The Captain's Doll.*

The story *The Ladybird* floats like a romance as an unsigned reviewer observed in *Times Literary Supplement* in 1923.

In *The Ladybird* (1921-22), Lawrence told Middleton Murry he had "the quick of a new thing." The "quick" lies chiefly in the character of the Bohemian Count Dionys, who is a resurrected man in a more intellectual, varied, and charming way than Hepburn. Dionys, of course, is purposefully named; but he is the magic Pan, not the vulgar Bacchus.

Again, as in the two previous stories, there is a contest for the neutral soul: the soul of Lady Daphine. But the forces in this contest are not in each case single figures. Lady Beveridge and Basil are a team—the fully civilized or naturally repressed characters, bound to the old civilized kind of selfless love. This is in contrast to Lord Beverdige and Lady Daphine, who are unnaturally repressed, that is, in opposition to their own natures.

Perhaps the most remarkable scene in the active contest is the long debate on love between Count Dionys and Basil, the champion of conventional love, who has told Daphne that his love for her now is a sacrament, and that he considers himself an eager sacrifice to her, and could happily die on her altar. These champions of different attitudes toward love carry on their debate with Daphne sitting between them, finding it curious that while her sympathy was with the Count, it was her husband whose words she believed to be true.

The very nature of them makes the stories obscure in argument. They are for telling at length. In *The Ladybird,* Lady Daphne Apsley, not unhappily married, but with repressions, and Count Psanek belong to each other only in the dark. Their conscious selves are, if not slightly hostile, at least ironically polite. He has a philosophy of the matter, expressed with some not very convincing references to Egyptology and the 'ladybird' which is the crest of his family, but it is a commentary rather than an explanation.

Charles Marriott observes about the collection: "Different as they are in character, incident, and setting, all three stories, *The Ladybird, The Fox,* and *The Captain's Doll*, deal with the same inexhaustible theme-the conflict between that compromise of habit and circumstance which is conduct, and that inner meaning of the individual which is life."

St Mawr (1924)

Again, of course, the story is on a central analogy between a human being and an animal. But the horse St. Mawr defines Rico not by similarity but by contrast.

Rico is all fraudulent play, never the real thing. Mr. Leavis has pointed to the significance of his playing at being an artist. Even his sexuality is bogus. His marriage with Lou is "a marriage...without sex"; and so there is brutal irony in the circumstance that he wears a ring, sent him by a female admirer, bearing a "lovely intaglio of Priapus under an apple bough." What Lou requires—and Rico is not at all—is a Dionys, the Pan of the dinner table conversation with the painter Cartwright.

This is particularly true of the long conversation between Lewis and Mrs Witt during the cross-country ride they take together to save St. Mawr. The ride culminates with Lewis's refusal of Mrs. Witt's offer of marriage; but before this offer, which ends all exchanges between them. Lewis has shown himself another of the Lawrence characters endowed with other-worthy magic. Mrs. Witt, who in her relations with every other man she ever knew had "conquered his country," feels that Lewis looks "at her as if from out of another country, a country of which he was an inhabitant, and where she had never been."

Monroe Engel observes, "*St. Mawr* is an ambitious story. In the disaster in which St. Mawr is disgraced, he is the figure of unrepressed man ridden by repressed man, Rico. The accident occurs, not fortuitously, when the horse shies at a dead snake. Ant-supporting the same suggestions—this precipitates for Lou an overwhelming vision of evil."

The horse St Mawr has ancestors, notably in the *Bush*, and in the apocalyptic animals of *The Rainbow*. Yet the figuration is new. Lou's marriage to Rico, the disoriented American woman to the Anglo-Australian hollow man, is also of a familiar type, the exhaustingly nervous, frictional, peaceless union. What distinguishes it is the density with which Rico's half-life as man and artist and friend is rendered; and his relationship with St Mawr, which is one of hatred between primitive male blood-knowledge and the highly strung parody of maleness that the man represents. The narrative shows how the different, brutal life of the horse—so insistently representative of "another world," the non-human world of Pan—damages Rico and changes Lou's world to one of separateness in an inhuman landscape.

Karmode observes, "The conclusion of *St. Mawr* is one of Lawrence's most fully imagined pieces. The landscape is more splendid and awful than a man-god, a saviour; beautiful and brutal, it has horrors which are not those of civilization and its 'Augean stables of metallic filth.' On a ranch subject to natural catastrophes—drought, packrats, disease—Lou passes beyond Law and Love, far beyond decadent sex sensation, choosing instead the wild America where 'a wild spirit wants me.' Her aspirations are questioned by her sckeptical mother; but the mother is on the side of death, Lou on the more terrible side of life."

Mr. Sherman thinks *St Mawr* carries on, from there, Mr. Lawrence's "criticism of life." It carries on his moving representation of the soul's fiery struggle for independent self-hood, for individuality. In this case the chief protagonists are women. From the first Mr. Lawrence has been a feminist—of a sort.

The magic and visionary qualities emerging through all the preceding short novels, dominate the middle and end of *St. Mawr*.

The final pages –marred only at times by Lawrence's preachy vein—give an affecting picture of the beauty and effort of man's attempt to bring order into chaos.

The Princess

The Princess which Lawrence wrote immediately after 'St Mawr' is in a way its negative. During their stay in London the previous December in 1925 the Lawrences had stayed with Catherine and Donald Carswell, whom they had met before the war. Catherine told Lawrence of a novel she had in mind: "The theme had been suggested to me by reading of some savages who took a baby girl, and that they might rear her into a goddess for themselves, brought her up on a covered river boat, tending her in all respects, but never letting her mix with her kind and leading her to believe that she was herself no mortal, but a goddess." Lawrence was fired by the idea, and offered to collaborate. Indeed, he sketched an outline the same day. Catherine felt inadequate, and left the story to Lawrence, who later completed it as 'The Princess.'

Keith Sagar accounts the story as follows: According to his original outline, Lawrence had at first intended to begin with the story of the girl's parents—material he later dropped. After the death of the mother, leaving a baby girl, the outline continues:

"Then it seems to him [the father] the mother was not mortal. She was a mysterious woman from the faery, and the child, he secretly believes, is one of the Tuatha De Danaan. This idea he gradually inculcates into the people round him, and into the child herself. It steals over them all gradually, almost unawares."

The girl accepts from the start a difference between herself and the rest of people. She does not feel quite mortal. Men are only men to her: she is of another race, the Tuatha De Danaan. She doesn't talk about it: nobody talks about it. But there it is, tacit, accepted.

Her father hires a poor scholar to be her tutor, and she has an ordinary education. But she has no real friends. There is no one of her race. Sometimes she goes to Glasgow, to Edinburgh, to London with her father. The world interests her, but she doesn't belong to it. She is a little afraid of it. It is not of her race.

When she is 17 her father is suddenly killed, and she is alone, save for her tutor. She has an income of about three hundred a year. She decides to go to London. The war has broken out; she becomes a nurse. She nurses men, and knows their wounds and their necessities. But she tends them as if they were lovable animals. Their blood is not her blood, their needs are not the needs of her race.

Men fall in love with her, and that is terrible to her. She is waiting for one of her own race. Her tutor supports her in the myth. Wait, he says, wait for the Tuatha De Danaan to send you your mate. You can't mate with a man. Wait till you see a demon between his brows.

At last she saw him in the street. She knew him at once, knew the demon between his brows. And she was afraid. For the first time in her life, she was afraid of her own nature, the mystery of herself. Because it seemed to her that her race, the Tuatha, had come back to destroy the race of men. She was terrified of her own destiny. She wanted never again to see the man with the demon.

So for a long time she did not see him again. And then her fear that she would never see him any more was deeper than anything else. Whatever she wanted, she wanted her own destiny with him, let happen what might.

It is not at all clear from this outline whether the woman's destiny is to be an escape into a more real world, 'the man with the demon between his brows being the 'mystic new man' who will perform for her the function performed for Lou by St Mawr, or whether it is to be suicidal, like that of the Princess or the woman who rode away. Certainly, the other world from which St Mawr is a messenger could easily have been linked to that of the Tuatha De Danaan, the pre-Christian nature deities of

Ireland, as it is linked by Lewis to Celtic folklore. The outline could have gone either way, towards rebirth or madness.

Thus Catherine Carswell's story could be seen as the germ of all three stories Lawrence wrote in the summer of 1924. Her sense of what makes her different from other people is her sanity, her openness to life, her deep need for a meaningful relationship with the living universe.

But the story itself is open to life: we cannot predict what will happen to Lou. In a sense, however, the very fact that she has answered the call is her salvation, although Lawrence was well aware of the dangers of cutting oneself off from one's fellow men and retiring to some wilderness place. It could be escapist. It could be a temptation to egotism, narcissism or solipsism; a way of closing oneself to life until one becomes a sealed monad and goes mad like the Princess, or dies of it like the man who loved islands.

The Virgin and the Gipsy

In September 1925, Lawrence left America for the last time, to spend the remaining five years of his life in Europe. At last he was reconciled with Frieda's daughters. Barby, in particular, stayed often with the Lawrences in Spotorno, and told Lawrence many stories of her life in the Weekley household. In January 1926 he wrote *The Virgin and the Gipsy*, based largely on those stories.

The Virgin and the Gipsy as a short novel, is more like a conventional novel than the other novelettes, full of characters, family and social relationships presented in scenes and moral judgements evinced through a finely modulated ironic tone, like a more direct, barbed and colloquial Jane Austen.

The mode is realistic, with no dominant symbol, emblem or myth, except insofar as the gipsy himself may be regarded as a symbol. Indeed, he functions on two levels, like St Mawr. He is a real gipsy, hawking his brooms, saucepans and copperware, with several brats to maintain; but for Yvette he is much more than that. He is messenger from a world free from all the stifling hypocrisies of her home.

According to Keith Sagar the integrity of the story can be measured by the extent to which it does not fulfil the expectations aroused by its perhaps unfortunate title. The relationship between virgin and gipsy never becomes overtly sexual. We do not know, and it does not matter, whether at the end she is still a virgin or not.

Nor is the gipsy blown up to figure as a mystic new man, a man with a demon between his brows or a noble savage, except to a slight degree in Yvette's adolescent imagination. Lawrence beautifully captures that phase of a girl's life—the infuriating selfishness, the sulks and outbursts of revolt, the general vagueness and wryly romantic longings.

Again, the ending is open. It is unlikely Yvette will ever see her gipsy again; certainly she pins no hopes upon him. There is no doubt much conflict and suffering ahead for her; but she has found the courage to live her own life, and is unlikely to let go of that.

The Man Who Died (The Escaped Cock, 1927)

Lawrence called this "The Escaped Cock" – a title that stresses on analogy. The theme of the resurrected man (and the Pan-Christ) had occurred in several of the other short novels, in different degrees of importance. Dionys is a resurrected man, coming back to life after being near death, and after considering himself dead and wishing his death. So too is Captain Hepburn in *The Captain's Doll*. In *St. Mawr*, Lou Witt—writing to her mother—says she wishes no more marriages, and understands "why Jesus said: *Noli me tangere*. Touch me not, I am not yet ascended unto the Father.... That is all my cry to all the world." And this, of course, is the repeated cry of the man who had died.

Frank Karmode calls this story a parable of rebirth. Like *St Mawr* it is a more finished work of fiction. The plot is this: A peasant's cock escapes its leash: Jesus awakes in the tomb. Lawrence's *noli tangere* now returns to its source; the reborn Jesus, "beyond loneliness," returning to the life of nature after the disillusion of death. He captures the cock and lodges with the peasant. The cock, and the colours and vitality of the sprint landscape, persuade him of the "surge of life." He encounters Mary Magdalene ("Don't touch me, Madeleine") and tells her that his mission is over, that his business is now his "own, single life." He remembers his own past complicity in treachery and egotism, and looks forward only to meeting a woman "who can lure my risen body, yet leave me my aloneness," the aloneness of the cock he has carried with him. Meanwhile he preserves himself from the touch of others, the egotists, fearers of death. In the second part of the tale he meets a priestess of Isis, her reborn husband. Thus "the man who had died and the woman of the pure search" come together; "I have risen naked and branded. But if I am naked enough for this contact, I have not died in vain. Before I was clogged." At last he rises into life, and is ready again to touch and be touched. When the priestess has conceived he withdraws: "I have sowed the seed of my life and my resurrection."

This remarkable parable is the best demonstration of a belief always held by Lawrence, and a good belief for a writer: that rebirth is into this life, and that eternity is the fullness of this life-what he sometimes called its fourth dimension.

Lawrence was dying. What he thought of death he put into *The Man Who Died* and into such poems as 'Bavarian Gentians' and 'The Ship of Death.' He wrote:

> All that matters is to be at one with the living God to be
> a creature in the house of the God of Life.

The passage of oblivion which the dead must take, and the untouched apartness of that death-in-life which is the preparation for rebirth, come together. *The Man Who Died* is an assertion of life in death; so is the work of Lawrence as a whole, which is why people like to say, inadequately, that even if he was on the side of many things they dislike; he was also on the side of life, of creation against dissolution. He speaks of a New Age, calling it 'Third Age.'

Lawrence's Short Stories

First published: *The Prussian Officer and Other Stories*, 1914; *England, My England*, 1922; *The Ladybird*, 1923; *St. Mawr, together with The Princess*, 1925; *The Woman Who Rode Away*, 1928; *Love Among the Haystacks*, 1930; *The Lovely Lady and Other Stories*, 1933; *A Modern Lover*, 1934

The short stories of D.H. Lawrence are many and varied; in the complete edition they fill three volumes. If anyone of these stories can be singled out as central to the art of Lawrence, however, one must invariably choose 'The Prussian Officer.'

Lawrence's first three stories were written for a local Christmas competition. Unlike the other two, the winning story, 'A Prelude'(first published in *Nottinghamshire Guardian*, 1907) was left unrevised. It is simple, rounded, and prettily sentimental. In 1907, when Lawrence was 22, the *Nottinghamshire Guardian* offered a prize of three pounds for the best Christmas story. There were three categories, an Amusing Adventure, a Legend, and an Enjoyable Christmas, and Lawrence wrote a story in each: 'The White Stocking', 'Legend', and' A Prelude to a Happy Christmas'. One person was allowed to enter only one story, but Lawrence cheated by J1ersuading Louie Burrows to submit 'The White Stocking' in her name and Jessie Chambers 'A Prelude' in hers, while Lawrence himself submitted 'Legend'. 'A Prelude' won and was published in the *Nottinghamshire Guardian* on 7 December 1907.

More strange, vivid, and elaborately constructed is 'A Fragment of Stained Glass.' Told by a vicar with archaeological interests, in explanation of a passage in imaginary fifteenth-century records which described the Devil's face 'flaming red like fire in a basket' and glowering down on the choir, the story is centred in Beauvale Priory, the main character being a mad serf who in his rage has killed a horse, and set fire to the stables in revenge for his punishment.

'The White Stocking,' the third of these stories, was probably extended. It evolved from an incident which happened to Lawrence's mother before her marriage, when she went to a ball at Nottingham Castle, and found she had taken a white stocking in mistake for a handkerchief. The main scene is a Christmas Eve dance at the Castle, but the story is one of jealousy which leads to a brutal quarrel, from the deception and bravado of a young wife who does not wish to upset her husband or renounce the attentions of a man to whom she was helplessly drawn at the ball. The narrative is neatly unfolded, and terrible in its probability from first to last.

'Goose Fair' (1909) another Nottingham story, is set in a period of depression which Mrs. Lawrence remembered. It was written in 1909, two years after the original of 'The White Stocking,' and has a slight similarity of construction, Lawrence starting at a point midway in the story and creating suspense.

By the summer of 1911 Lawrence had written several stories. The writing of the early part of *Sons and Lovers* suggested some, the greatest (and probably the first) being 'Odour of Chrysanthemums'(1911). The places in the story are actual, and the tragedy is based on that of Lawrence's Aunt Polly; the main scenes are imagined in a cottage not far form where his grandfather lived. To some extent Lawrence owed his inspiration to Synge's 'Riders to the Sea,' but it was the lively vigour of the opening description which convinced Ford Madox Ford that Lawrence had genius. The story echoes to the infinite, with Lawrence's conviction that division in life leads to eternal apartness.

The moral poverty of middle-class values is the theme of the more extended 'Daughters of the Vicar.' F.P. Pinion thinks the conciseness and thrust with which Lawrence presents the effect of socio-economic factors on feeling and personality are remarkable from the outset.

One story that serves to indicate this fact is 'Daughters of the Vicar.' Here there is no elemental confrontation of force against force, yet the opposing principles are the same. Love opposes hatred, fertility revolts against frigidity. The Reverend Mr. Lindley is the vicar of the story; he harms no one directly, but the terms of his life prove to be damaging in the extreme to those with whom he lives. He is what may be called a mechanical Christian; he tends his parish with care, respect, and objectivity. Yet he is careful at all times to maintain a distance not only between his social class and that of his coal-mining parishioners, but between his sense of self and their very identities. The story is as same as 'The Prussian Officer' both in its theme and treatment.

The Reverend Mr. Lindley is not only a fierce snob but also a person devoted to extinguishing the unconscious needs and passions of all life. In this he may be compared to another moral invalid, Sir Clifford Chatterley. His household is a monstrosity: his wife becomes a neurotic invalid, he himself is a kind of machine, and his daughters are slowly squeezed into the inhuman mold of his design. They enter, unwillingly to be sure, the same life of obedience to all the codes, rules, customs, and negations he imposes. Yet one daughter, like the orderly of 'The Prussian Officer,' breaks through to reality. In this story too the effort is not without its cost. She falls in love with a collier and, in a scene that is a triumph of domestic hatred, she is exiled from her family and her class to live with him. But the severance is a kind of liberation. Her mother cries out that the daughter thinks only of herself, while the daughter thinks at this moment of the love that has enabled her to do just that. It is love in action, she realizes, that has made her awaken. In this case, as in *Lady Chatterley's Lover,* the protagonists are forced to live for a time under the normal conditions of society, circumstances which, conceived in terms of rules and regulations, carried out under the sanctions of family, caste, and class, reduce individuals to extensions of withered ideals. It is love that brings them back to individual life—not the traditional love of things spiritual, but, in Lawrence's cosmology, the love that is primitive, dark, and bodily. They awaken to life after they awaken to their bodies.

The Croydon stories often show pleasing, colourful observations, but their general tone is artificial. 'Lessford's Rabbits' (*Phoenix*, 1968) and 'A Lesson on a Tortoise' (*Phoenix*, 1968) suggest that there were times when Lawrence the teacher looked round desperately for something to write about. More unconvincing is 'A Fly in the Ointment' (*New Statesman,* 1913) in which he imagines writing to Muriel (Jessie Chambers) after receiving primroses from her. They had made him dreamy and vacant all day at school, and he was oblivious of everything around him when he finished a letter to her late at night, to be confronted by a housebreaker in his landlady's kitchen. 'The Old Adam' *(A Modern Lover,* 1934) has the same Croydon setting, and is undoubtedly based on the jealousy Lawrence aroused in his landlord Mr. Jones. The Carnal symbolism of the iris recalls a scene in *Sons and Lovers*.

'The Witch à la Mode' (*Lovat Dickinson's Magazine*, 1934) is more subtle, and there is an appropriateness in its cold artificiality, its subject being Lawrence's relationship with Helen Corke.

Shortly 'before the death of his mother, in December 1910, Lawrence had ended his long engagement to Jessie Chambers and become engaged to Louie Burrows. He continued to see Jessie, and also formed an intimate relationship with Helen Corke in London. But Lawrence was not able to bring any of these relationships on to a satisfactory sexual footing. The frustration contributed to the breakdown in his health at the end of 1911 which forced him to leave the teaching profession. Lawrence's overwrought state at this time is evident in both 'The Old Adam' and 'The Witch a la Mode.'

Perhaps the humour of 'Delilah and Mr Bircumshaw' (*Virginia Quarterly,* 1940) is too near the serious side of married life to be popular. The husband is a mild bully, and his wife becomes "a little, uncanny machine" when she and her friend engage in ridiculing him. He can cow one woman, but he is afraid of two, and goes off to bed, hoping to inflict "the penalties of ill-humour on his insolent wife." Mr. Bircumshaw is a bank clerk with 'unspent energy turning sour in his veins'; he is degenerating, and there is nothing at the end of the story to suggest he will change.

'Second Best' is neatly contrived, with an eye to the detail of rural background; for its narrative it relies on a rather unpleasant analogy which creates a kind of symbolism.

A rarefied quality emanates from 'The Shadow in the Rose Garden.' It is a haunting story of a woman who married below her, and goes with her husband for a seaside holiday, privately to see the garden where she had been courted by the rector's son, an officer who had left the army. She returns to her husband, "absent, torn, without any being of her won." He insists on an explanation, and is filled with hate; when her story is concluded, the hate gas gone but shock has reduced their relationship to a sate of impersonality.

Strike conditions when Lawrence returned to Eastwood in February 1912 prompted a number of sketches, the most moving being 'A Sick Collier,' the story of a devoted young husband who suffers from a mining accident during the national strike.

'Strike-Pay' is in a lighter vein. It begins with an amusing scene as strike-money is handed out by a Union official in the Primitive Methodist Chapel. A group of miners walk to Nottingham to see the football match, and ride on pit ponies in a field between Nuttall and Bulwell as a diversion on the way. One of them finds he has lost his-sovereign dole, but the other three give him two shillings each, and they go to the match. When he returns home and hands over five-and-sixpence, it is not his wife but his mother-in-law he has to fear. After giving him a piece of his mind, she sails out to her other daughter's, and his wife asks if he would like his dinner warmed up. She is not a meek woman, but he is *her* man, not her mother's.

'Her Turn' (*Saturday Westminster Gazette*, 1913) may be based on some occurrence the truth of which is a little stranger than fiction. A woman of character shows her husband that, though he is on strike-pay, he must remember her housekeeping money. He restrains his anger; he has a heart, is tender to his doves and tortoise, and writes poetry. 'The Miner at Home' (*Nation*, 1912) is a more serious satire, and presents a scene familiar to Lawrence from his early years, the mother washing her husband's back as she tries to manage the children. 'The Miner at Home' and 'Her Turn' were occasioned by the strike situation of February 1912, and 'Delilah and Mr Bircumshaw' was written about the same time.

'The Christening' is a story of ironies. Hilda, a teacher at the British School and the eldest of the Rowbotham sister, calls at the baker's to buy cakes, unaware that the baker's man is the father of her unmarried sister's child. She feels responsible for the conduct of her family, and means to "keep up the prestige of her house in spite of blows." The child is to be baptized at home; there is a special high tea to mark the occasion. The larger irony is with the aged father who prays at great length after the christening, and asks the Lord to be the Father of the child, and take away "the conceit that our children are ours."

In 'A Modern Lover' (originally a book of short stories published in 1934) and 'The Shades of Spring' Lawrence returns to his love of Jessie Chambers, combining the Haggs Farm setting with fiction. The first opens with colourful, highly figurative description, provides an interesting list of the lovers' reading, refers to their "dreadful strenuousness," and stresses the hope of the lover, on his return from London, that they will begin again-living, not speculating and poetizing together.

'The Shades of Spring' is mainly fictional, with much natural description. The returning lover is married, and the girl is far more assured than he had known her. It was she, he says, who wanted him tc be highly educated, when she tells him that he cast her away on finding he had no further use for her. She is now in love with a gamekeeper. The story has a sting in its tail.

'Love Among the Haystacks' (originally a book of short stories published in 1930) is woven round an incident which took place when Lawrence assisted the Chambers in the two fields by the vicarage where Baron von Hube lived above Greasley Church. His Polish origin suggested the lively Polish governess who creates the jealously on which the fiction is founded. The movements of the stackers are conveyed in varying rhythms, Geoffrey's expressing his feelings; but the finest features of the story are based on scenic memories, in sunshine and twilight, from some of the happiest days in Lawrence's life.

'A Chapel Among the Mountains' (first published in the volume *Love among the Haystacks,* 1930) and 'A Hay Hut among the Mountains' are predominantly autobiographical interest. Four other stories arising from Lawrence's elopement with Mrs Weekley are related to the German army. As the narration suggests, the central story of 'Once' could have been told by Frieda when she and Lawrence were in the Tyrol; it may derive from her own experience, for 'Anita' is "an Answer" to the young officer who draws an armful of roses from under his cloak and throws them over her as she lies on her bed, just as Frieda is 'the call' and Lawrence "the answer" in the 'Bei Hennef.' Details in the setting are obviously fictitious, and there is much altogether that looks like the literary décor of invention.

'The Mortal Coil' (*Seven Arts,* 1917) provides a finer story, from an experience of Frieda's father when he was a young officer. Lawrence thought it first-class and one of his 'purest creations' when he made a copy of it. The young officer of the story has nothing to live for, since he has lost his honour by incurring large gambling debts; his mistress Marta, the daughter of a tradesman, cannot understand his lack of resolve. As he sits watching a candle flame, he realizes it is a "travelling flood, flowing swiftly from the source into the darkness." Marta loves him, and his faith restored. Keith Sagar writes, 'The Mortal Coil,' written in Italy before the war and based on an experience of Frieda's father, was rewritten in October 1916. The protagonist, Friedeburg, like Skrebensky in *The Rainbow* and Gerald Crich in *Women in Love*, suffers and causes suffering because he lacks the Lawrentian strengths—independence and integrity. Nevertheless Lawrence writes of him with an unusual depth of inwardness, understanding and compassion. Although in this story Lawrence specifically exculpates God, we seem to be in a Hardy like world where tragedy, oblivious of human values, hunts down the truly living and leaves the dead to inherit the earth. Lawrence called 'The Mortal Coil' "a first-class story, one of my purest creations" yet it was never included in any of the collections of short stories published in his lifetime.

Lawrence had reason to remember the fortifications at Metz, and the experience of the solider who had no head for heights is excitingly told in the first part of 'The Thorn in the Flesh.'

By contrast the psychological vividness of 'The Prussian Officer' (formerly called 'Honour and Arms.' This was a book of stories published in 1914) is sustained throughout; Lawrence thought it the best story he had written. It is highly imaginary, the starting-point being Frieda's recollections what she had heard from a corporal friend who told her about bullying in the army, and how he hated it. The original title was 'Honour and Arms.' Lawrence was annoyed when Garnett changed it and used the new title for his first published collection of stories.

The best of Lawrence's short story 'The Prussian Officer' begins under the aspect of nature; its protagonists are soldiers moving down a German country road surrounded by thickets of trees, ripe and heavy crops, green meadows, and tall black pine woods. Everywhere there is a sense of ripening, and the men are at the mercy of a harsh and brilliant sunlight. The orderly and the Captain are the principals of this story: the former moves slowly and painfully across our field of vision on foot, the latter moves quickly and savagely on horseback. The Captain has the look of a man at odds with life. He is solitary, bitter, a figure of the soldier for whom there is no reality but war. Significantly, he is unmarried. Although now and then he finds a mistress, he is sexually isolated: after the event he goes back to duty tense, hostile, and aggressive. However latent at this point, the Captain is a sexual deviate. As the story unfolds we see that he is in fact a sadist.

In decided contrast, the orderly is one of Lawrence's perfectly heterosexual heroes. He is in a sense the male counterpart of Lady Chatterley: strong, heavy, swarthy, full of animal vitality. The orderly appears to be a figure of an ideal kind, perhaps of Laurentian nature. What evidently matters about him is that he is capable of giving and sustaining love. The great difference between him-and-his isolated superior is that he is in love, or perhaps the difference may be the fact that he is capable of experiencing and inspiring love.

It is this quality which motivates the hatred of his superior. With increasing fury the Captain senses the difference between the full humanity of his orderly and his own desiccated and withdrawn being. This realization drives him to a passion of hatred, and to the action which is central to the narrative. In a passion of hatred both for the orderly and for himself, he beats the orderly furiously, kicking him until he collapses. The orderly is covered with enormous bruises but, even more pointedly, he himself experiences a kind of hatred foreign to him before that moment. From this point the action of the story really begins. In a semi-delirium of outrage and pain, under the terrific pressure of the heat of the march and his awakened hatred, the orderly attacks his superior and strangles him. The story is simply told: a principle of evil has attacked a work of nature; in turn it is destroyed. The orderly himself dies after he has proved this point.

In many of the short stories there runs this theme of the confrontation of primitive nature with civilized corruption. In these stories character serves a double function, that of realism and that of symbolism.

Lawrence's 'The Prussian Officer' reminds us Kafka's story 'In the Penal Colony.' Kafka 'In the Penal Colony' is a bit sado-masochistic. The story recounts the visit by an "explorer" or "voyager" to a tropical penal settlement where an officer is keen to demonstrate his instrument of punishment, called "the harrow." "Whatever commandment the prisoner has disobeyed is written upon his body by the harrow," the officer explains. Punishment is determined without fuss; there is no trial and the sentence is decided arbitrarily: "My guiding principle is this: guilt is never to be doubted." The condemned knows neither the sentence nor even the fact that it is to be carried out. "There would be no point in announcing it to him. You see, he gets to know it in the flesh." The long-standing debate about whether Kafka foresaw the fate of the Jews in Nazi Europe is revived by this story.

Lawrence's feat in transmitting his sensations is comparable to Stepehn Crane's in *The Red Badge of Courage*. Hyperaesthetic effects vary from near to far, from the knocking which announces the tapping of a small bird overhead to the wonderlight of the mountains.

'New Eve and Old Adam' presents a situation which might be more effectively illuminated in the context of a novel. Lawrence was amused by it, although his typist thought it unworthy of him. It illustrates the battle so many married people fight, without knowing why. The new Eve seems to love protestations of love; the old Adam is restive because he has lost that pride and pleasure in his own physique which the first months of married life had given him. Each thinks the other self-seeking. In 'New Eve and Old Adam' the characters are again clearly Lawrence and Frieda, though the incident is probably fictional. The best text for Lawrence's dramatic sketch is to be found in Blake's 'The Cold and the Pebble.'

'The Primrose Path' is the last of Lawrence's pre-war stories, and reveals much in the life of his mother's brother Herbert Beardsall, the black sheep of the family. The imaginary journey from Nottingham to Watnall is a device for presenting him, as taxi-driver, face to face with the bedridden, consumptive, first wife he abandoned when he emigrated to Australia with a sentimental young woman who read Browning. His bullying manner is seen later with the girl who shares his home.

'The Thimble' (*Seven Arts,* 1917) was occasioned by the wounding of the Prime Minister's son, Herbert Asquith, early in the war. Lawrence sent the manuscript of the story to his wife Lady Cynthia Asquith for approval, confident that she would find his sketch of her "better than Sargent or Watts in paint." The next day he stressed the theme resurrection, and said that we should give up everything "so we may save the hope of a resurrection from the dead, we English, all Europe. What is the whole empire, and kingdom, save the thimble in my story?" Lawrence was trying to say in symbolic narrative what he had said in 'The Crown.'

In 'England, My England' (originally a book of stories published in 1922) Lawrence is frequently heard as a direct commentator. This is most subtle and most long composition in the book. Here two episodes stand out: the history of Joyce's crippling for life, and the vivid sensations of her father just before his death on the battlefield in Flanders. The opening presents the Meynell families at Greatham as representative of old English stock; Greatham is "secret, primitive, savage as when the Saxons first came." Joyce is Sylvia Lucas; her mother, Madeline Meyline, had married Perceval Lucas, and he, as

Egbert, is at the centre of Lawrence's satirical analysis of one class of English society. With blue, Viking-like eyes and agile figure of an English archer, he has no profession; his main interest is folklore. An inheritance of one hundred and fifty pounds a year is fatal; he busies himself, but is amateurish in everything he does. He has plenty of friends in town "of the same ineffectual sort as himself," but he prefers to ignore the world, and go his way "like a casual pilgrim down the forsaken sidetracks." For him his wife, home, and garden are everything. "The story is the story of most men and women who are married today of most men at the War, and wives at home," Lawrence wrote. An unsigned reviewer in the New York Times wrote in 1922 that the Crockham Cottage, a relic of the old England of hamlets and yeoman with its small, glowing garden scooped out in the hollow among the snake-infected commons, is an appropriate setting for all the fierce sense of suppression and bafflement and despair. The reviewer adds about this book *England, My England* (1922), which had 10 stories and about Lawrence's craft "They are not tales for those who wish merely to be amused, to read and enjoy without their own brains, these tales of Lawrence's. He is one of those writers who demand more than a little co-operation from their readers. But to those able and willing to give that cooperation England, My England will prove a fruitful and long-enduring source of pleasure."

Lawrence wrote two rather unusual stories in Cornwall at the end of 1916, after completing *Women in Love.* The story of 'Samson and Delilah' (*Virginia Quarterly*, 1940) would have appealed to Thomas Hardy, but he would have presented it with more humour. In its surprising sequence of unusual events, it is not typical of Lawrence. Perhaps, when he wrote it, he was reminded of reconciliations which followed violent quarrels with Frieda. The husband, who has been bound at Deliah's bidding and thrown out of the inn, finds that the door, which had been locked and barred, is open when he returns. He enters, and finds his wife by the kitchen fire. Having worked as a miner in Montana for nearly sixteen years, after deserting her, he has some admiration for her toughness. The happy ending is secured by the power of touch, reinforced by the news that the husband has brought home over a thousand pounds.

The admixture of comedy at the end contrasts with the romanticism of the second story, 'The Horse Dealer's Daughter' (*The Miracle*) which Lawrence preferred. His brief description shows that its first title was 'The Miracle.' The setting is Eastwood, and the original of the Pervins' home is that of 'The Hollies.' The doctor had been irresistibly fascinated by the girl whose life he restores after rescuing her from the pond where she attempted suicide, but the climax depends on the complete change which takes place in him after he has undressed and dried her, and wrapped her naked in blankets before a fire. On recovering consciousness and learning what has happened, she shuffles forward on her knees, clings to him, and then, looking up with 'flaring, humble eyes of transfiguration,' murmurs in strange transport, "You love me, I know you love me, I know." He is horrified. To steady himself, he grasps her shoulder, and a flame seems to burn him. As her eyes fill with tears, he can bear no more, and holds her face to his throat; when he kisses her, he knows he has "crossed over the gulf to her." Both have entered a new life. The story is movingly narrated.

'The Blind Man,' another story of touch, was planned when Lawrence was staying with Carswells in the Forest of Dean. Isbel Pervin is based on Catherine Carswell, and her cousin Bertile Reid, on her husband Donald. The farm, which gives Isabel's husband Maurice, blinded and disfigured in Flanders, a real joy through contacts with life, has the charged atmosphere of the Brangwens.

Five other stories seem to have been written at Mountain Cottage, Middleton, Derbyshire. 'You Touched Me' is rather sketchy, and has all the air of a fabricated, conventional plot with a Lawrentian ingredient. The setting is Bromley House, Lynncroft, Eastwood; and the crucial turn of events depends less on the power of touch than on the despotism of a father who threatens to disinherit his daughters unless the eldest marries his adopted son Hadrian (who, with the indomitable courage of a rat, seems to fore shadow Henry in 'The Fox'). But for the quirkishness of Matilda's father and his position would be untenable. Her sudden acceptance of him is unmotivated, unless one assumes that the power of touch is magical. F.B. Pinion says Lawrence fails to give the story inherent probability.

Shortly after finishing 'The Blind Man,' Lawrence visited his sister Ada at Ripley, leaving the train in Butterley, where he saw the flamelurid spectacle which invests the opening of 'Fanny and Annie'. Other impressions, from his walk into Ripley, enter this rather tragic story of 'second best.' It reaches a climax when Harry, Fanny's first love whom she has returned to marry, is denounced in chapel, at the end of the harvesc anthem in which he has sung solo, by the mother of the promiscuous Annie. The narrative loses none of its cogency, even if one ignores the dubious Lawrentian nub that Harry's kisses of long ago had lived in Annie's blood and "sent roots down into her soul." We are told she is doomed.

'Tickets, Please' is on the same theme, but is more subtle, more true to life, and the most successful of the stories written at Mountain Cottage. The most curious of the Mountain Cottage stories is 'Wintry Peacock.' It developed from Lawrence's dream of a young blue peacock which fell to the ground after being mauled by two dogs in the air. It kept crying, and a woman came out of a cottage, saying it would be all right.

Lawrence wrote a short version of 'The Fox' (Lawrence expanded it into a short novel later) at Mountain Cottage. Its setting is Berkshire, like that of 'Monkey Nuts,' which belongs to the period when the Lawrences were living at Hermitage in 1919. Rather a commonplace story, 'Monkey Nuts' shows how a shy young man who had been singled out by a resolute land girl, eventually plucks up courage to withstand her domination, so suddenly and shockingly that she never appears again. His release brings him greater relief than the Armistice cease-fire.

'The Captain's Doll' (Lawrence expanded it into a short novel later and an American publisher published a book of that under this title) has amusing situations, but is unduly prolonged. "I have just got it high up in the mountains of the Tyrol, and don't quite know how to get it down without breaking its neck," Lawrence wrote. The second half is based on recollections of a holiday at Thumersbach.

'The Countess Hannele' and 'Baroness Mitchka' owe something to Frieda and her sister Johanna; the Herr Regierungsrat may be a sketch of the latter's husband, and the Scottish captain, of Donald Carswell. After losing his wife, who lived for adoration, and leaving Hannele, who made a doll of him literally, the captain becomes a changed man. When he returns, and finds his doll reduced to part of an arrangement in a still-life (which he purchases), he tells Hannele, who is engaged to the adoring Herr Regierungsrat (though he makes her feel like a queen 'in exile').

Lady Cynthia Asquith and the thimble story are adapted to strange effect in 'The Ladybird' (Lawrence expanded it into a short novel later). This story first appeared in a book of that name in 1923. Then the book had three tales: 'The Ladybird,' 'The Fox' and 'The Captain's Doll.' Lawrence expanded them into short novels later. Realistically the narrative ridiculous; allegorically, it presents the romantic mystique of Lawrence's dark love.

Although almost contemporary with 'Pan in America,' 'The Overtone' is a youthful, Swinburnian affirmation, in some of Lawrence's most poetic prose. Past and present are fused principally by images, some of which recall Virginia Woolf.

By contrast 'None of That' tells the horrible story of an American woman of tremendous will-power, who made the mistake, first of seeking a new husband to match her remarkable and epoch-making energy and character in the wrong country, and then of being captivated by the wrong man. Living for imaginative experience, she stimulated men's minds and thwarted them physically. In Cuesta, the Mexican bull-fighter, she chose a man with neither imagination nor intellect. Being physically attracted but imaginatively balked, she behaved irrationally, giving Cuesta the impression she was playing with him.

The havoc created by dissociation of mind and body in sex is even more the subject of 'The Princess' (Lawrence expanded it into a short novel later). Ethel Cane in 'None of That' is betrayed by their imagination; Dolie Urquhart, by her will.

Brought up in splendid isolation by her crazy father, she becomes imprevious as crystal. Having read Zola and Maupassant, she seemed to understand things in a cold light perfectly.

Earlier in 1924, at Kiowa Ranch, Lawrence had written 'The Woman Who Rode Away' and 'St Mawr' (Lawrence expanded it into a short novel later). The former combines impressions of the silver mines he visited with Gótzsche near Minas nuevas, Sonara (on his second journey into Mexico), with those made on an excursion with Mabel Sterne to the ceremonial cave above Arroyo Seco. The significance of the story is spiritual; it is a sustained metaphor expressing renunciation of western values. As the story is a kind of allegory, the woman who rode away is generic and anonymous. Behind 'The Overtone,' 'The Woman Who Rode Away' (Lawrence published a book of stories under this title in 1928) and the conclusion of *The Plumed Serpent* is a sense of the deadness of England which Lawrence felt in London. The spirit of revulsion rather than of laughter in which 'St Mawr' is written is centred symbolically in hoof-revolt. Dorothy Brett noticed the sheer delight of Lawrence and Frieda's indignation as he read the account of St Mawr's revenge on Rico.

Lawrence's annoyance with Murry arose partly jealously, but mainly from disagreement with his views. It finds expression in his letters and more maliciously in short stories. 'The Border Line' is based on Lawrence's visit with Frieda to Baden; it records his impressions even more vividly than 'A Letter from Germany,' with prescient hints of emergent Hitlerism. The 'border line' has various connotations: it is the war-front crossed in the Marne country; it is the boundary between future peace and war; between France and Germany; and between life and death. In Philip, Katherine, and Alan one can see Murry, Frieda, and Lawrence. Far more creative genius is found in the mocking fantasy of "the Last Laugh." The red-bearded Lorenzo (Lawrence) announces a new world when he sees the new-fallen snow, as he bids farewell to his visitors Marchbanks (Murry) and Miss James (Dorothy Brett) at midnight. Like the heroine of 'Daughters of the Vicar' the woman Katherine of 'The Border Line' lives in a state of suspended animation. Although she is the picture of the sensual, feminine type, she is tied to a husband who is thin, ill, and feeble of constitution. She is described as soft-fleshed and voluptuous, while he, in a kind of aesthetic and ultimately existential opposition, is physically inconsequential. This opposition is in actuality one of Lawrence's moral categories. His protagonists are another version of the Sir Clifford-Lady Chatterley opposition, and what represents good in the mind of the novelist is the act that separates them rather than the sanctions which bind them together. Katherine begins to live only after her husband dies, and with a logic and boldness peculiarly his own Lawrence writes of the death scene that the departure of the husband is the release of the wife. The sick man does not awaken pity, but only contempt for not being strong and sexually potent. As he dies, the woman is drawn to another bed by her lover. It is an immoral act, but one symbolic of Lawrence's conception of reviving life.

'Smile' is Lawrence's last fictional gibe at Murry. The Italian setting is based, according to Merrild, on the memory of Lawrence's visit, at her father's request, to see a Mexican girl on her death-bed. Lawrence imagines Murry's grief over the death of Katherine Mansfield; his face "would have done for Christ on the Cross, with the thick black eyebrows tilted in the dazed agony."

Two satirical stories were prompted by Lawrence's calling on Faith Mackenzie early in 1926, and finding that her husband was away on the Channel Island. Whatever their particular reference, neither can be regarded as venomous; they have sufficient universality to raise them above the personal. the Blue Birds is a delightful sketch, ending with a dramatic crescendo of artful bitchery against the devoted secretary by the jealous wife who spends so much of her husband.

It is clear that the three islands of 'The Man Who Loved Islands' were imagined in the English Channel; at the island author gets his typist with child and deserts her, it is not surprising that Compton Mackenzie threatened a libel suit unless derives, however, from Lawrence's recurrent moods of revolt from the civilized world. Whatever appeal the life of isolation had for him, he shows no illusions about it here or in 'The Man Who Was through with the World'.

One of Lawrence's last stories 'Things' was suggested by the Brewsters' habit of 'picking up' bric-à-brac in their travels. They are recognizable in the freedom-lovers whose souls climb towards "the sun of old European culture or old Indian thought," only to find the props supporting their idealistic veins fall one after another, while (unknown to themselves) their horizontal interest make them clutch at 'things.' Exaggeration and fiction are artfully introduced to create a storv of delightful comic ironies, impersonal, and without malice. Indirectly it reflects the love of freedom which made Lawrence scorn the impediments of possessions.

'Sun' is not a success. Up to a point it is a *Lady Chatterley* story, the wife feeling a blood intimacy with the Mediterranean peasant which makes her wish that her next child could be his and not her husband's.

'The Virgin and the Gipsy' (Lawrence expanded it into a short novel later) was hurriedly written at the opening of 1926, and its setting in hilly Debyshire is rendered unidentifiable by many misleading place-names. The opening develops slowly, with some vitriolic sketches of the Weekley family based partly on Barbara's recent gossip; and the fascination the gipsy has for Yvette ensures that the question whether she will disgrace her family at the rectory as her mother had done remains in suspense. On realistic grounds the story is rarely convincing; symbolically, it achieves little imaginative significance.

The reverence with which Lawrence treats his theme in 'The Man Who Died' is expressed in cadences which are often Biblical. There is a parallel between the tied cock and the unnamed Jesus, bandaged and swathed in the bomb, but the escaped cock story could have been reduced without any symbolical loss. Like the silken green wheat, the red anemones, and the flamelike new leaves of the fig-tree, the bird is but a "wave-tip" in the tide of "the swaying ocean of life." The man who died had been dead in life; he had offered only the corpse of love, even as he had been served with it. His desire to compel had caused his death, but he has left his striving self in the tomb. The teacher and saviour are dead; his business is with his single life. The story is about Jesus's resurrection and what Jesus does after returning to life. It is a bewildering experience for the son of God. Here Lawrence make Jesus a human being and Jesus falls in love with the pagan goddess Isis and understands for the first time what "God is love" means. Christ who emerges from this book is a demythological one, shorn of all his God-like paraphernalia.

The most important expression of this cosmic wholeness recalls 'The Flying Fish,' "the greater day" being constrasted with "the little day" of little people and unregenerate slaves. The man made whole escapes out to sea from the danger which "the little life" threatens, promising to return as "sure as spring" when "the nightingale calls" from the "valley-bed" of his healer. He has become like the cock, a wave-tip in the swaying ocean of life.

'Rawdon's Roof' is a slight venture in the Boccaccio style, with no Lawrentian overtones, the main story being that of a man who confirms his boast that no woman shall ever again sleep under his roof but remains ironically ignorant of what goes on in the servants' quarters. 'The Rocking-Horse Winner' is one of those rare stories which is like a parable that speaks for itself and almost defies commentary. Its subject is the will for worldly success which eats the heart out of the mother's life, and drives her anxious boy to frenzy and death.

'The Lovely Lady' (Lawrence's one book of stories was published under this title in 1933) is a contrived story with symbolism at many points. Pauline Attenborough seems to have the secret of perennial youth. Its connection with the sun is superficial, for she takes her sun-bath within thick dark yew hedges.

In 'The Blue Moccasins' emotions are generated by a call-up result in the marriage of a young man to a woman socially superior and more than 20 years his senior. After the war his married life becomes increasingly negative, and he finds happiness in the company of a war widow of his own age. There can be no doubt where Lawrence's sympathies lie.

In 'Mother and Daughter' the satire is unqualified. The two stories have much in common. One mother is ready to 'put the lid on' her sons' marriages, the other on her daughter's. Both are dehumanizing circes who are finally defeated.

What is important to Lawrence is not the morality-immorality contrast, or the indecency displayed: he thinks only of the symbolic oppositions. The husband is for him simply useless, while the lover is a carrier of the life force. What matters ultimately is that one man stands for the force of death, and the other for that of life. Lawrence's male characters stand or fall in so far as they are committed to his own gauge of moral action.

The Reverend Mr. Lindley, the Prussian officer, Sir Clifford Chatterley, the dying husband of 'The Border Line,' are all the creatures of life as we know it. Their contrasts and enemies-the gamekeeper in Lady Chatterley's Lover, the coal miner in 'Daughters of the Vicar,' the orderly of 'The Prussian Officer,' the lover in 'The Border Line' are creatures of another kind of life. Their virtues are not moral but simply existential. It is intentional that the lover in 'The Border Line' comes from out of the rocks and the forest. The first adulterous love takes place among the rocks, and the woman finds there an experience she had never known before. What unites these existential heroes is the fact that they do come from out of the "real" world of nature. They have, so to speak, absolutely no intellectual dimensions. Like the woodcutter hero of 'The Fox,' they are signalized by a stubborn refusal to abide by rules and a terrible cleaving to the flesh. The heroines of these stories are inevitably attracted, repelled, and eventually transformed by these men. A good deal of implicit social commentary is involved because the men are invariably from a class below that of their women. The union is symbolic, perhaps too evidently so. A Freudian might put it this way: the Ego becomes fully constituted only by accepting the burden of the Unconscious. In order to do so, it must first reject the artifices of the Super-Ego.

This search for the identity of the force at the heart of life, the essential quick of nature, was to take Lawrence on a journey which would involve him in torments of urgency as he "saw" the world poised for self-destruction. His understanding of the real quickness of life, his intuition, drew him to a belief that human beings were not the gainers through material progress but the dangerously sad losers. Only by restoring to ourselves that which we had totally abandoned—a sense and spirit he discovered in the Mexican Indians, for example, in their closeness to Nature, the sense he had from them of the power of being alive—could we hope to live a life worth the name and survive.

Lawrence always had an ineradicable preacher/prophet streak in his character.

Melvyn Bragg in his introduction to Cambridge edition of Lawrence's stories *The Prussian Officer and Other Stories* observes, "One of the delights and confirmations of Lawrence's short stories is the description of nature. Lawrence is one of the greatest nature writers in the English language. It is not silly to compare the exactness of his knowledge with that of Shakespeare and the resonance of his descriptions with that of Wordsworth's. In the stories which are of love—whether it is the unacknowledged homoerotic love of 'The Prussian Officer,' the lost love of 'Shades of Spring,' or even the dead love of 'Odour of Chrysanthemums,'—nature is there, a confirming presence. Not only adding to the pleasure of the story but directly cradling it: reaffirming Lawrence's faith in the indivisibility of our own relationship with the natural world.

"The critics? Well. I don't think it is doing very well," he wrote of the volume, "the critics really hate me. So they ought." " The main reviews—*Times Literary Supplement,* the *Standard,* the *Manchester Guardian*—all made similar points: the stories were described as ugly, morbid, unpleasant: "...it must be understood that this is not a gentlemanlike book, wrote Allan Monkhouse in the *Manchester Guardian*. Yet the volume was not entirely without support: Gerald Gould in the *New Statesman* wrote of its "power": yet on the whole the reception was a forewarning of the anti-Lawrence feeling which was to erupt over *The Rainbow*. Lady Ottoline Morrell liked it. A grateful and angry Lawrence replied to her, "One wants the appreciation of the few."

5

D.H. Lawrence's Poetry

First published: *Love Poems and Others*, 1913; *Amores*, 1916; *Look! We Have Come Through*, 1917; *New Poems,* 1918; *Bay* 1919; *Tortoises*, 1921; *Birds, Beasts, and Flowers,* 1923; *Pansies*, 1929; *Nettles*, 1930; *Last Poems,* 1932; *Fire and Other Poems,* 1940; *The Complete Poems of D. H. Lawrence*, 1964.

The following are some of Lawrence's books of poems that were analyzed in his times.

Love Poems and Others (1913)

Edward Thomas observes of Lawrence's first book of poems *Love Poems and Others* (1913): "Lawrence's poetry is intense and known for amorousness and Mr. Lawrence is fearless in treatment as in choice of subject. He will be exact in defining an intuition, a physical state, or an appearance." Ezra Pound says in 1913, "Lawrence's *Love Poems* (1913) is the most important book of poems of the season. He has realized that contemporary poetry must be as good as contemporary prose if it is to justify its publication."

Amores (1916)

Francis Bickley observes, "In one poem Lawrence writes, 'A woman's rejection of what passes for sex in the modern world, her acceptance of separateness and authentic contact with the cosmos-stated thus the theme sounds almost too familiar.' But the book says much more. 'I will sift the surf that edges the night, with my net, the four Strands of my eyes and my lips and my hands and my feet sifting the store of flotsam until my soul is tired or satisfied.'"

Such things are the fruit neither of theory nor of caprice. They are obviously the direct rendering of sensations really felt. Lawrence is an impressionist, and a wonderfully successful and vivid one. His effects, though nearly always surprising, are nearly always right.

Yet poetry, rather than prose, is his true medium. He is so subjective and so intensive that, whatever the form his writing takes, he is always essentially a lyric poet. That is why his novels, powerful and beautiful as they are, are difficult to read.

Lawrence's philosophy is a synthesis of paganism and Christianity, the pagan ideal of absolute being and the Christian ideal of not being. Lawrence writes, "What is really Absolute [he writes] is the mystic Reason which connects both Infinites, the Holy Ghost that relates both natures of God. If we now wish to make a living State, we must build it up to the idea of the Holy Spirit, the supreme Relationship. We must say the pagan Infinite is infinite, the Christian Infinite is infinite: these are two Consummations, in both of these we are consummated. But that which relates them alone is absolute... a superb bridge, on which one can stand and know the whole world, my world, the two halves of the universe."

In *Amores*—poems of loves which are not all sexual—one may find glimpses of this perfect relation of opposites; but more evident are traces of their secular antagonism.

Edward Garnett observes, "Mr. Lawrence in his two volumes, *Love Poems and Others* and *Amores*, comes today to redress the balance. As a poet rehabilitates and sets before us, as a burning lamp, passion—a word which, in the sense of ardent and tumultuous desire, has almost shed to the vulgar mind its original enrooted implication of suffering."

Look! We Have Come Through! (1917)

John Fletcher writes in *Poetry,* Chicago, that the English press has felt that Lawrence is a dangerous writer to their society, and it has neglected his poetry, angering him. According to him, Lawrence's message is this:

> "That everything which we call spiritual is born and comes to flower out of certain physical needs and reactions, of which the most patent is the reaction of sex, through which life is maintained on this planet. Lawrence therefore stands in sharp contrast to the Chiristian dogma of the Middle Ages, and to those writers of the present day who still maintain an attitude of respect to the Christian view, which is that we are each endowed with an immortal soul, at strife with our physical needs, which can only be purged by death. Lawrence, like a recent French writer, 'does not desire to spit out the forbidden fruit, and recreate the Eden of the refusal of life.' He is frankly pagan."

This brings him into close connection with Walt Whitman, who similarly spent his life in preaching with puritanical fervour a most unpuritan gospel. Indeed, if one examines closely Lawrence's latest technique as shown here in such poems as 'Manifesto' and 'New Heaven and Earth,' one is surprised to see how close this comes in may respects to that of the earlier Whitman, the Whitman of 'The Song of Myself.' For example, note the selfsame use of long, rolling, orchestral rhythm in the two following passages:

> When I gathered flowers, I knew it was myself plucking my own flowering,
>
> When I went in a train, I knew it was myself traveling by my own invention,
>
> When I heard the cannon of the water, I listened with my own ears to my own destruction.
>
> When I saw the torn dead, I knew it was my own torn dead body.
>
> It was all me, I had done it all in my own flesh.
>
> Every kind for itself and its own, for me, mine, male and female,
>
> For me those that have been boys and that love women,
>
> For me that man that is proud and feels how it stings to be slighted,

> For me the sweet-heart and the old maid, for me mothers and the mothers of mothers,
>
> For me lips that have smiled, eyes that have shed tears,
>
> For me children and the begetters of children.

The difference is that Lawrence is more delicate, more sensitive, more personal. He deliberately narrows his range, to embrace only life. Unlike Whitman, he has a horror of the infinite, and he could never bring himself to 'utter the word Democracy the word *en-masse.*'

Conrad Aiken adds in *Dial* in 1919, "The poetry of Mr. D.H. Lawrence is a case very much in point. His temperament is modern to a degree, morbidly self-conscious, sex-crucified, and affair of stretched and twanging nerves. He belongs, of course, to the psychological wing of modern poetry. Although we first met him as an Imagist, it is rather with T.S. Eliot, or Masters, or the much gentler Robinson, all of whom are in a sense lineal descendants of the Meredith of *Modern Love*, that he belongs. But he does not much resemble any of these. His range is extremely narrow-it is nearly always erotic, febrile, and sultry at the lower end, plangently philosophic at the upper. Within this range he is astonishingly various."

Bay (1919)

'Piano,' from the last volume of the rhymed poems, *Bay*, is one of Lawrence's best-known poems but is often dismissed with the charge of sentimentality. His tormenting love for Frieda is well expressed in 'A Young Wife,' from *Look! We Have Come Through!* The experiences reflected in this volume begin in 1912 and extend to the winter of 1916. In the poem the ambivalent feelings, the tension between love and fear, is expressed in images of darkness and night. The darkness becomes a favourite image for Lawrence, as it appears to symbolize or suggest both death and the profound, mysterious, and instinctual inner life. Lawrence, who grew up in the raped countryside of the Midlands, whose father was a victim of the mines, became in "philosophy" a primitivist who felt that modern society had buried man's instinctual, most human self.

He advocated a retreat from rationality and a rediscovering of the primitive "blood-consciousness" of emotional and instinctive being. His novel *The Plumed Serpent* depicts a revolution in Mexico, behind which lies the revival of the ancient Indian god Quetzalcoatl, whose return is accompanied by rituals which include the shedding of blood. The forms of modern culture were to be swept away; and the original man, including his cruelty, was to be resurrected. In Lawrence's view it is that modern voice of education which must be overcome, so that men can live as men again, and not as machines such as Lady Chatterley's symbolically crippled husband.

Birds, Beasts And Flowers (1923)

There are in this volume more astonishing strokes of natural genius, and in greater number, than in any other volume of contemporary poetry.

It is this sincerity, in which the mists between the poet and the object are cleared away and both have unsullied light around them, which translates intuition into art. This makes great poetry of simple lines like

> O they rade on, and farther on,
> And they waded rivers abune the knee,
> And they saw neither sun nor mune,
> But they heard the roaring of the sea,
> and Wordsworth's
> My apprehensions come in crowds;
> I dread the rustling of the grass;
> The very shadows of the clouds
> Have power to shake me as they pass.

Collected Poems (1928)

When Lawrence's *Collected Poems* edited by J. C. Squire appeared in 2 vols in 1928, this criticism followed. The publication was â laudable effort.

The two volumes are headed, one *Rhyming Poems* and the other *Unrhyming Poems.* It well exemplifies Mr. Lawrence's logic that the second volume contains a considerable number of the poems in rhyme. He did not notice. He is too febrile, hectic, full of blood and haunted by dreams to be precise about title-pages and the arrangement of books.

He writes his poems on theory, and he judges them on theory. He is afraid of what he likes; and he is anxious that what he writes should be interpreted in the light of his life. J.C. Squire writes of this: "Mr. Lawrence must be read in the light of these statements; and of his other statement that 'the things the young man says are very rarely poetry. So I have tried to let the demon say his say, and to remove the passages where the young man intruded.' He is, in other words, a limited, a writhing, a bewildered poet: honest, muscular, out of touch with ordinary mankind, afraid of himself and afraid of others, at one moment surrendering to beauty, at the next tortured by the thought that the surrender may have been too easy. A philosophy nobody but a solemn ass will ever get out of Mr. Lawrence: he is a poet, a brooder, an introspective sensualist: a man capable of violent flights towards the ideal and violent revulsions against it: but quite incapable of philosophic generalization, or any such understanding of other people as would make him feel that his experiences were universal. His form is not usually lyric: but for what he is worth he is in the category of Heine, Burns, and Catullus, though these were all better artists than he: the interest goes out of his work if there is no interest in himself."

Pansies (1929)

One unsigned reviewer in the *TLS* in 1929 observes of Lawrence's poetry, with reference to *Pansies*: "With the same fascinated loathing with which Swift railed at man's animal nature and animal actions, and 'with a no less passionate hatred, Mr. Lawrence attacks everything in modern life which deprives man of his animal delights and checks the noble and beautiful savage. And yet we hesitate to say that it is the noble savage whom Mr. Lawrence exalts.' "

Lawrence thinks man is lopsided on the side of the angles. He hates money civilization.

But there are some women who seem to epitomize all that Mr. Lawrence dislikes:

> Will no one say hush! To thee,
> Poor lass, poor bit of a wench?
> Will never a man say: Come, my pigeon,
> Come an' be still wi' me, my own bit of a wench!

Mr. Lawrence is a master of the pathetic, and the lines are written in the little language of Swift.

These pansies and passions of hatred directed against the lilies and languors of virtue are called pansies because, as Lawrence tells us, "they are rather *pensées* than anything else," and he wishes them to be taken as "casual thoughts that are true while they are true, and irrelevant when the mood and circumstance changes."

Lawrence uses with great sensibility a metre which is perhaps derived from translations of Chinese poems, and has been of much use to gnomic poets.

Nettles (1929)

The confiscation from the Warren Gallery, London, of thirteen of Lawrence's paintings made him write a sequence of even more disagreeable poems, all dating from July and August 1929, called *Nettles*. Lawrence continued to write 'Pansies' throughout 1929, and a collection of no less than 205 was published, with other work of greater moment, in *Last Poems* after his death.

Last Poems (1929)

In one's recollection, all the *Last Poems* tend to be coloured by their greatest achievements. They seem like a song-cycle tempered to the pitch and quality of the deepest voice, the *basso profondo*, descending lower and lower to the ultimate C. But in fact there is a good deal of energy and bite in these poems. This is so even though Lawrence was fatally ill, in Bavaria and the South of France, when he wrote them. There is, in no bad sense, a carry-over from the more positive of the *Pansies*.

Consider 'The Greeks are Coming'; 'Red Geranium and Godly Mignonette'; and 'Demiurge':

> as if any Mind could have imagined a lobster dozing in the under-deeps, then reaching out a savage and iron claw!

It is questionable how far many of these *Last Poems* are separate one from another. Interdependence is obvious in the last two quotations. Nevertheless there are some poems articulated enough to stand by themselves. One thinks, in the Homeric 'Man of Tyre,' of the lyrical yearning for a beautiful girl wading in the water:

> Oh lovely, lovely with the dark hair piled up, as she went deeper, deeper down the channel, then rose.
>
> Shallower, shallower, with the full thighs slowly lifting of the wader wading shorewards and the shoulders pallid with light from the silent sky behind. . .

Philip Hobsbaum thinks yet this poem, self-sufficient though it is, relates to other poems about the sea: 'They Say the Sea is Loveless', 'Whales Weep Not!' 'Mana of the Sea'. And these, in their turn, relate to one of the most secure of Lawrence's masterpieces, 'The Ship of Death.'

The Complete Poems of D.H. Lawrence (1964)

In a note to his *Collected Poems* of 1928, D.H. Lawrence explains that he tried to arrange the poems in chronological order "because their personal nature made them, in effect, a biography of inner life and experience." This is good. Like Thoreau's poetry, Lawrence's poetry is rough and crude yet alive. Also his poetry is simple and understandable. His poems open to the gusts of emotions—anger, bitterness, tenderness, outrage, nostalgia, regret, love—which make up their form and content, and which are artistically controlled and expressed chiefly in haunting thought generally a metrical rhythms.

The poems, up to 1923, revolve around Lawrence's early love, and his mother. They recall us the theme of his first novel *Sons and Lovers.* Then there is the death of his mother in 1910, which completes the volume of rhymed poems and forms. Chronologically overlapping these poems, which run through the war into 1918, are the unrhymed poems of *Look! We Have Come Through!* deals mainly with the love and torments of his marriage to Frieda, who left a husband and two children to marry Lawrence, and their life in Austria and in England during the World War I. The poems in *Birds, Beasts and Flowers* (1923) are mainly of the Mexican and New Mexico sojourn of 1920-1923, and conclude the first volume. Beyond these, Lawrence's poems, most notably in *Pansies* (1929) and *Nettles* (1930), beccme stridently political and anti-social. Rough-hewn and full of disdain, anger, and even hate, often near hysteria, full of preachings and pronouncements, these poems are mostly ephemera. Then, with last poems like 'The Ship of Death,' he reaches the apex of his poetic career. Haunting, mysterious, religious, the poem is a unique contribution to modern verse.

Frank Magill thinks that it is nearly impossible to illustrate the nature of Lawrence's poetry with short quotations, for the poems build slowly from a perception, an image, to a hash of realized emotion. They are deceptively simple. They are organic growths, and the art with which Lawrence can build a poem to a climax is disarming. Details are introduced; they slowly become focused and symbolic as a persona, a viewpoint, is established, a conflict—emotional, sexual—is gradually engaged and developed through incremental repetition. Then the full experience blossoms forth, usually directly stated, and the poem, a little drama built out of the countercurrents of image and response, is completed. There is, therefore, more intensity and significance in the cadences and reiterations of detail than in memorable lines. The poems grow, develop; they are not set pieces.

At his best, however, the accumulating reiteration of line, image, and thought has the effect of a chant. The poem becomes, as in "The Ship of Death" or in "Bavarian Gentians," a kind of ritual; or, in a poem like "Snake," it is as if the poet's nerves were laid bare, quivering. In one of his early poems, "The Scent of Irises," Lawrence displays the facility with which he can develop a response, in this case to a jar of iris in the classroom where he was teaching. The iris and his lonely slavery as a schoolteacher take him back to an earlier time, in the country, with a girl. The internal rhyme and alliteration, the way the lines are rove-over, the strongly cadenced anapestic-like rhythm with the beautifully manipulated double stresses, the repetition of syntactic phrases and clauses, may, in their chanting effect and syncopation, remind one of Hopkins or Whitman or Dylan Thomas, and rightfully so. The developing tensions between the girl and the Rowers, between sexual blossoming and the reminder, in the last line, of death, illustrates, in part, the manner in which Lawrence characteristically works. There is strife here, between the "you" of the girl and the "me" of the poet; the tone is half-nostalgic, half-bitter. The love and the simultaneous hate vie for precedence with desire and scorn: cross currents of emotion. The 'Scent of Irises' is a very typical and compelling poem, as are the better-known 'Love on the Farm,' 'Lightning,' and 'Monologue of a Mother,' all from the early poems.

Lawrence's movement, in his verse, toward themes dealing with ancient myth and ritual is evidenced by this first stanza from 'Middle of the World,' one of his last poems. Here is cadenced verse, working very close to prose, but highly poetic in its control, in its patterning of syntax, and the movement of symbolic images. Dionysos is, of course, a symbol and the repository of the life of passion, of instinct, and of freedom from the bindings of rationality. The sea is a symbol of life.

Lawrence searched the globe for a place where he could feel the ancient pulse of life still beating, but perhaps nowhere did he feel it more than in the burial caves of the ancient Etruscans; the vaults are vividly decorated with images of hunting and of other activities. From the Etruscan caves Lawrence drew the main images and primitive conception of death which informs 'The Ship of Death.' Perhaps his greatest poem, it was rewritten many times, but the reader will find it fully rewarding simply to read as one poem. It is a ritual chant in praise of death and man's journey toward obliviousness. Lawrence refers to the Etruscan belief in a kind of rebirth, when souls will need their tools and crockery, and the ship, which sails to oblivion, sails on through to a new life, where peace is renewed within the heart.

No quotation can communicate the poem. Alternately elegiac and joyful, the cadences subtly modulated to fit the moods, Lawrence here plumbs, as it were, his vision of death and touches on the rock of belief he found in ancient ritual and culture. The poem 'The Ship of Death' begins thus:

> Now it is autumn and the falling fruit and the long journey towards oblivion.
>
> The apples falling like great drops of dew to bruise themselves an exit from themselves. . .

But this is preliminary. It is the second strophe that brings in the central idea:

> Have you built your ship of death, O have you?
> O build your ship of death, for you will need it . . .

Reinforced by, what we don't have in the draft, a rich autumnal imagery:

> The grim frost is at hand, when the apples will fall
> thick, almost thundrous, on the hardened earth.
> And death is on the air like a smell of ashes!
> Ah! can't you smell it?
>
> And in the bruised body, the frightened soul finds itself shrinking, wincing from the cold that blows upon it through the orifices. . .

There is no room in this structure for a meditation upon the souls crying upon the shore. That idea is relegated to the ancillary poems. Instead, Lawrence goes on to play imaginatively with the Shakespearian word, mentioned only in passing "quietus":

> And can a man his own" quietus make with a bare bodkin?
>
> With daggers, bodkins, bullets, man can make a bruise or break of exit for his life; but is that a quietus, O tell me, is it quietus?

> Surely not so! for how could murder, even self-murder ever
> a quietus make. . .?

The word becomes further subdued, into "quiet," and this provides the opportunity to restate explicitly, what has been implied throughout, the main theme:

> O let us talk of quiet that we know, that we can know,
> the deep and lovely quiet of a strong heart at peace!
>
> How can we this, our own quietus, make?
>
> Build then the ship of death, for you must take the longest
> journey, to oblivion. . .

This poem is said to be one of the best poems in the English language.

'Bavarian Genetians' also depicts an imaginative journey to the underworld, where in the mysterious life in darkness Lawrence chants, in images of Pluto's hell and of Persephone, his mythic sense of death and rebirth in the darkness of lost and legendary time.

6

D.H. Lawrence's Plays

Lawrence's plays include: *A Collier's Friday Night* (1906, 1909), *The Widowing of Mrs Holroyd* (1910, 1913), *The Merry-Go-Round* (1911), *The Married Man* (1912), *The Fight for Barbara* (1912), *The Daughter-in-Law* (1913), *Touch and Go* (1918), *Altitude* (1924), *Noah's Flood* (1925), and *David* (1925).

Mr. Lawrence, the playwright, is a very different subject. Philip Robinson observes, "Lawrence wrote ten plays. They must be considered as overflows from his central work. But they do have points of particular interest. *A Collier's Friday Night* (1906, 1909) is a conflation of several scenes which were to occur in *Sons and Lovers;* it seems to relate to an early draft of that book." Climactic to the play is a scene when the Lawrence-figure (Ernest) pays so much attention to the Miriam-figure (Maggie) that he burns the bread he should have been watching.

Mother: It's all very well, my son—you may talk about caring for me but when it comes to Maggie Pearson it's very little you care about me—or Nellie—or anybody else.

Ernest: (*dashing his fingers through his hair*) You talk just like a woman! As if it makes any difference! As if it makes the least difference!

Mother: (*folding her hands in her lap and turning her face from him*) Yes, it does.

Ernest: (*frowning fiercely*) It doesn't. Why should it? If I like apples, does it mean I don't like bread? You know, Ma, it doesn't make any difference.

Mother: (*doggedly*) I know it does.

The Morel-figure, the old miner of the title, is finely achieved in speech whose vivacity of dialect shows what was to be Lawrence's especial forte in drama, "It's a nice thing as a man as comes home from th' pit parched up canna ha'e a drink got 'im . . ." There is, in this dislocation of accepted syntax, a noticeable freedom from the conventional language of the drama of the time.

The Widowing of Mrs Holroyd (1910, 1913) relates to Lawrence's story 'Odour of Chrysanthemums.' The dramatic speech, as ever, is alive in its rhythms. Thus the wife, sponging the face of the dead miner: "My dear, my dear, oh, my dear! I can't bear it, my dear. You shouldn't have done it, you shouldn't have done it. Oh, I can't bear it, for you. Why couldn't I do anything for you?, the children's father? I wasn't good to you, but you shouldn't have done this to me . . ."

Distantly, there is David's lament over Absalom in the Authorized Version; nearer home, the cadences of J. M. Synge in *Riders to the Sea*. It is no accident that Lawrence's gift for dialogue was praised by two great Irish playwrights, Bernard Shaw and Sean O'Casey.

Just as the first two plays relate to the early fiction, so *The Daughter-in-Law* (1913) foreshadows 'Fanny and Annie' which is a work of 1919. Here we see the life of the well-bred young woman after she has married an artisan; a miner, coddled by his overbearing mother. In this case, the daughter-in-law does not find out about the impending child the miner has given to another woman until well after her marriage to him. The marriage has not so far been successful but this circumstance, together with the fact that the husband has been hurt while picketing a colliery-strike, brings the couple closer together, though uneasily so:

Luther: (*He sways as he takes his cap off*) Minnie

Minnie: My love, my love!

Luther: Minnie, I want thee ter ma'e what tha can o' me. (*He sounds almost sleepy*.)

Minnie: (*crying*) My love, my love!

Luther: I know what tha says is true.

Minnie: No, my love, it isn't, it isn't.

Luther: But if ter' lt ma'e what ter can o'me-an' then if ter has a childt, tha'it happen ha'e enow.

Minnie : No, no, it's you. It's you I want. It's you.

These three plays have obvious crudities: contrivances of entry and exit, jerks and disjunctions in plot. But their virtues in the linguistically exiguous twentieth-century theatre are rare indeed. They are written in a language which demands to be spoken and which turns vernacular into something very like dramatic poetry. And their concerns are the stuff of life: the social mores of what had been the submerged classes, the estrangement between husband and wife, or, as here, their painful attempt at reconciliation.

The rest of Lawrence's dramatic output can be dealt with morern tersely. *The Merry-Go-Round* (1911) is a Derbyshire *As You Like It* —rapid changes of partners, scenes of pantomime farce. *The Married Man* (1912) retails the embarrassments of a local philanderer who conceals from various willing ladies the fact that he already has a wife and child. *The Fight for Barbara* (1912) shows Lawrence in a very different vein—drawing upon his experience of life with Frieda after their elopement. There are stirring scenes of conflict between the guilty couple on the one hand and Barbara's mother, father and deserted husband on the other. *Touch and Go* (1918) shows Gerald Barlow, director of a colliery, contending against a miners' strike. The play has a degree of interest as a footnote to *Women in Love*, and the strike-leader bears more than a fugitive relationship to the Aaron of *Aaron's Rod.*

Altitude (1924) is a sketch of the people surrounding Lawrence's patroness, Mabel Dodge Luhan, in Taos: its interest is mainly biographical. *Noah's Flood* (1925) is the beginning of a morality play in which the men of earth conspire together to overthrow the power of Noah. And *David* (1925) is an ambitious historical tragedy, based on the Biblical hero but giving considerable extension to the role played by David's wife, Michal, and to the stormily romantic figure made of Saul. But, unlike the early realistic plays, the Biblical cadences of *David* are not mediated through local speech and so lack colour and emphasis: "I will wait and watch till the day of David at last shall be finished, and wisdom no more be fox-faced, and the blood 'gets back its flame. Yea, the flame dies not, though the sun's red dies. . . ." According to Robinson, "As the follower of Synge and the contemporary of O'Casey, Lawrence occupies no negligible place in the underpopulated pantheon of modem dramatic masters. It is hard to think of Lawrence as a playwright because his most achieved works in this genre seem to be appendices to successes in his chosen area of prose fiction. What one can say is that in a National Repertory, if anything of the sort existed, there would be found a place for three of Lawrence's plays: *A Collier's Friday Night, The Widowing of Mrs Holroyd* and *The Daughter-in-Law*."

It would be hard to beat *David* for sobriety, for the deliberate and well-managed archaism of its diction, for clarity of thought and beauty of detail.

Edward Sackville West thinks for Mr. Lawrence Saul is a better man than David. He sees in Saul the possessor of that Power, which we of the modem world have lost; but in David he sees the incarnation of Will, as opposed to the blind Power-the cunning, cautious, foxy ability that is the curse of contemporary civilization.

It is interesting to compare this play with another on the same subject, Andre Gide's *Saul*. M. Gide's conception of the story and its protagonists is a totally different one; he also has his theory, but it is a far more literary one. He makes of Saul a sort of feeble Baron de Charlus, assailed by the demons of neurosis, and the interest of the play is frankly erotic. Mr. Lawrence's Jonathan is rather a strong character, a 'lithe stripling', and in his relations with David he takes the ascendant. The rivalry between Saul and Jonathan for David's affection makes the central theme of the play.

Perhaps the best of Lawrence's play lies in the last two scenes the abnegation of Saul at the hill of sacrifice, and the scene of the shooting of the arrows and the parting of David and Jonathan. The final scene is one of great emotional solemnity.

7

D.H. Lawrence's Travelogues

Philip Robinson observes, "One cannot classify the non-fictional prose of Lawrence into neat compartments; not even the compartment called non-fiction. There is literary criticism in his travel sketches and philosophy in his criticism. The popular journalism of his later career often intensified into prophecy; the prophecy that characterizes the last stage of his life is criticism of a very high order indeed. As much as his verse, Lawrence's prose is the record of a flow of thought; and, as with his verse, components can be separated from the surrounding plasm and discussed as independent entities." The following is an account of Lawrence's travel accounts as a major non-fictional output.

Twilight in Italy (1916)

This is Lawrence's travel work. It is the author's travel essays of the places like the Tyrol and Lago di Garda in Italy of the period of 1912-1913. The work involves the Lawrences, the Signora, Il Duro, an Italian peasant, John Giovanni, an Italian immigrant to America and others.

Twilight in Italy is a small book of travel essays, worth reading for the light they throw on the context of Lawrence's work.

D. H. Lawrence was a prolific and versatile writer whose plays, poems, novels, novellas, and short stories — more than forty volumes produced in a writing life of twenty years — often need to be read in the context of his essays, pamphlets, and travel books. There are four of these last, excluding the passages of description in his letters recording his expatriation in Europe, America, and Australia. The first of these journeys is recorded in his first travel book, *Twilight in Italy*.

Both journey and book came at an important time in his life. Thereafter the gift for natural description and for the "felt" characterization which distinguishes his fiction was so broadly used as to make him geographically the most universal English writer of the twentieth century.

In August, 1912, Lawrence and Frieda, then Mrs. Ernest Weekley, walked south from Icking, near Munich, to Riva on Lago di Garda, which was then in Austrian territory, and later, in September, to the Italian Gargnano, farther down the lake. They stayed there till April 1913, while Lawrence worked at his writing. There he completed the final draft of *Sons and Lovers*, wrote the German stories, collected in *The Prussian Officer*, and began the poems published in *Look! We Have Come Through*! To this versatile performance he added the first versions of the travel essays published in first the *English Review* and in 1916 as *Twilight in Italy*. The first of the essays deals with a walking trip in the Tyrol before the journey south to Italy; it is entitled "The Crucifix Across the Mountains." The key word "strange" is employed on the first page and thereafter frequently, for that was not only a strange country in its people and its language, but also in customs, such as wayside crucifixes, new to Lawrence's Congregationalism.

The release of Lawrence's fancy on strange objects stemmed from his decision not to return to teaching after his illness in 1912, but to live by his pen. This courageous decision gave him three novel sensations in Gargnana. He was living with Frieda as a married man, his time was his own, and he was in a foreign country. He completed several old manuscripts which would be published in the next two or three years and he began new work. The completion of *Sons and Lovers* marked the first stage in his withdrawal from his Nottinghamshire material, a withdrawal continued in *The Rainbow* and effected in Aaron's visit to Italy in *Aaron's Rod*. Placing his personal material in clearer artistic focus marked also the beginning of his major phase as a writer. He changed the style of his writing, as first seen in the poems in *Look! We Have Come Through!* and this change accorded with the growing resolution of his ideas into what is usually called his uphilosophy." The effect of these changes was to break the first draft of his next novel into two novels, *The Rainbow* and *Women in Love*, but the ideas behind these changes are apparent in *Twilight in Italy*, the first groping statement of the Lawrencian mystique.

The essays in the book are four, of which the second, 'On the Largo di Garda,' is divided into seven short sketches amounting to more than half the book. Lawrence records conversations with chance acquaintances on his hike across the Alps and his walks around Gargnano. More than a picture of foreign people, the essay records Lawrence's reflections precipitated by novel surroundings and time to think; his developing consciousness of the dark sun. His cheerfully free use of the material of *Twilight in Italy* is shown by the three versions of 'Christs in the Tyrol' or 'The Crucifix Across the Mountains,' by his reference to this material at the conclusion of *Women in Love*, and by the exclusion of at least two travel pieces belonging to this period, sketches published posthumously in *Love Amongst the Haystacks* in 1930.

Although Frieda Weekley appears fleetingly as "the Signora" (as she was to appear as "the Queen Bee" in *Sea and Sardinia*), her interest in the bambini—she had recently left her own children for Lawrence-is a clue to the deeper influence she had on this book and lawrence's writing. By her act Lawrence moved from childish observer in the rites of married love to full participant; the currents he had felt in married couples he now knew at first hand, and could graft his insights on to the Italian. But although there is also observation of parents and children, as in the story of "John," the main interest is in individuals. Where their individuality is respected, the observation is sufficiently keen, as in 'The Spinner and the Monks,' to present a vivid and poetic picture; the individual male characters, such as the padrone in 'The Lemon Gardens,' tend, however, to become either "Italians" or "males," and the glib use of national or universal labels tends to make them meaningless.

The total value of *Twilight in Italy* to Lawrence was threefold: first, it established his technique of obtaining his material by rapidly "glimpsing" his objects; second, he glimpsed for the first time the "dark sun" or "dark god" in strange objects; third, from this vision he worked out his philosophy of the "demon" which drove him and his characters to do what they did not consciously want to do, giving his work its characteristic harshness and truth to life. Only New Mexico was to provide an equally valuable novelty.

Sea and Sardinia (1921)

Beautiful is the right word for *Sea and Sardinia*. "I like Italian newspapers," says Mr. Lawrence, "because they say what they mean, and not merely what is most convenient to say. We call it naivete-I call it manliness. Italian newspapers are read as if they were written by men, and not by calculating eunuchs."

This is certainly Sardinia. That is the subject of the book. This is naturalness, a willed naturalness. Lawrence apparently suffers a great deal from the supposed unfriendliness and resistance of the world. He has still, in a remarkable state of preservation, the ordinary English middle-class horror of having his privacy invaded by a "bounder." Sardinia notebook gives one an excellent idea of Lawrence. We have him for a week, close-up, with a pointedly seen and swiftly changing background of Sardinia. Also we have a silhouette of his accompanying wife, a mere outlander who prices vegetables and shops for saddle-bags and wants to go to the marionette show and is rather annoyingly interested in the native. She is a German. He calls her the q-b, queen bee. Had he come from Peoria he would indicate her as the squaw. But in essence if not in the idiom of his facetiousness, D.H. Lawrence does come from Peoria. He is the Middle Westerner athirst for beauty, aflame with imagination, and aching with ideas as with apples devoured green.

Because what D.H. Lawrence communicates is his own feeling. He gives us the stone-damp houses, the innkeeper with a wine-dripped shirt-front, the nerve-drained bus driver who is yet such a smooth master of his machine, the priest with a long nose who spits the young wife restless from her bridal bed, the little cabin in the ship with a panelled slide-door and no room to move, the icy dawn that is like the kiss of a corpse, the kid roasted in front of a roaring oak-root fire, the impudent peddlar packed with aqua vitae, the Italians sugary with sympathy and linked together in fondness, with feelings as nude as sausages. Whatever Lawrence experiences he experiences with full savour, and he has retrieved an astounding number of his experiences in this book of Sardinia.

France Hackett observes, "Yet it is the book of an aesthetic parvenu, just as Jan Juta's striking poster-like illustrations are parvenu illustrations."

Lawrence's travel writings are many and varied. And this is most true of his *Sea and Sardinia*. Lawrence writes as he sees, and what he sees is marvelous: natural scenery in all its grandeur and variety; people, alive and vital, mimicked exquisitely; houses, inns, railways all delineated with such intimacy and gusto that they seem to speak to us.

Even so, yet more remains, for interspersed throughout *Sea and Sardinia* are brief areas of introspection where Lawrence mused over the issues which constantly concerned him, Sardinia is a kind or remote island with a life and identity of its own against which Lawrence projects deeper questions.

R.H. Poole thinks 'Mandas' contains brilliant portrayals: a traveler's vividly drawn, clearly-observed etchings. Lawrence offers us a glorious comic-opera-sketch of the wife who missed her train, of her woebegone husband, of the inn-keeper who tamed the eccentric candle, and of the three station officials.

R.H. Poole observes, "What we also encounter is *Sea and Sardinia* is Lawrence's self-portrait, in the sense that we know instantly what is like to be Lawrence faced with day-to-day situations, as, for example, when he is annoyed at a demand for an excessive tip. In Lawrence's descriptions of natural scenery we notice a similar modulation towards inwardness. At times Lawrence's natural descriptions are written with a felicitous economy and sharpness of outline, but often we have richness, rhythm, and symbolic depth."

Critics thinks *Sea and Sardinia* is Lawrence's most unified travel-book. This is one of the least-read of Lawrence's major writings. In many ways it deserves to be set beside his tales. It is a characterization in depth of a confidence trickster *malgre lui*: The whole memoir deserves to be set among Lawrence's classics.

Mornings in Mexico (1927)

Lawrence's New Mexico travel book revolves around the idea of contact, which is basic to Lawrence's philosophy of life. The stranger (Jesus) of *The Man Who Died* is resurrected to a deeper life by contact with the priestess of *Isis*. Lawrence defends that tale saying: "And Church doctrine teaches the resurrection of the body; and if that doesn't mean the whole man, what does it mean?" It is the Roman world (symbolic of materialism) which destroys the idyll of the stranger and the priestess and so, in 'New Mexico,' it is the materialist American world that destroys the Indians' sense of contact. The modern world is wrapped so carefully like a sweet in transparent paper that we cannot achieve contact. Travellers (packaged tourists) hardly come into contact with the life around them. Certainly Lawrence was not one to yield before the barren.

Lawrence thinks the American materialist society ruined native life. It is true that a native tribe may be more creatively educated than a Western race. The man who spends his Sunday mornings worshipping his car through ablutionary rites may be less educated than the native carving his statuette. This view is one Lawrence voices most definitely: "All we posses is life-weaving, carving, building— this is the flow of life, life flows into the object—and *life flows out again* to the beholder. So that whoever makes anything with real interest, puts life into it, and makes it a little fountain of life for the next comer. Therefore a Gandhi weaver is transmitting life to others-and that is the great charity."

Yet everywhere we see Western society advancing so that we must recognize that people are losing contact. Most of us are probably not prepared to lose the fruits of materialism, and neither, seemingly, are the emergent nations.

At the end of the essay Lawrence seems to envisage an apocalyptic end for America, but surely this is not how history develops; not even Jesus produced an apocalypse, at least, not yet. Materialism is not wholly contemptible, its way of life does not necessarily lead to oblivion. It is the material mental outlook which is dangerous.

R.H. Poole who has worked on Lawrence's travelogues observes, "This quality of insight is typical. In 'The Mozo' the obsidian knife, which we also meet in *The Woman Who Rode Away,* symbolizes the 'instant moment' outside of which nothing exists. The difference between Indian and Western civilization is shown as a difference between the timelessness of the former and the precision of the latter. In 'Indians and Entertainment' Lawrence elaborates this point, suggesting that there are two mutually exclusive kinds of consciousness."

Lawrence's point that the two consciousness are mutually exclusive cannot mean that to accept the Indian consciousness the Westerner must be as an Indian, but that no resolution of the two is possible.

Mornings in Mexico, for example, is basically very Dickensian: it is a series of walks. On Friday morning Lawrence tells us he tried to write but was distracted by the parrots making a mockery of the dog ('Corasmin and the Parrots'). On Saturday morning he went to the market and found himself among black-hatted Indians from the hills and sarape men who whistled like ferocious birds ('Market Day'). On Sunday morning the sunshine drew him out of town and into the hills for a picnic under the guava trees ('Walk to Huayapa'). And on Monday morning his servant Rosalino— who had seemed quite happy on the Sunday walk—decided to leave for his native village. "He gave off a black steam of hate, that filled the patio and made one feel sick. . ." ('The Mom'). All these "mornings" were written in December 1924.

Philip Robinson observes, "But there were more considered essays dating from the April and the August of that year. They include 'Indians and Entertainment' and the much admired 'Hopi Snake Dance.' These, however, tend to obscure the simple lineaments of the book and add to it an unwelcome layer of pretension. 'The American-Indian sees no division into Spirit and Matter, God and not-God. . .' "

Etruscan Places (1932)

Another aspect of the duality we have seen in Lawrence's reactions to the countries he visited is seen in his handling of Etruscans. Against their natural flowering is set Roman self-assertive morality. We are reminded of the New Mexico Indians whose life was a living symbol: sprouting corn grows and its growth is symbolic of the life urges. That dual tension of life force termed by Lawrence "the Holy Ghost" existed also for the Etruscans who represented it as the *patera* or *mundum*: "the round saucer with the raised knob in the centre, which represents the round germ of heaven and earth." Lawrence's imagery recalls us Wallace Stevens's poem 'Anecdote of the Jar:'

> I placed a jar in Tennessee,
> And round it was, upon a hill.
> It made the slovenly wilderness
> Surround that hill.
>
> The wilderness rose up to it,
> And sprawled around, no longer wild.
> The jar was round and bare
> And tall and of a port in air.
>
> It took dominion everywhere,
> The jar was gray and bare.
> It did not give of bird or bush,
> Like nothing else in Tennessee.

Towards the end of *Etruscan Places* Lawrence refers to a decline of the power of the symbol among the Northern Etrucans. As with the Indians, the power of the symbol is physical, but here with the northern Etruscans Lawrence already sees mental consciousness supplanting the physically-centred religion of the Southern Etruscans. We are looking towards the same Roman world that came to destroy the new-formed life of *The Man Who Died,* and the modern equivalent of the Roman world is our own Western civilization. The point is further made in his poem *Cypresses*:

> Tuscan cypresses,
> What is it?
>
> Folded in like a dark thought
> For which the language is lost,
> Tuscan cypresses,
> Is there a great secret?
> Are our words no good?
>
> The undelivered secret,
> Dead with a dead race and a dead speech, and yet
> Darkly monumental in you,
> Etruscan cypresses.

This journey through time is remarkable one. We are not competent to judge the archaeological scholarship of the work, though Lawrence went to considerable trouble to prepare himself for the undertaking, but his poetic descriptions, re-creations, and interpretations are so intuitive that scholarship takes second place. Lawrence breathes into these monuments a new life so that they assume perhaps a richer consciousness than their distant makers possessed in the flesh.

Philip Robinson comments, "In *Etruscan Places* Lawrence sketches the life of the people who flourished before the mechanistic Romans and the idealistic Christians. He sees the Etruscans as a people who developed neither gods nor nationhood; who kept life fluid and changing; whose pictures on the walls were an evocation of all we have lost."

8

D.H. Lawrence's Letters

Frank Magill observes, "One's understanding of D.H. Lawrence cannot be considered complete without a careful perusal of *The Collected Letters*. For there is a side of Lawrence that, while it is found elsewhere, receives its fullest expression only in the letters—a side that, beneath all the tensions of his life, is cheerful, optimistic, affirmative. Lawrence's belief in the ultimate sanctity of physical being finds its embodiment not only in formal essays and narratives, but in these informal meditations that reflect his day-to-day existence."

This aspect had already been revealed in 1932, when Aldous Huxley published an impressive collection of Lawrence letters. Harry T. Moore draws heavily on Huxley's edition in the expanded collection in 1962. Appearing less than two years after Lawrence's death, the Huxley book was a great achievement, and many Lawrence scholars have an almost sentimental attachment to the pioneer volume of letters. But the time has long been ripe for a more comprehensive collection, one that would include not only many unpublished letters, but items in the myriad volumes of memoirs and biographies. *The Collected Letters*, however, is scarcely complete; no collection could be. Many letters will still have to be consulted in the Huxley volume and from other sources; secondary items and duplicative letters were, as Moore ruefully points out, excised.

The earliest item is a postcard dated 1903, shortly after Lawrence had turned 18. Then he was still very much the miner's son seeking a way out by attending a pupil-teacher center. The girl to whom the postcard is addressed is one of a group of friends known as the Pagans. The last letter, dated 1930, is from a sanatorium at Vence, France, a few days before his death. The intervening pages form the most complete epistolary record we have thus far of a major modern writer: his private life, his struggles with public and publishers, his friends—who often came and went in a rather kaleidoscopic way—his thoughts and his mind. They remind one most forcefully of the extent to which a writer is an intuitive register of his time. Depressed and disgusted with the outbreak of World War I, Lawrence, from the beginning, is concerned with what is to follow, and in his musings he foreshadows the disillusionment of the 1920's. The society that could produce such a war is obviously sick, wrote Lawrence.

The Collected Letters creates a distinct persona of the author. Rarely do his letters provide us with the sort of immediate, unfiltered reactions to experience that we find in other letters. His are more mediative and reasoned in tone. Nevertheless, the Lawrence we get is clearly a genuine Lawrence, one who persists below the surface of daily events. This Lawrence possesses the serene face of the man who has the capacity and the courage simply to face life in all of its manifestations. Oddly, for the comparison would be shunned by the earlier author, he reminds one in these pages of an earlier idealist, Henry David Thoreau, who asserted: "I wished to live deliberately, to front only the essential facts of life." Thus, in one letter, we find Lawrence asserting that one ought to fulfill as the deepest of all desires the wish to avoid the extraneous, to live only for pure relationships and living truth.

Lawrence's desire is a general wish 'to distinguish between what is life and what is not-life, between being and not-being (Lawrence likes to quote Hamlet here). It is as part of this general desire that we get the specific ideas with which Lawrence has been identified and that we discover that those ideas are scarcely as specialized as they might seem to be in other contexts, as in his *Fantasia of the Unconscious*. Here we find the very important letter of January 17, 1913, to Ernest Collins, a letter containing the first relatively systematic statement of Lawrence's belief in the sense of physical being, as against the abstract knowledge of life provided by the intellect. Here we find his attacks Freudianism as being too abstract, in their approaches to man's hidden life. Here, in another important letter of July 16, 1916, to Catherine Carswell, we find Lawrence distinguishing his own views from those of Christianity, accepting the Christian ethic as the greatest historical force ever to sweep through mankind, but seeing it, as did George Bernard Shaw, as something to be surpassed. A new ethic is now needed, he claimed, one that will encourage the fulfillment of bodily as well as spiritual desires. Developed and modified in essays, fiction, and later letters, these concepts ultimately become the center of Lawrence's final statement on man and his time in *Lady Chatterley's Lover*.

Lawrence's letters provide us his sense of optimism that could turn on occasion into an almost aggressive affirmation. It is scarcely a Pollyanna-like optimism. In one of the most haunting letters in the collection, written to Lady Cynthia Asquith, in January, 1915, Lawrence describes the depths of despair and hopelessness into which the news of the war had plunged him. Only now is he beginning to rise from his grave; he begins to hope that something may emerge from the war. Lawrence begins to hope, as did many of his generation, that the very destructiveness of the war may lead to the sort of smash-up that will require a social reconstruction, and the world may then be ready to listen to him. As it becomes evident that the smash-up is not going to take place, Lawrence falls back on his affirmation of the roots of life itself. He asks us for spontaneous existence.

Even the suppression and censorship of his novels, embittering and demeaning as they were, failed to crush Lawrence. After *The Rainbow* was suppressed, we find him correcting proofs, collecting early poems for a book, trying out the idea of a subscription scheme for *The Rainbow*. He believed in his books as he believed in life and in himself.

The following are two of Lawrence's letters which he wrote to Bertrand Russell from Greatham, Pulborough in 1915 and Mabel Dodge Luhan from Kandy in 1922.

Lawrence's friend Lady Ottoline collected authors and artists at her homes in Bloomsbury and Garsington, Oxfordshire. One of these was Bertrand Russell, whom she brought to Greatham to meet Lawrence. He and Russell agreed that the war was a monstrosity, and for a while a strong sympathy existed between the two men. But Lawrence was working out his anti-intellectual theories about the power of "blood-knowledge," and such ideas ultimately caused Russell to shrink from him. Russell says in *Portraits from Memory* (1956), "it was only gradually that we discovered that we differed from each other more than we differed from the Kaiser." At the time however, Russell thought so highly of Lawrence's opinions that he thought of killing himself after some harsh criticism from Lawrence. In early 1916 he broke off the friendship, and years after Lawrence's death, wrote an essay about him with a pen dipped in poison. Look at Lawrence's letter:

"In your lecture on the State, you must criticize the extant *democracy,* the young idea. That is our enemy. This existing phase is now in its collapse. What we must hasten to prevent is this young democratic party from getting into power. The idea of giving power to the hands of the working class is *wrong*. The working man must elect the immediate government, of his work, of his district, not the ultimate government of the nation. There must be a body of chosen patricians. There must be woman governing equally with men, especially all the inner half of life. The whole must culminate in an absolute *Dictator*, and in equivalent *Dictatrix*. There must be none of your bourgeois presidents of Republics. The women's share must be equal with the men's. You must work this out in your own way. But you do it."

"Can't you see the whole state is collapsing? Look at the Welsh strike. This war is going to develop into the last great war between labour and capital. It will be a ghastly chaos of destruction, if it is left to Labour to be constructive. The fight must immediately be given a higher aim than the triumph of Labour, or we shall have another French Revolution. The deadly Hydra now is the hydra of Equality. Liberty, Equality and Fraternity is the three-fanged serpent. You must have a government based upon good, better and best. You must get this into your lectures, at once. You are too old-fashioned. The back of your serpent is already broken."

"A new constructive idea of a new state is needed *immediately*. Criticism is *unnecessary*. It is behind the times. You must work out the idea of a new state, not go on criticizing this old one. Get anybody and everybody to help—Orage, Shaw, anybody, but it must be a *new* State. And the idea is, that every man shall vote according to his understanding, and that the highest understanding must dictate for the lower understandings. And the desire is to have a perfect government perfectly related in all its parts, the highest aim of the government is the highest good of the *soul*, of the individual, the fulfilment in the Infinite, in the Absolute."

"In a fortnight I shall come and take account of you."

"[P.S.] Don't be angry that I have scribbled all over your work. But this which you say is all social criticism: it isn't social reconstruction. You must take a plunge into another element if it is to be social reconstruction."

"Primarily, you must allow and acknowledge and be prepared to proceed from the fundamental impulse in all of us towards The Truth, the fundamental passion also, the *most fundamental* passion in man, for Wholeness of Movement, Unanimity of Purpose, Oneness in Construction. *This is principle of Construction.* The rest is all criticism, destruction."

"*Do, do* get these essays ready, for the love of God. But make them more profound, more philosophical. Make them no popular, oh, not popular. The best is to attack the spirit, then proceed to the form. You call the spirit Subjectivism. Do go to the root of this: kill it at the root. Show how everything works upon this great falsity of subjectivism now. I like it where you take them one by one, The State, Marriage, etc. But you *must* put in the *positive idea.* Every living community is a living State. You must go very deep into the State, and its relation to the individual."

Lawrence and Frieda were going to America in 1922 because they had been invited to Taos, New Mexico, by Mrs Mabel Dodge Sterne (Mrs Luhan), a wealthy hunter of celebrities who felt that Lawrence could express in verse and prose the wonder she felt in New Mexico. In February 1922, the Lawrences sailed for Ceylon, where they stayed a month with the Brewsters in their bungalow in the hills above the Kandy Lake. There Lawrence did not admire the Asiatic people nor its Buddhism. Lawrence's one letter addressed to Mabel from here is as follows:

"Dear Mabel Dodge Sterne: I have your two letters, but still no sign of book or necklace. *Speriamo.*

"No, the East doesn't get me at all. Its boneless suavity, and the thick, choky feel of tropical forest, and the metallic sense of palms and the horrid noises of the birds and creatures, who hammer and clang and rattle and cackle and explode all the livelong day, and run little machines all the livelong night; and the scents that made me feel sick, the perpetual nauseous overtone of cocoanut and cocoanut fibre and oil, the sort of tropical sweetness which to me suggests an *Untertang* of blood, hot blood, and thin sweat: the undertaste of blood and sweat in the nauseous tropical fruits; the nasty faces and yellow robes of the Buddhist monks, the little vulgar dens of the temples: all this makes up Ceylon to me, and all this I cannot bear. *Je m'em vais. Me ne vo.* I am going away. Moving on."

"I have cabled for money from New York, and anxiously await the return cable so that I can book berths on the *Orsova,* on the 24th of this month, for West Australia: about 10 days from Colombo to Fremantle. The address there will be c/o Mrs. Jenkins, Strawberry Hill, Perth, W. Australia. I don't know how long we stay there: but I shall take my steamer-ticket right to Sydney. I want to look at Australia, and try what it's like. If I don't care for it, then I can very easily come on. There are steamers every fortnight from Sydney to San Francisco; and San Francisco is not far from Taos. And I shall be fulfilling my real desire to approach America from the West, over the Pacific. I hope I shall arrive in Taos with ten cents left in my pocket-ten cents left to me in the world, even. Knees of the Gods."

"I still of course mistrust Taos very much, chiefly on account of the artists. I feel I never want to see an artist again while I live. The Indians, yes: if one is sure that they are not jeering at one. I find all dark people have a fixed desire to jeer at us: these people here-they jeer behind your back. But heavens, I don't see much in them to admire, either. They seem to be built round a gap, a hollow pit. In the middle of their eyes, instead of man, a sort of bottomless pit. That's Buddhism too. Buddhism seems to me a very conceited, selfish show, a vulgar temple of serenity built over an empty hole in space. No, no, these little darkie people don't impress me, upon actual contact. The place, Ceylon, is a real prison to me, oppressive, and I want to get out. Two weeks today, pray God."

"I wish I could come to America without meeting the awful 'cultured' Americans with their limited self-righteous ideals and their mechanical love-motion and their bullying, detestable negative creed of liberty and democracy. I don't believe either in liberty or democracy. I believe in actual, sacred, inspired authority: divine right of natural kings: I believe in the divine right of natural aristocracy, the right, the sacred duty to wield undisputed authority. Naturally I find myself in diametric opposition to every American – and everybody else, beside Americans—whom I come across. Nevertheless, there it stands."

"Well, so far so good."

9

D.H. Lawrence's Paintings

Lawrence's paintings were exhibited at the Warren Gallery, Maddox Street, London from 14 June 1929. On 5 July the exhibition was raided by the police who took away thirteen of the pictures that were considered to be obscene. At the subsequent court hearing, presided over by Mr. Mead, the Marlborough Street Magistrate, the pictures were ordered to be returned to their owner on condition that they would not be re-exhibited. *The Paintings of D. H. Lawrence* is a volume of reproductions of these paintings which was put on sale at the exhibition. It includes an Introduction by Lawrence.

This book contained an introduction in which Mr. Lawrence stated his views on painting, and they, apart from the censored pictures, are worthy of consideration. As a phase of his general outlook, expressed in the prose which is his real medium, they form an important section of his philosophy.

The English, says Mr. Lawrence, have produced few good painters because the national spirit became atrophied with fear at the time of the Renaissance. This fear was caused by the wave of venereal disease which then swept over Europe. High and low alike were tainted—Mr. Lawrence gives a lurid account of the Tudor and Stuart dynasties—and the result was a shuddering, universal attack of sex-repression, which obliterated 'Merry England' and has continued with gathered strength to the present time. It was reflected in literature by the morbidity of the Elizabethans, the emasculated intellectualism of the cavalier poets, and the coarseness of Restoration comedy. Thus a mental attitude towards life took the place of an intuitional one. By the time English painting really got started with Gainsborough and Reynolds the English had lost their imagination and freedom of expression. France, because it had affected some sort of rational compromise with sexual necessity, was a little better off. This sex-repression, caused by the fear of disease, has by now robbed the English of the power both of artistic creation and appreciation. "We, dear reader, you and I, we were born corpses and we are corpses." Such is Mr. Lawrence's general thesis, and such his general nonsense.

Blake, as we can well understand, Lawrence appreciates, for much of his own work is an embroidery on *The Marriage of Heaven and Hell*. He praises the classic English landscape-painters, too, though he blames them for not being figure-painters instead. And the French Impressionists painted light admirably—though why paint light? In fact, Mr. Lawrence really wishes to get from painting such satisfaction as one gets from his novels.

The art critic W. Earp observes, "In Cezanne's apples Mr. Lawrence finds the first and only successful attempt for centuries to portray actual matter. Mr. Lawrence's eulogy of the Master of Aix is noble and moving; though obviously his conception of Cezanne himself as an heroic character—a literary figure—has much to do with it, and makes a strong appeal to Mr. Lawrence, the romantic novelist. And because he is so good a novelist we are interested in his views on painting."

For painting to Mr. Lawrence is simply what the violin was to Ingres. It may be a delightful hobby, but the exhibition as a whole showed no signs of a vocation. The honesty of Mr. Lawrence's effort is not questioned, yet the pictures, although there were no desire to shock, were really shocking from the point of view of art. The magistrate remarked that the most beautiful picture in the universe might be obscene, but if Mr. Lawrence's pictures had been beautiful it is doubtful whether they would have been prosecuted. The offensiveness lay in the bad painting.

Lawrence's pictures took second place to his writing, yet when he learned that the Condon magistrate might order them to be burned, he wrote to tell Dorothy Warren that he did not under any circumstances, or for any cause want his paintings destroyed. He was willing to do his bit to help the cause of English liberty, but "to admit that my pictures should be burned, in order to change an English law, would be to admit that sacrifice of life to circumstance which I most strongly disbelieve in." He would not be a martyr.

H.T. Moore and Warren Roberts comment, "Perhaps his best painting is one of those now in Texas: *Boccacio Story*. This canvas has a living quality, with Lawrence's rich colouring; and it presents a dramatic human picture (the gardener, sexually exposed, lying asleep, and the startled nuns discovering him): the positions of the gardener's legs and arms form balanced angles, the nuns appear in juxtaposition to two white dogs on the opposite side of the picture, and the furrows of earth running in somewhat different directions in the centre and background of the painting give it a rhythmic quality. This is heightened by the rows of delicately coloured, plumy trees in the background. There is an almost equally fine effect in "*Red Willow Trees*" in the Karavas collection: three naked men in the foreground bathe in a stream that winds among hills and vermilion willow trees, with a slope full of umbrella pines beyond. Again the composition has balance and wonderful colour. Many of the paintings, however, are fairly crude— Lawrence was particularly bad at drawing arms— but most of them strike the attention forcibly, and the colouring is often as rich as in Lawrence's poetry and prose."

10

D.H. Lawrence's Criticism

Lawrence has these to his credit: *A Study of Thomas Hardy* (1914), *Psychoanalysis and the Unconscious* (1921); *Movements in European History* (1921); *Fantasia of the Unconscious* (1922); *Studies in Classic American Literature* (1923); *Reflections on the Death of a Porcupine* (1925); *Pornography and Obscenity* (1929); *Assorted Articles* (1930); *Apropos of Lady Chatterley's Lover* (1930); *Apocalypse* (1931); *Phoenix* (1936); *The Symbolic Meaning* (1962); *Phoenix* II (1968)

A Study of Thomas Hardy (1914)

According to Robinson the years between *Twilight in Italy* and *Mornings in Mexico* saw the march of a series of tracts, not large in scale but amorphous in form, which Lawrence generically called his "philosophy". The years 1914-19, in particular, formed a period of mounting bitterness when practically everything he wrote was liable to be invaded by this curiously contextless manner of writing. He was confined to England by the war, and such work may well have proved a defence mechanism.

By no means all this 'philosophy' got published in its period. *A Study of Thomas Hardy* (1914), for example, did not appear (apart from its third chapter) until 1936, when *Phoenix*, a collection of Lawrence's papers, was brought out. *The Study*, like several of its successors, lacks coherent shape. Indeed, the most cogent remark that can be made about it is that its title seems a misnomer. Nisbet & Co. had commissioned a little book on Hardy for a series intended for students, and they must have been sorely puzzled by what they received. At any rate, they refused to publish it. One must say that, when the *Study* condescends to discuss Hardy, it does so to some effect; picking out the central figures of his books with sharp particularity. This, however, was not the line that Lawrence's criticism was to take; it contrasts greatly with the theoretic overtones that lend resonance to most of the later critical writing. Consider his account in the *Study* of *The Return of the Native*. Eustacia Vye is said to have a romantic imagination bounded by Paris and the beau monde; Wildeve is always attracted from outside and never driven from within; while Clym Yeobright thought his map of the static surface was the thing itself. Contrast this with the interpretation of Harold Child, who wrote the book that replaced Lawrence's in the series. He turns the novel into a species of novelette: "Clym Yeobright is left alive, indeed, after Eustacia and Wildeve have been whirled by desire to death. . . but his suffering and humiliation had been terrible. . ." Clearly Child's prose wasn't up to interpreting Hardy's novel. That of Lawrence certainly was; but it is necessary to add that his particular exposition is confined mainly to Chapter III, the chapter that got published independently, and that the *Study* as a whole is best read as Lawrence's attempt to work out the elements of his "philosophy".

He begins the *Study* with a thunderous attack on various systems in society that, he considers, prevent man from attaining the fulfilment of his nature. He goes on to propound, as a positive value, a reconciliation between the sexes. As ever with Lawrence, the particulars he adduces by way of illustration—his sense of joy in the simple life of the poppy—come across sharply. The statements about Being and Not-Being, however, do not. And the more positive those statements are, the weaker they seem.

The positives are vague, too, in the *Study's* immediate successor, *The Crown* (1914-15). They achieve a partial realization only in certain images, such as this, of the Woman.

Movements in European History (1921)

The conceptual works of the First World War and its aftermath are a kind of crypto-fiction: a criticism without texts, a series of disquisitions starved of concrete reference. It is this that makes one prefer the decent pot-boiling of Lawrence's schoolbook, *Movements in European History* (1918-19), to the effervescing rhetoric of 'Love', 'Life' and 'The Reality of Peace' (1916-17).

One can find indications of specific experience in certain of these works, and this it is that gives them what being they have. In *The Education of the People* (1918, 1920), for instance, Lawrence's practical knowledge as a teacher powers his shrewder observations. One particularly warms to his remarks upon the position of the schoolteacher crushed between the educational theorists above him and the doggedly resisting pupils below. Yet the problem is given to us far more graphically in the narrative of Ursula's conflict with both her headmaster and her classes in Chapter XIII of *The Rainbow*. Further, for all its incidental insights, *The Education of the People* is more than a little bedevilled by the peculiar psychology Lawrence worked out between its first drafting in 1918 and its final version in 1920.

Psychoanalysis and the Unconscious (1921)

Lawrence in the Foreword to his book *Psychoanalysis and the Unconscious* (published along with *Fantasia of the Unconscious*) in 1923 speaks of these things:

"Only let me say, that to my mind there is a great field of science which is as yet quite closed to us. I refer to the science which proceeds in terms of life and is established on data of living experience and of sure intuition. Call it subjective science if you like. Our objective science of modern knowledge concerns itself only with phenomena, and with phenomena as regarded in their cause-and-effect relationship. I have nothing to say against our science. It is perfect as far as it goes. But to regard it as exhausting the whole scope of human possibility in knowledge seems to me just puerile. Our science is a science of the dead World. Even biology never considers life, but only mechanistic functioning and apparatus of life."

"I honestly think that the great pagan world of which Egypt and Greece were the last living terms, the great pagan world which preceded our own era once, had a vast and perhaps perfect science of its own, a science in terms of life. In our era this science crumbled into magic and charlatanry. But even wisdom crumbles."

"In that world men lived and taught and knew, and were in one complete correspondence over all the earth. Men wandered back and forth from Atlantis to the Polynesian Continent as men now sail from Europe to America. The interchange was complete, and knowledge, science was universal over the earth, cosmopolitan as it is today."

"I do not believe in evolution, but in the strangeness and rainbow-change of ever-renewed creative civilizations."

"Exactly the fire resided in the Tree of Life. That is, life itself. So we must read: 'It must have appeared to the ancient Aryan that the sun was periodically recruited from life—which is what the early Greek philosophers were always saying: And which still seems to me the real truth, the clue to the cosmos."

"One last weary little word. This pseudo-philosophy of mine—'pollyanalytics,' as one of my respected critics might say—is deduced from the novels and poems, not the reverse.

"And finally, it seems to me that even art is utterly dependent on philosophy: or if you prefer it, on a metaphysic."

Fantasia of the Unconscious (1922)

J. M. Murry says, "'Mr. D. H. Lawrence is the outlaw of English literature, and he is the most interesting figure in it.' The cultivated people who wagged their heads and called him 'mad,' now nod their heads and murmur 'genius.' Their real feeling is, of course, unchanged."

Lawrence is primarily a novelist. He is also a notable poet. He has written two books of psychological criticism—*Fantasia of the Unconscious* and *Psychoanalysis of the Unconscious.* These represent a reaction against the psychology of Freud with its emphasis on sex and the incest-motive. Lawrence tried to counter Freud by propounding a psychology of his own based upon an equally individual view of physiology. He argued that there were four major nerve centres in the body. The thoracic ganglion related to the spine and shoulders and was associated with matters intellectual. The lumbar ganglion related to the spine and buttocks and was concerned with excretion and rejection. The cardiac plexus related to the nipples and was associated with breathing, eyesight and, by extension, concern for others. The solar plexus was the basis of the sensual life of man and was the seat of instinct.

Indeed, it was instinct largely that guided Lawrence's classification. For example, his feeling about the solar plexus is based on his sense of the intimate connexion between mother and child via the umbilical cord. The solar plexus is the seat of a creative knowledge to be valued more highly than the cerebral sort of knowledge associated with the thoracic ganglion. And the theory has, in Lawrence's hands, a certain beauty. But it is spoiled by his intermittent insistence that it is exact science, to be taken literally. The nerve centres that he specifies are four out of many which have to do with the activities he denotes, and it is clear that in all these activities he considerably underestimates the role of the brain.

Philip Robinson thinks *Fantasia of the Unconscious* philosophizes this physio-psychological theory and takes it to extremes.

There are many things which might be said of Lawrence's *Fantasia of the Unconscious*. The book has been published in America, and not in England. And the meaning of this is that Lawrence-an Englishman of the English, born in a Midland mining village, where the grim Black Country fades into some of the most beautiful rural scenery that England possesses-is, or has been, in a state of rebellion against his native land. By a monstrous abuse of the law in 1915 one of the most significant of his novels, *The Rainbow*, was suppressed on a fantastic charge of immorality. Shortly after, so soon, in fact, as the material opportunity offered-the suppression of the one book made publishers fearful of accepting work from him—he shook the dust of England from his feet and began a slow and haphazard journey round the world. This was the period of his outlawry in spirit and in fact. Lawrence was anathema to English criticism.

Both of Lawrence's expository or philosophical volumes start from a psychoanalytical basis. Lawrence was the first man in England probably in Europe also, truly to realize the scope of the problems of which psychoanalysis has touched the fringe. This knowledge he had not as a student of Freud or Jung, but directly and instinctively by his own intuitive apprehension of life.

The professional psychoanalysts had discovered that in modern civilization some great primal urge—"Sex" for Freud, something less simple, Libido, for Jung—was thwarted and contorted with disastrous results to the individual. They began, clinically, to elaborate a subtle technique for liberating these suppressions. If man becomes a machine, he also acquires some of the numbness of a machine. To make him aware of his own deep discomfiture, his lack of true satisfaction, his poverty of being, is only to increase his pain and his impotence, unless you can give him something new and true to live by. Psychoanalysis, without knowing what it is doing, has assumed the responsibilities of a religion without having religious duties to impose or religious satisfactions to offer.

This then is the cardinal issue which Lawrence has faced continuously during his life as a writer, in moods that have passed through anger, embitterment, dismay, to a final serenity. It is the conclusion of the great minds of modern times—of Dostoevsky, of Tolstoy, of Nietzsche, of Whitman. But how? In *Fantasia of the Unconscious* Lawrence gives, with a joyful spontaneity of language which is itself an augury of the newness of life he proclaims, his answer to the question. D.H. Lawrence is the only writer of modern England who has something profoundly new to say; and finally that he must inevitably become a figure of European significance.

Studies in Classic American Literature (1923)

D.H. Lawrence's *Studies in Classic American Literature,* at first glance a puzzling book, survives nonetheless for its powerful insights into American literature. It is puzzling because of its style, so informal, so impulsive, and so seemingly self-contradictory. It is full of exclamations, words all in capital letters, choppy sentences. But it is impressive in the great task it undertakes, and it will leave the reader shaken with new ideas about American literature, upset enough to force him to a reconsideration and re-evaluation not only of American classics, but also of the quality of the American experience. Lawrence believed that criticism, like literature in general should be written with passion and with moral purpose. Lawrence sees American literature in a fresh way, as an outsider looking with a special perspective. In this extended essay the works of eight American authors are studied: three novelists (Cooper, Hawthorne, and Melville), three prose writers (Franklin, Crevecceur, and Dana), and two poets (Poe and Whitman), all but two belonging to the first seven decades of the nineteenth century. The selection follows what has become since Lawrence the standard authors or classics of the beginnings and the renaissance of American literature, except for the surprising inclusion of Dana and the omission of Jefferson, Irving, and the Transcendentalists. The selection was probably dictated by the origin of the articles which after periodical publication came to make up the book. In about 1915-1916 Lawrence, contemplating emigration to the United States, reread some of the American books of his youth and wrote out his findings in some salable articles. Also, being Lawrence, he used his reading of the texts to propound his ideas, this accounting for the important opening chapter 'The Spirit of Place' which more or less directs the argument, and probably for the omission of Emerson, who must have been anathema to him.

It is Lawrence's only book of literary criticism; it is the only writing on American literature by a great English writer; and the essay on "The Spirit of Place" is significant in the study of Lawrence, the most world-wide geographer in English fiction.

The different extant versions of this opening essay are described in Armin Arnold's *D.H. Lawrence and America*. The general argument of the essay, developed in the book, is typically an exhortation to Americans to become Americans by responding to the spirit of the place, America.

Lawrence said in letters that this work was a kind of psychoanalysis of literature, and he spent much time polishing the essay but not rereading his texts-before publication in *The English Review* in 1918-1919 and before their appearance as a book. But just as there is a little clarification of the principal term "American" (meaning Americans as they are and as they were or ought to be), so there is still difficulty with the critical terms "knowledge" and "consciousness"; the distinction between the two meanings Lawrence employs is usually represented as the difference between thinking and feeling.

Stuart P. Sherman, the editor of *New York Herald Tribune* in his review of Lawrence *Studies* entitled 'America is Discovered' writes this: "I will admit that Lawrence has even what certain of our own critics would call a 'messianic' purpose. He has borrowed our language and discussed our classics in order to deliver, in a style intelligible to us and with illustrations suited to our comprehensions, his own message. This book, like his novels and his philosophical works, has a thesis."

In this book Lawrence surveys the American literature. First of all, he speaks of Benjamin Franklin as a boar. Franklin is the grandshire of American literature. Lawrence, as a cave-man thinker dislikes Franklin's utilitarian philosophy.

Next, Lawrence seizes upon Hector St. John de Crevecreur, and explains why, with all his faults, he takes to 'Hector.' The good fellow prated, to be sure, about Nature and the Noble Savage in the perfumed terms of eighteenth-century sentimental illusion.

In Fenimore Cooper, two men: outside, a simulacrum of a man, a white man, an American citizen, a democrat and equalitarian, inflated by a hobnobbing with European aristocracy. Leatherstocking novels-poetic escape from the vast unendurable humbug of the Founders of the Republic.

Poe-poor Poe! He was not a cave-man; but he was the next best thing to it. He was a dissolvent of the rotting old European ideals by the fierce excess of his attachment to one of them. Bah! In Ligeia, in Eleanora, in *The Fall of the House of Usher*, Poe unconsciously proved the necessity for the return and revival of cave-man philosophy by demonstrating the ghastly stench of decaying personality which results from the abandonment of it.

"Hawthorne, you little blue-eyed darling," says Mr. Lawrence in effect—the epithet is his you were a cave-man; but you fooled them. Your *Scarlet Letter* was conceived in irony, in deep satirical irony, which passed over the heads of your commentators, leaving them blandly unscathed. *The Scarlet Letter* is not a tract on behalf of irretrievable marriage. It is a strange, symbolical, yearning plea of the blue-eyed darling's suppressed hunger for passion, voluptuousness, Oriental richness and colour.

Lawrence likes Dana and Melville. Brothers, they were of his blood. In their youth, at any rate, the heavy chains of intellectualizing, conventionalizing, idealizing New England could not hold them. They cruised under a fanatical captain (i.e., Puritanism) in quest of Moby Dick, the White Whale here interpreted as "the deepest blood-being of the white race." But they could not kill it. The White Whale got them; and with a flick of his fantastic omnipotent tail he scattered them in a gorgeous truancy from Puritanism among the dusky, scarlet-hibiscus-garlanded daughters of the South Pacific foam.

Finally, Whitman. In him again, two men, one detestable, the other a captain to follow into the unknown. The detestable Whitman is the enamoured democrat, the intoxicated equalitarian, the decadent lustre for the ecstasy of dissolution into union with anything and everything. "I am he that aches with amorous love," quotes Mr. Lawrence.

Mr. Lawrence is an interesting fellow, perceptive, receptive, inquisitive, sincere, violent, and vengeful. But he is far less of a cave-man than he would have his feminine readers believe.

Stuart Sherman thinks it may be safely assumed also that Lawrence's attack upon American intellectualism and idealism proceeds from a reaction for the recovery of his own balance. Indeed, he himself declares flatly against any real reversion to the cave. One of his mystical certainties is that the destiny of the white man points him ever forward into a larger and larger conscious self-realization.

Lawrence does not appreciate the Transcendentalists. As a thinker of blood knowledge he did not like rationalist philosophy of life. His appreciation of the fine wild things in the American genius is perhaps unequalled by any of American native writers except Whitman. His book will doubtless stimulate other explorers to a fresh psychoanalysis of the national spirit. It will probably be welcomed by all American critics of the Party of Nature and condemned by most of their critics of the Party of Culture.

The hero of his whole study is Natty Bumppo (whom Europeans usually prefer to Huckleberry Finn) because Bumppo acknowledges the "spirit of place" and allows it to guide his actions. One suspects that there are further reasons. Bumpo remained a bachelor and a virgin; Hester Prynne's villainy consists in wearing that scarlet letter and thus denying, to Lawrence at least, her "blood-consciousness" of her paramour, Dimmesdale. Lawrence's preference for the lack of women in Melville, Dana, and Cooper, and his particular approach to Walt Whitman make him appear to suffer the "Boy Scout" complex. Leslie A. Fiedler analyzes in *Love and Death in the American Novel,* a work which bears a certain superficial resemblance to Lawrence's essay.

The villain of the book is Franklin, whom Lawrence reluctantly admires and actively dislikes as the originator of the latter-day American delight in gimmickry and the denial of the Adamic past.

The most interesting essay is that on Two Years Before The Mast, by Richard Henry Dana, Jr. This study introduces the works by Melville on the sea, as against those on the land by Crevecreur, Cooper, and Hawthorne (concluding with his study of *The Blithedale Romance*), and the change of subject enabled him to sum up the relation of Americans to their soil.

This discussion prepares the ground for the final essay on Whitman and its noble conclusion on the soul, which by this time Lawrence has come to accept as an equivalent to "blood-consciousness": the soul is freed in Whitman's primary symbol of the open road to achieve a "democracy" of naked relationships which Lawrence promptly converts into "the love of man and woman" and "the love of comrades," thus triumphantly discovering in the last of his studies the overt expression of what he had insisted all along lay hidden in "classic American literature."

Reflections on the Death of a Porcupine (1925)

Edward Sackville West writes, "Lawrence's physiological mysticism runs straight up against scientific fact, but he is a poet and succeeds." Lawrence thinks that the religious state of mind is disappearing from Western Europe, as a result of the progress of scientific knowledge:

Without God, without some sort of immortality, not necessarily life-everlasting, but without something absolute, we are nothing. Yet now, in our spitefulness of self-frustration, we would rather be nothing than listen to our own being. Again, Mr. Lawrence writes, 'Your spirit will be like a dead bee in a cell,' if you 'set up as absolute' scientific facts. So, for lack of this religious spirit, this smokeless flame that should burn in every man, modern civilization is decaying inside its own shell, wherein it seeks to reform itself, turning and turning upon itself in a vain effort to bring good out of evil. It is only when we have broken the shell that the new shoots of life will spring up and we shall be born again. As Zarathustra, Mr. Lawrence's spiritual father, beautifully said: 'One must still have chaos in one, to be able to bring forth a dancing star.' Christianity has exhausted itself and has died a natural death; it is time that the old gods of Power came back to us—of Power that is not the same as Will, but the force that made Sardanapalus, and Saul, and Caesar. The sense of values, all but destroyed by (I) Scientific Materialism, and (2) the War, must once again be cultivated. The Heroic Idea will reappear.

Edward Sackville West thinks the remaining essays in the book, all much shorter, belong to more recent years and exhibit the inequalities already referred to. We cannot but admire the intensity of the writer's conviction and the occasional brilliance of the language in which he expresses it, but he too frequently takes the step which lies between the sublime and the ridiculous. On the subject of the novel he has much to say that is both interesting and original; but, unfortunately, here as elsewhere, strength of feeling leads him, as it often led Swinburne, into vociferation and our prejudice is aroused at the outset by having our ears assaulted by prose resembling the back-chat of a guttersnipe. A good case can be made out against Tolstoy the man, on the ground that his philosophy was unconscious humbug. We may agree that his novels succeed triumphantly in spite of their author's otiose pietism. But there are ways of expressing the attack.

Robinson thinks later philosophical disquisition uses images of animal life to illustrate its theme. And it is to those images we return; not to the disquisition at large. *Reflections on the Death of a Porcupine* (1925) is an attempt to justify man's need to kill in order to hold his place in the universe. But it is the portrait of the porcupine that lives: "a great aureoled tick. . . a pallid living bush. . . his white spoon-tail spiked with bristles. . .' Similarly, 'Love Was Once a Little Boy" (1925) attempts to put forward a concept of individualism—an individualism that is not merely egotistic. The prose strains and cracks in the attempt, and the one effective part of the essay is the unforgettable portrait of Susan—not as the embodiment of this individualism, but as Lawrence's wilful domestic cow. She "flings her sharp, elastic haunch in the air with a kick and flick, and plunges off. . . her udder swinging like a chime of bells. . " Portraits like the Porcupine and Black-Eyed Susan really belong to *Birds, Beasts and Flowers*. It is strange Lawrence did not realize that he had already shown in those poems what he was endeavouring to conceptualize in 'Reflections on the Death of a Porcupine' and its attendant essays.

Pornography and Obscenity (1929)

Messrs. Faber and Faber published a remarkable pair of pamphlets. One is called *Pornography and Obscenity* and is written by D.H. Lawrence; the other is called *Do We Need a Censor?* and is written by the late Home Secretary, Lord Brentford.

Mr. Lawrence's pamphlet is profound and original in a very high degree. Lord Brentford's contains an exceedingly competent and complete exposition of the attitude of those who cultivate the very common human desire to enforce their own ideas of morality upon their fellowmen.

Mr. Lawrence in our opinion is abnormally obsessed with all those questions which centre round the crude facts of sex. His definition of pornography, though not comprehensive, is admirably simple and convincing. He says in effect that pornography is that sort of writing or painting which tends to stimulate or encourage the practice by either sex of private masturbation. His definition explains succinctly what has puzzled many people, namely, why Rabelais and Boccaccio and Ovid and all the other great indecent writers are somehow not pornographic. Their works are calculated to produce perhaps a certain amount of sexual excitement, but it is of the right sort, not of the wrong sort; such books, frank as they are, could not injure the mind of a child.

On the immediate subject of discussion-the existing or threatened censorship—Mr. Lawrence is we think entirely in the right. Pornography should be suppressed. But what is too commonly called indecency should not be suppressed.

An unsigned reviewer in *New Statesman* wrote in 1929 "We must say again that in this pamphlet Mr. Lawrence has hit the nail on the head. His analysis of the factors of the sexual problem might well be suppressed by any Home Secretary of what he calls the 'grey' type; but for all its vehemence and extravagances it is one of the most powerful and sane and penetrating pieces of writing that we have read for very many years. This pamphlet is the work of profound thinker. His pamphlet is a pamphlet which, if it wins understanding, may well mark an epoch in the history not only of censorship but of the reasonable appreciation of the realities of sexual morality and sexual honesty and decency. Perhaps Mr. Lawrence has never before written anything quite so powerful or so effective. The whole question, he says, of pornography seems to me a question of secrecy. Without secrecy there would be no pornography. And again: 'Sentimentality is a sure sign of pornography.'"

E.M. Forster thinks of Lawrence and Lord Brentford thus: the first common characteristic is an emotional uncertainty which threatens them whenever they generalize about the public. Their second common characteristic is that each of them detests indecency, and desires to suppress it. Lord Brentford's opinion is familiar, but it is Mr. Lawrence, not he, who writes, "I would censor genuine pornography, rigorously."

Of course, as soon as we try to define 'genuine pornography' the battle opens; still, both disputants feel that there is something in sex which ought to be prohibited. "It would not be very difficult," adds Mr. Lawrence, but he has not yet been Home Secretary. Lord Brentford, who has, did not find it very easy.

Forster writes, "What, then, is our remedy? Free speech? Not altogether. To say, as has been said above, that by defining filth Mr. Lawrence hopes to sterilize it, is not quite to express his attitude. He does not wholly believe in free speech. However much we speak out and denounce our repressors, we shall still be imprisoned in the circles of self-consciousness, we shall merely be the grey denouncing the grey. To escape into salvation and colour, something further is needed: freedom of feeling, and how is that to be attained? He does not tell us, except by mystic hints which only the mystic can utilize, and in this direction his pamphlet comes to a standstill. But as a polemic it is remarkable. He has brought a definite accusation against Puritanism, and it will be interesting to see whether Puritanism will reply."

One might sum up the conflict by saying that Lord Brentford wants to suppress everything except marriage, and Mr. Lawrence to suppress nothing except suppression; that the one sounds the trumpet of duty, the other the trumpet of passion, and that in the valley between them lie the inert forces of the general public.

Apocalypse (1931)

Likewise, a hypothetical text gave rise to the other great positive myth in this last stage of Lawrence's life. In 1924 he had reviewed an ingenious reconstruction by John Oman of the Book of Revelation. Dr Oman's edition attempted to clarify the text in terms of Christianity, but it suggested to Lawrence that other inferences were possible. His interest was also quickened through his association with Frederick Carter from 1923 onwards. Carter's manuscript on the subject of Revelation resulted in Lawrence writing two introductions to what eventually became Carter's book, *The Dragon of Revelation*. But neither introduction was used for its original purpose. One (January 1930) was published as an independent essay in *The London Mercury*; the other (December 1929) became a separate book, *Apocalypse*.

Lawrence wrote *Apocalypse*, a piece of spiritual writing, as a sick man about four months before his death. A sample of it runs thus:

> "...What man most passionately wants is his living wholeness and his living unison, not his own isolate salvation of his 'soul'. Man wants his physical fulfillment first and foremost, since now, once and once only, he is in the flesh and potent. For man, the vast marvel is to be alive. For a man, as for flower and beast and bird, the supreme triumph is to be most vividly, most perfectly alive. Whatever the unborn and the dead may know, they cannot know the beauty, the marvel of being alive in the flesh. The dead may look after the afterwards. But the magnificent here and now of life in the flesh is ours alone, and ours only for a time. We ought to dance with rapture that we should be alive and in the flesh, and part of the living, incarnate cosmos. I am part of the sun as my eye is part of me. That I am part of the earth my feet know perfectly, and my blood is part of the sea. My soul knows that I am part of the human race, my soul is an organic part of the great human soul, as my spirit is part of my nation. In my own very self, I am part of my family. There is nothing of me that is alone and absolute except my mind, and we shall find that the mind has no existence by itself, it is only the glitter of the sun of the surface of the waters.
>
> So that my individualism is really an illusion. I am part of the great whole, and I can never escape. But *I can deny* my connections, break them, and become a fragment. Then I am wretched.

> "What we want is to destroy our false, inorganic connections, especially those related to money, and re-establish the living organic connections with the cosmos, the sun and earth, with mankind and nation and family. Start with the sun, and the rest will slowly, slowly happen" (*Apocalypse,* pp. 222-4).

In Robinson's view Apocalypse is a form of criticism that has intensified into prophecy. Just as in earlier work Lawrence differentiated between the integrity of the material and the will of the author, so here he shows how the vision of a pagan universe can be overlaid and obscured by a mechanistic system. Even if we do not accept his interpretation, we may find that it serves to alert and focus some of the dissatisfactions we feel with the society about us. It may even help us towards our own positive re-assessment.

In some of his works Lawrence discovered mythologies through travel: observing the open-air life of the Sicilian peasant and the ritual dances of the Mexicans, and visiting the ruined Etruscan tombs. In other works he traverses a text: "the bright book of the novel", Melville, Verga, the Apocalypse. And, in their turn, all these prose works, whether travel or criticism, link up with those most astonishing revelations of his genius: the later Tales.

Lawrence wrote a lot of work, fiction, plays, poetry, travels and letters. His essays are vast and ferlite with his tastes and temperament. Richard Aldington thinks the term 'essays' is a poor word for Lawrence's brilliantly-varied writings, since an essay unhappily implies something formal and academic and highbrow, whereas Lawrence was always intensely personal and spontaneous, with such a horror of pedantry and the university manner that he vastly preferred to be slangy and jaunty. 'Non-fictional prose' is worse than "essay," so until somebody coins a better word we must stick to essays, though in Lawrence's case the word is more like a reference number than a description of literary form. The following is a brief analysis of Lawrence's essays.

The essay on Thomas Mann (1913) has often been termed unfair to its distinguished subject. Undoubtedly Lawrence is idiosyncratic and uses his texts in a manner calculated to advance his own concerns rather than those of Thomas Mann. What he has done is assimilate the German author to a concept of "art for art's sake." Der Tod in Venedig becomes, in this context of argument, an exploration of sickness whose main validity is the skill with which it is done. Lawrence's essay exists to define a kind of novel, the kind which exists as craving for form in fiction, that passionate desire for the mastery of the medium of narrative, that will of the writer to be greater than and undisputed lord over the stuff he writes, which is figured to the world in Gustave Flaubert.

According to Philip Robinson, in his major criticism, Lawrence is concerned to make a distinction between the author's intuition and his mind. He usually expresses the former in terms of the work itself or of the world which it describes. The latter is usually expressed in terms of the pressures of society, economics, the general average of the human masses.

A representative statement, even though the terminology is not as achieved as it might be, is the essay on John Galsworthy (1927). The basic material of *The Man of Property* is applauded: Galsworthy has described beings merely social, the Forsytes. They have no process of existence other than the scraping together of money; they are parasites upon life. But, Lawrence goes on, the author has falsified his intention. He puts forward, as an alternative by which to judge the Forsytes, the love affair of Irene and Bosinney. Irene, however, is a parasite even upon the parasites; while Bosinney is no more than an anti-Forsyte, a rebel whose rebellion can be described only in Forsytean terms as a grudge against property. It is as though, in launching a satire against the Forsytes, Galsworthy finds nothing but Forsytes in the wide human world. The artist's intuition has succumbed to his mind; a mind formed by the pressures of the surrounding society.

Robinson writes, "What Lawrence is particularly against, in life as in letters, is the mind as social entity. In a fragment to be found in *Phoenix*, a kind of emission from the Galsworthy essay, he writes, 'The moment the human being becomes conscious of himself, he ceases to be himself. 'Lawrence works out this apercu in terms of authors and characters alike. For example, there is a penetrating review (1927) of *The Social Basis of Consciousness* by Trigant Burrow. This is a book well worth reading in itself: it advocates group therapy and the importance of developing a tactile consciousness. Lawrence's crucial comment is this: 'The real trouble lies in the inward sense of "separateness" which dominates every man.' He claims that man has made a 'picture' of himself—what, in other contexts, Lawrence calls a 'social being' and that this picture relates to living reality as a two-dimensional pocket-camera photograph relates to the person it claims to portray. In other words, Lawrence puts forward a distinction between the intuition which is in touch with the universe and the 'social being' which is a prisoner of its own society."

Lawrence's positive position is defined even further in a remarkable series of essays written in 1925. They benefit by being studied together. 'Surgery for the Novel—or a Bomb' criticizes the so-called realism to be found in such novelists as Joyce and Proust. This, for Lawrence, is yet another example of the novelist acting as mind; the social form of ego. It is also liable to give rise to a restricted form of moralism: this development Lawrence discusses in another essay in the series, 'Art and Morality'. Here he defines such moralism as an inability to see things as living by their own laws; it imposes on them a kind of Platonic Idea "in all its photographically developed perfection".

As an antidote to all this Lawrence puts forward serious claims for a kind of novel other than that written by Joyce and Proust. He sees it as "a perfect medium for revealing to us the changing rainbow of our living relationships" ('Morality and the Novel'). His word is "medium" as distinct from "moral"; for the kind of novel he admires resists philosophy. "You can develop an instinct for life, if you will, instead of a theory of right and wrong" ('Why the Novel Matters'). In yet another of these related essays, 'The Novel and the Feelings,' Lawrence carries the distinction further; seeing the reader not as listening to the "didactic statements" of the author but to the 'calling cries' of the characters.

These essays are very much literary theory: one may feel the need for more examples of writing in practice. However, in more clearly practical criticism, Lawrence's judgments tend to be pejorative. For example, he claims that Emma and Charles Bovary are too insignificant as characters to carry the full weight of Flaubert's "profound sense of tragedy". And the Russians, by whom Lawrence seems especially to mean Dostoyevsky, "escape the non-heroic dilemma of our age by making every man his own introspective hero.' These remarks are culled from an essay (1922) on the Sicilian novelist, Giovanni Verga; the better of the two versions is in *Phoenix* II. And it is Verga whom Lawrence sees as a modern classic; a classic, that is to say, in an age that fights against the existence of such things.

This sense of the heroic thwarted by the meanness of modern society runs through and links together Lawrence's late tracts. Predominantly they are concerned with matters of sex, literature and censorship. He claims that a movement against the instincts took the form of a morality in all countries after the inception of syphilis ('Introduction to These Paintings', 1928). He finds in Cezanne, however, an instinctual intuition akin to that which he applauds in Verga.

The fear of touch and of being touched resulted, says Lawrence, in a kind of Puritanism which condemned as obscenity the natural flow of sex and which censored as pornography its celebration in literature and art ('Pornography and Obscenity', 1929). The banning of *Lady Chatterley's Lover* and its subsequent dissemination at the hands of pirates gave Lawrence a brilliant opportunity to expatiate upon this theme. In 'A Propos of Lady Chatterley's Lover' (1929) he traces the

Puritan heresy back to a past far predating that of Sir William Joynson-Hicks who condemned his paintings.

Many of Lawrence's articles are collected as *Assorted Articles*. Instances that come to mind are 'Nobody Loves Me,' 'We Need One Another,' 'The State of Funk' and 'The Real Thing.' It can be seen, too, in the Introduction (1930) to his translation (with Koteliansky) of 'The Grand Inquisitor,' that 'poem' which is one of the climactic points of *The Brothers Karamazov*. Lawrence sees this as an essential criticism of Christ, that Christianity is too difficult for the mass of mankind. 'The Grand Inquisitor' (whom Lawrence identifies with Dostoyevsky himself) "finds that to be able to live at all, mankind must be loved more tolerantly and more contemptuously than Jesus loved it . . . loved for itself, for what it is, and not for what it ought to be . . . ".

Lawrence was a persistent metaphysical and reforming thinker, and produced works which he loosely called philosophical. But in trying to express ideas Lawrence never bothered to acquire the language of philosophy, and almost always discussed abstruse ideas in terms of myth and symbol. Interesting and sometimes beautiful as these writings are, they are baffling and irritating to any unprepared reader.

How much Lawrence detested the pompous quasi-philosophical sort of criticism which was the vogue in his day! Lawrence used to say that such critics merely looked at a book in order to paint their own portraits from the mirror, and referred to that 'ad' on the old South-Eastern Railway of a simial looking at himself in a burnished frying pan with the stern caption: "Monkey Soap Won't Wash Clothes. It won't you know."

One must know Lawrence was a fine, though controversial journalist, and wrote essays like 'Sex Versus Loveliness,' 'Nobody Loves Me,' 'Democracy' and others. *The Spirit of Place*, which was an important conception to Lawrence, seemed a reasonable title to hold together his essays on Nature and travel and foreign countries. The three pieces on England 'Whistling of Bird,' 'Nottingham and the Mining Country,' and

'Dull London' may give the impression that Lawrence had little but hostile criticism to make of his native island, but all his earlier novels and stories abound with passages of the tenderest love for country England, and even in Australia he longed for the primroses and bluebells of an English spring. But his hatred of the blind industrial destruction of the old rural England was vehement and implacable.

11

D.H. Lawrence's Worldview: His Concept of Love, Sex and Religion

Lawrence and Love and Sex

Although it is even less true of Lawrence than it is of Freud that he thought "everything comes from sex," there can be no doubt that, from the beginning of his career to the end, sexual relationships were a dominant theme not only of his novels and poems, but also of his miscellaneous prose, including the letters. For Lawrence, the dance of the atoms is a sexual dance, the sway of wheat in a field, an aphrodisiac; while sex as a vital principle in the Lawrentian universe seems at time to affect even the stars in their courses.

The common saying is that sex for Lawrence is a "sort of religion." Lawrentian view implies that to take a woman will it self ensure a man of his salvation. Nor is sexual to be equated with carnal. In spite of Lawrence's respect for the human body, his attitude towards physical sex is essentially healthy in that it involves the whole personality. There is a great deal about sex in Lawrence's fiction, but he hated anything sexy. Theoretically Lawrence had a puritanical streak. This will not surprise those who have found a similar trait in Freud. At times Lawrence, in passages of superb prose, which form a kind of appendage to works like 'The Golden Bough,' revels in the pagan and the phallic, the teeming foison of Mother Earth.

Critic are of the view that considered historically, Lawrence's attitude to sexual relationships between men and women has changed the face of the English novel and added abundantly to the literature of married life.

The Elizabethan view of women alternates between bawdy and breathless wonder. In the nineteenth-century novel, sexual passion for the most part disappears underground, with occasional irruptions as in *Jane Eyre.* It begins to emerge in *Tess of the d'Urbervilles,* though muted and obscured by imagery. With Lawrence, the whole subject is out in the open, and its treatment is frank and fearless. There can be no wonder that Lawrence is a popular author with women. Like the great nineteenth-century novelists such as Tolstoy and George Eliot, Lawrence has shown that women are worthy of analysis on exactly the same terms as men and that they are neither more nor less inexplicable than men.

Lawrence's treatment of sex is uninhibited rather than brutal.

Lawrence's refusal to idealize love, his insistence on passional experience, and his idiosyncratic use of visceral words like "blood," "belly," "lions"—it has been well said that Lawrence "put the loins into literature"—should not blind us to the very real tenderness and even refinement in his treatment of love. It should come as no surprise that Lawrence, with no ironic intent, thought of calling Lady Chatterley's relationship with Mellors is a refining experience. The refinement is of feeling. Connie's relationship with Mellors gives meaning to sexual act which before has been null and void. She did not know what it was. He was able to give her physical satisfaction.

Love, for Lawrence, is a kind of aesthetic exploration. Through the highly complex but creative process of love, men and women discover not only each other but also themselves. In this process the sense of touch is of paramount importance. Through touch people get to know each other. This is evidenced in his story *The Blind Man.* To savour life at one's finger tips would seem to be for Lawrence valuable in itself. Even the trucks at the mine in *Sons and Lovers* acquire dignity because they are sanctified by human touch. Lawrence's view of human touch is startlingly illustrated in the story 'Glad Ghosts' where a character says: "Think how ghastly for Jesus, when He was risen and wasn't touchable! How very awful, to have to say *Noli me tangere!* Ah, touch me, touch me *alive*!"

In the Lawrentian universe, the forces of *darkness* are the creative, dynamic forces. The unconscious from which these forces emerge is not the unconsciousness of the psychoanalyst in search of cure. There are no neurotics in Lawrence's world, only the spiritually live and the spiritually dead.

It is in the sexual relationship that, for Lawrence, the individual is best enabled to reach down into the mindless centres of his personality.

When Lawrence describes men and women, we learn a great deal about their physical sensations, little about their physical shape. For Lawrence, the word beautiful is pretty meaningless if applied to the body in isolation. Beauty is not a question of lineaments, but of soul, of spontaneous and vital movement.

P.S. Shepherd observes, "Before Lawrence, sexual relationships as described in the greatest novels had never been simple: after him, they became indescribably complex. As, in life, sexual love is a source of conflict, of passion that lies near to hate, as well as of exaltation, of calm, and of ennobling tenderness, so, in Lawrence's work, it is a source of confusion and obscurity, as well as of psychological insight, of unsurpassed lyrical beauty, and of blinding illumination. Above all, Lawrence showed that sexual love, besides being the most thrilling experience known to man, is also the most creative."

One is not surprised at Lawrence's protest in an early letter: "But why do you persist in separating soul and body? I can't tell, in myself, or in anybody, one from the other." He was never tormented, like Aldous Huxley, with a body-spirit problem. For Lawrence, the human soul is no fiery particle imprisoned within its walls of flesh. One can understand why he was not attracted to oriental philosophy. Even in his most exalted mood, he neither rejects, nor tries to by-pass the body. This recalls us Whitman's ideas about man's physical life. The twelfth century south Indian thinkers called *Sharanas* enunciated the view that body and sex are as important as the soul and spirit in man's transcendence.

It is true, however, that Lawrence saw sex as something to be surpassed. From *The Rainbow* onwards, and particularly in *Women in Love,* the authentic Lawrentian characters are striving not merely to retain their individuality in the face of a threatened absorption by a partner, but to reach out towards a condition for which Lawrence had several names—"the unknown," "the creative beyond," etc. Love as a means and not as an end becomes the one meaningful goal. The "lone singleness" of the Lawrentian hero is not a tragedy but a triumph.

There is another side to the question-less visionary, more domestic. Even *Lady Chatterley's Lover* may be seen as a novel of domestic life.

Finally, there is plenty of evidence, particularly in the short stories, that Lawrence's preoccupation with tumultuous passions was no bar to the operation of his highly refined sensibility or his sense of humour.

Lawrence and Religion

Aldous Huxley, in his perceptive introduction to his edition of the letters of D.H Lawrence, recounts an anecdote in which Lawrence passionately refused to accept evolution: "'But look at the evidence, Lawrence,' I insisted, 'look at all the evidence. His answer was characteristic. 'But I don't care about evidence. Evidence doesn't mean anything to me. I don't feel it *here*.' And he pressed his two hands on his solar plexus.'

This story shows something of the temper of Lawrence's religious attitudes. He is an intensely religious writer. At the outset of *Fantasia of the Unconscious* Lawrence states: "...the essential religious or creative motive is the first motive for all human activity."

The most obvious example of this *Apocalypse* where he re-casts in his own mould biblical and Christian themes, while the most obscure example is the nevertheless significant Foreword to *Sons and Lovers* where Lawrence reverses St John's famous statement from "And the Word was made flesh" to "The Flesh was made Word." This reversal lies at the core of Lawrence's religious experience.

He saw no use in such abstract terms as "supreme Being," and the "fixed law" he regarded as anarchical. His plea was for "complete imaginative experience." Elsewhere he calls the term "God" a fetish-word. For Lawrence the "will of God" is an "inrush of pure life."

On one occasion Lawrence did explicitly say: "The Greeks, being sane, were pantheists and pluralists, and so am I." Naturally Lawrence turned towards those geographical regions where he thought he saw religion expressed through its purest form – the physical.

Lawrence's God is different from other Gods: the good God, the *moral* God, the personal God, the God of the Jew, the pill of the Roman Catholics. Likewise Lawrence's Jesus is different from the Jesus of the reveled religion.

Lawrence considered that revealed religion denied man's creative urge by fencing him in with a framework of mental requirements. The religious faculty was, for Lawrence, the inward worship of the creative life mystery and mental consciousness only a great indicator and instrument. It is when Lawrence the prophet attempts to belittle mind that he cuts the frantic figure of his dispute with Bertrand Russell, causing the latter to comment, acidly, years later: "His descriptive powers were remarkable, but his ideas cannot be too soon forgotten."

Repeatedly we find Lawrence admiring Christianity but crying that it had outlived its time. Lawrence has made an important distinction between "will" and "power." The former he regarded as an attribute of the ego, as an agent or accelerator, whereas the latter is that which comes from beyond, something which is part of the natural order.

In society Lawrence saw an increase in mere sensuality, trivia and material greed. The pages of Lawrence are full of examples of life-denying, ego-inflicting people, as, for example, the clerical shams in 'Daughters of the Vicar' and 'The Virgin and the Gipsy.'

Writing to Gordon Campbell Lawrence draws a distinction germane to his distaste for the Crucifixion story, a distinction that serves an introduction to his own Jesus, the stranger of *The Man Who Died.* Lawrence finds the death of Jesus unsatisfying because there is no suggestion that he had suffered a "dying into life." Hence Lawrence's essay, *The Risen Lord*, and the fable, *The Man Who Died,* where Lawrence's final position is revealed in all its power and tenderness. Lawrence regarded as petty the idea that resurrection was a matter of morality, sin and salvation. In *Why the Novel Matters* Lawrence has a brilliant paragraph commenting pertly on the text, "The Grass withereth, the flower fadeth, but the Word of the Lord shall stand for ever."

What Lawrence wanted was a tearing apart of the Christian fabric and weaving of a new mythology. It was the Risen Lord, not the crucified one, who revealed life's potency.

When we consider the amazing way in which, throughout the ages, sexuality has become a moral fetish, it is hardly surprising that Lawrence felt that society needed to reorientate itself radically. Lawrence frequently rejects accepted values. One example of Lawrence's reversals (and *Lawrence in Brief* reveals tellingly the sharpness of his unorthodox insights) may be found in the opening of his letter to Catherine Carswell where, in line with his later *The Man Who Died,* he denies the need for the renunciation of desires, maintaining instead that Christianity should be based on the fulfillment of desire. Related to this are his criticisms of Christianity in *Apocalypse* and in his preface to S.S. Koteliansky's translation of Dostoievsky's *The Grand Inquisitor* from *The Brothers Karamazov*. In the former he exclaims that pure Christianity cannot fit a nation or a society at large, it can only fit individuals. The argument is that Christianity took insufficient account of man's nature.

R.H. Poole observes, "Two important Lawrentian ideas are involved here. One is the importance of touch (whether of the act of sex merely touching, as in *You Touched Me* or *The Blind Man* as means of awakening to life, and the other is the power of pre-Christian religion represented by priestess of Isis. It is significant that in *Apocalypse* Lawrence also views *Revelation* as complementary to the 'pure Christianity' of Jesus. Part of the argument in *Apocalypse* is that *Revelation* is a mixture of Christianity and pre-Christian mythology."

Nietzsche follows Dostoievsky in finding the life of Jesus possible only for the few. Nietzsche had a contempt for the Christian concern for rewards, retribution and salvation consequent upon the resurrection. There follows from Lawrence's sense of the incompleteness of Jesus an appreciation that traditional Christian moral values were also incomplete. Lawrence views Vronsky's taking of Ann Karenina in Tolstoy's novel of that name, not as a sin but as a necessary consummation.

Lawrence thinks mankind is not in a state of sin but incompleteness. In *The Rainbow* occurs an episode when Ursula, after a quarrel with her sister, Theresa, goes away feeling "unchristian, but clean." Lawrence seizes upon the keystone of the Adam and Eve creation myth, inferring that its knowledge of the act that constitutes the sin. From his earliest days Lawrence maintained the humanity, not the divinity of Jesus. God was incarnate in nature but not specifically in Jesus. In his *Study of Thomas Hardy* Lawrence expands these concepts making use of another pair of polarities, the 'Will-to-Inertia' and the "Will-ot-Motion." The former he describes as female and the latter as male. The psychology of this is clear enough; more unusual is Lawrence's establishment of two opposite concepts which he entitles the 'two great conceptions, of Law and of Knowledge or Love' which are contradictions yet complementary to each other. When the two act together "then Life, something is created." He continues: "Now the principle of the Law is found strongest in Woman, and the principle of Love, in Man." Law signifies the natural law: it is stable, conservative, fecund, it is the "Will-to-Inertia," whereas the male principle, the "Will-to-Motion" is spirituality, love, mobility, mental activity. Hence God as the great female principle because God is the dark source of natural law, of being. However, since man is the active force "the expression of God has always been left to the male, so that the supreme God is forever He." Jesus, Lawrence considers, exemplifies the male spirit continually acting, continually projecting spiritual love.

The idea of conflict is embedded in Lawrence, and pa.ticularly that of spirit and flesh. In his dualities, in his expression of the primacy of the body, in his attack upon Christianity, Lawrence resembles an earlier revolutionary, William Blake. The latter's *The Marriage of Heaven and Hell* (1793) propounds at the outset the vitality of contrarieties. Like Lawrence, Blake attacks human reason because it makes an abstraction of what should be a living force: the god within.

Religious people, the Bible, and sacred codes have been guilty, says Blake, of three errors: that man has a body and soul; that good is to be equated with (passive) reason and evil with (active) energy; and that God would torment man in eternity for following his energies.

Lawrence's response to the mystery of religion may be observed in *The Rainbow* when Will and Anna visit Lincoln Cathedral. Their reactions differ. For Will, entry into the cathedral is a kind of sexual consummation, with the stones leaping upward in clustered desire till they meet in the arching dusk of the apex. In *The Plumed Serpent* the Catholic Doña Carlota is a more sympathetic embodiment of Christian love than is the fulsome Kangaroo. Lawrence's antipathy towards abstract, fleshless Christianity is seen in Ramon's talk with the Bishop concerning the disestablishement of the Roman Catholic church in Mexico.

P.H. Poole thinks it is in his finest poems that Lawrence's religious feelings show themselves at their purest, at their most mystical, though always with Lawrence the way to the central mystery lay through sensuous experience. Even animals exercised a fascination for Lawrence.

The value of the *Birds, Beasts and Flowers* collection lies partly in Lawrence's penetration below the level of the conscious. In 'The Song of a Man who Has Come Through' Lawrence's theme is the resurrection of man and woman into a new order of life.

God is a mysterious power felt throughout the physical universe, throughout the past and within the living now. This is Wordsworth's pantheism. Finally Lawrence thinks death had to be accepted with calm resignation. The possibility of no hereafter had to be faced. Basava, a twelfth century Indian thinker observes that life here is all the life one can have, no life hereafter. If life is so urgent perhaps its force could survive even oblivion for, even as the arx of the Etruscans suggested to Lawrence the continuance of life in the midst of death, so the ship of death might not sail in vain. Resurrection comes, not through a literal belief in the pagan death of the godman, but through a rich awareness of life in all its forms.

12

D.H. Lawrence Studies and Criticism

Lawrence, a controversial figure in English literature became the cause of even greater contention. Many of the obituary notices were downright bad, hurting the future posterity. T.S. Eliot, Clive Bell, J.C. Squire and others wrote denigratingly of Lawrence. Lawrence was, however, staunchly defended in the press by such old friends as Catherine Carswell. Lady Ottoline Morrell, who had forgiven Lawrence for portraying her as Hermione in *Women in Love*, spoke up for him in a public letter signed by her initials; Murty was anonymous in his defence of Lawrence. E.M. Forster wrote of him with generosity and appreciation.

Almost immediately afterwards, volumes of memoirs began to appear, most of them presenting a debased portrait of Lawrence. Two exceptions were Richard Aldington's *D.H. Lawrence* (1930), a reprint of a pamphlet of three years earlier, which had mildly amused Lawrence, and Rebecca West's *Elegy* (1930), taken from a magazine article that appeared soon after Lawrence's death. Rebecca West said that she had first heard that Lawrence was gravely ill while she was attending a performance of the dramatization of Huxley's *Point Counter Point*. She immediately thought what a loss to the play it would have been. if the character representing Lawrence (Mark Rampion) had been omitted: "Even so did those of us who heard of Lawrence's death feel that from the spectacle of the universe, by the incredible stupidity of a destroying angel, the best thing had gone." Stephen Potter's little book, *D.H. Lawrence: A First Study* (1930), was a purely critical exposition of the writings, almost entirely favourable. Then came Murry's *Son of Woman* (1931), which Aldous Huxley spoke of as a "curious essay in destructive hagiology". Murry was one of the leading British critics of this century, but his *Son of Woman* was a mistake, though he partly rectified it in 1957, the year of his death, in *Love, Freedom and Society: An Analytic Comparison of D.H. Lawrence and Albert Schweitzer.*

Young Lorenzo: Early Life of D.H. Lawrence (1932), by Lawrence's sister Ada (Mrs W.E. Clarke) and a Nottingham journalist, G. Stuart Gelder, was a sympathetic picture of the author's youth. But Mabel Dodge Luhan's *Lorenzo in Taos* (1932) showed Lawrence through the eyes of a neurotic woman. Her book and Murry's did enormous damage to his literary reputation. Readers of such volumes as Mrs Luhan's would hardly be convinced that the Lawrence they showed could have written anything worth reading, and the damage was not undone by two friendlier volumes of reminiscence, Catherine Carswell's *The Savage Pilgrimage* (1932) and the Hon. Dorothy Brett's Lawrence and Brett (1933). Murry's *Reminiscences of D. H. Lawrence* (1933) was a reprint of his memoirs of his former friend. Anais Nin's *D. H. Lawrence: A Critical Study* (1932) reprinted in 1964 did some good. *Lawrence's Letters* (1932), edited by Aldous Huxley, indicated to a good many readers that Lawrence was a first-rate writer, and sent them back to his imaginative works; Huxley was a good friend of Lawrence.

Meanwhile, the biographies had continued to appear in the 1930s. *D.H. Lawrence: Reminiscences and Correspondence* (1934), by E. and A. Brewster, was a sensible and detached book. Frieda's vigorous biography, *Not I, But the Wind* (1934), plangently defended Lawrence. Jessie Chambers (writing under the initials E.T.) showed in *D.H. Lawrence: A Personal Record* (1935) how cruelly the friend of her youth had treated her, and she indulged in some self-justification, incidentally revealing how little she really understood the man she had futilely loved. When the collection of Lawrence's writings, *Phoenix*, appeared in 1936, Clifton Fadiman in *The New Yorker* was publicly amused that such a writer could have attracted so much attention in the 1920s; an appraisal in *The Nation* (New York) by Harry T. Moore said that Phoenix would be "an influential book," and indeed it has proved to be so. In 1938, another of the more sympathetic memoirs appeared, *A Poet and Two*

Painters, by the Danish artist Knud Merrild, who tried to make a book-length reminiscence by muddling together a number of Lawrence's printed statements and disguising them as conversation. Hugh Kingsmill's *D.H. Lawrence* (1938) muddled together all the memoirs in a way that made Lawrence look more ridiculous than most of the individual memoirs had done. William York Tindall's *D.H. Lawrence and Susan His Cow* (1939) used Lawrence's own writings applied genuine scholarship to the subject. Lawrence was safely forgotten in the interwar years.

The Revival began. Professor Tindall helped pave the way for a revaluation of Lawrence when, in *Forces in Modern British Literature* (1946), he courageously indicated in public a change of mind and said in effect that, since we all now faced the possibility of being blown up, Lawrence's prophecies sound useful. Richard Aldington's *Portrait of a Genius, But...* (1950) was not bad. A generation of writers began to deal with Lawrence with detachment: Anthony West in *D.H. Lawrence* (1950), Harry T. Moore in *The Life and Works of D.H. Lawrence* (1951) and *The Intelligent Heart* (1955), Father William Tiverton (Martin Jarrett-Kerr) in *D.H. Lawrence and Human Existence* (1951), F.R. Leavis in *D.H. Lawrence: Novelist* (1955), and Mark Spilka in *The Love Ethic of D.H. Lawrence* (1955). One last unfriendly memoir came out in 1951, Winer Bynner's *Journey With Genius*. In *D.H. Lawrence: A Composite Biography* (1959), Edward Nehls usefully brought together a number of the memoirs in perspective and added various new ones, in a three-volume work of the highest value to students of modern literature. Studies on Lawrence continued. A D.H. Lawrence Society started at Eastwood. The D.H. Lawrence Society of North America meets each year with the Modern Language Association, and there is an active Lawrence Society in Japan. Lawrence is taught in schools everywhere, and he has been recognized with a plaque in the Poet's Corner of Westminster Abbey.

A few of the many books published about Lawrence since 1966 are mentioned here. *The D.H. Lawrence Review* under the editorship of James Cowan has become one of the more distinguished of the many periodicals devoted to a single author. In 1984 with the publication of Volume 17 direction of the *Review* passed to Dennis Jackson who now edits it from the University of Delaware. A useful exploration of Lawrence's early experience is available in *D.H. Lawrence: L'Homme et La Genese de Son Oeuvre, Les Annees de Formation* (1969) by Emile Delavenay (English edition, Heinemann, 1972). Harry T. Moore's biography *The Intelligent Heart* was revised in 1974 as *The Priest of Love*. Martin Green's *The von Richthofen Sisters* (1974) offers new and important background material about Frieda Lawrence and her influence on Lawrence. Carl Baron of St Catharine's College, Cambridge, edited G.H. Neville's memoir of D.H. Lawrence, *The Betrayal* (1981). The 1963 *Soho Bibliography of D.H. Lawrence* by F.W. Roberts was revised for publication by Cambridge in 1982, and the first volume of James Cowan's comprehensive two volume annotated bibliography of secondary sources was published in 1981.

Many new Lawrence letters have been discovered, the two most important published collections being *Lawrence in Love: Letters from D.H. Lawrence to Louie Burrows,* edited by James Boulton (1968) and *D.H. Lawrence: Letters to Thomas and Adele Seltzer*, edited by Gerald Lacy (1976).

By far the most significant contribution to Lawrence scholarship is the monumental D.H. Lawrence project initiated by the Cambridge University Press in the early 1970s under the direction of Michael Black. The Press has undertaken the publication of a complete edition of Lawrence's letters and his complete works in some thirty-seven volumes.

James Boulton is General Editor for *The Letters of D.H. Lawrence,* volume IV, of which appeared in 1987. General Editors for *The Cambridge Edition of the Works of D.H. Lawrence* are James Boulton and Warren Roberts. Volumes published so far are: *Apocalypse and the Writings on Revelation* (1980); *The Lost Girl* and *The Trespasser* (1981); *The White Peacock* and *The Prussian Officer and Other Stories* (1983); *Mr Noon* which included the newly discovered manuscript of the second half of the novel, a publishing event of major importance, and *Thomas Hardy and Other Essays* (1985); *Women in Love, The Plumed Serpent* and *Love Among the Haystacks and Other Stories* (1987).

13

Conclusion

Richard Aldington who in his introduction to Lawrence's *Selected Essays* (Penguin, 1950) thinks Lawrence's great literary output is remarkable for its diversity in originality, its versatility. As the impulse took him he attempted different kinds of writing, and failed only as a writer of plays. His was not a long career, a quarter of a century of writing and less than twenty years of publishing at most; but he was inexhaustibly fertile. From 1911 to 1930 not a year passed without the publication of at least one and often several books, and the amount of material unpublished or lost in periadicals which has been recovered since his death exceeds the total output of more sterile authors. All this mass of writing is held together by no formal links but by the magical power of Lawrence's unique temperament.

Aldington observes, "Consider the variety of his achievements. *Sons and Lovers, Women in Love, Aaron's Rod, Kangaroo, The Plumed Serpent,* how different they are, what different worlds they explore, how unlike other novels of the time! Lawrence took up the short novel or novelette, and made it his own mouth-piece, from the curious psychology of *The Captain's Doll* to the virulent satire of *St Mawr*. In the short story he produced such masterpieces as *The Prussian Officer, England, my England* and *The Woman Who Rode Away*, and such scathing satires as *Jimmy and the Desperate Woman* and *The Man Who Loved Islands*. Think of his travel books, the matchless *Sea and Sardinia, Twilight in Italy, Mornings in Mexico,* and *Etruscan Places.* As poet, basing himself on Hardy and Whitman, he kept vividly alive and honest an art which is dying out in a series of parlour tricks. Yet it was after his death that some of his best work as a poet was revealed, and that he was discovered to be one of the most entertaining of English letter-writers."

Lawrence was really a great writer. He was both prolific and versatile. He was both original and controversial. His contribution to western literature and thought is immense.

Lawrence's writings as they were controversial provoked a lot of reaction and criticism. Many critics, including Murry sometimes, reacted against Lawrence much harshly. Some of the critics, particularly Aldous Huxley, Murry, Forster and Leavis spoke of Lawrence with sympathy and reality. Forster defended Lawrence boldly in a BBC interview.

According to E.M. Forster "in one of his recent talks Mr. Desmond MacCarthy remarked that D.H. Lawrence is a difficult writer. You cannot understand a writer without reading him-an obvious and painful truth, and one that is often forgotten. And the only real reward a writer can have is to be read. At present Lawrence is not being read enough or in the right way. He has two publics, neither of them quite satisfactory. There is the general public, who think of him as improper and scarcely read him at all, and there is a special public, who read him, but in too narrow and fanatical a way, and think of him as a sort of god, who has come to change human nature and society. His own public—a real public-he has scarcely found that yet. I regard him myself as one of the great writers of our time."

Lawrence belonged to the working classes. He grew up in a collier's cottage on the border of Notts and Derby, and he describes that country and the life there in his two early novels *The White Peacock* and *Sons and Lovers*, and in his play, *The Widowing of Mrs Holroyd*. He never worked down the mine himself. He was framed as a teacher probably owing to the influence of his mother: he was devoted to his mother; she had great character and intelligence and her death was one of the most terrible things he had to bear. For a time he was a schoolmaster at Croydon near London and perhaps this accounts for his mistrust of education. Then he took to literature. Shelley must have been a little like that, but Lawrence was a rougher, tougher than Shelley. The war developed. His health was already very bad, and exempted him from military service, but not from the terrors of the civilization. He suffered acutely; moreover his wife, to whom he was devoted, was German, and they were persecuted at Carnwall by stay-at-home patriots and driven from place to place. He has left a description of this in his Australian novel *Kangaroo*. Lawrence escaped from England at last, and never settled down in it again. For the rest of his life he moved from country to country Germany, Italy, Australia, Mexico, etc.-pursued by good advice from the admirers of his earlier work, and, greatly to his credit, never taking the least notice of it. His later work is less admired, as it is didactic.

Lawrence felt himself to be a teacher with a message to us to follow our instincts. It was his philosophy that liberated his imagination. His treatment of sex, for instance has raised such protests. But it does connect up with things. You cannot say, "Let us drop his theories and enjoy his art," because the two are one. Disbelieve his theories, if you like, but never brush them aside. And do not scold him, even when he scolds you.

Lawrence's dislike of civilization was not a pose, as it is with many writers. He hated it fundamentally, because it has made human beings conscious, and society mechanical. Like Blake and other mystics, he condemns the intellect with its barren chains of reasoning and its dead weights of information; he even hates self-sacrifice, and love. He believes in individuality—his mysticism is not of the Buddhistic, annihilistic sort—and, illogical as it sounds.

Murry and his wife, the New Zealand writer Katherine Mansfield were the friends of the Lawrences for long as hinted at it often. Murry liked Lawrence's writings, of course reviewing them often. Murry's reviews about *The Lost Girl* (1920), *Women in Love* (1920), *Aaron's Rod* (1922), *Lady Chatterley's Lover* (1928), and many more items encouraged Lawrence rather critically. Murry welcomed *Chatterley's Lover* calling it "a cleansing book," though for him it represented a half-truth. Later Eliot reviewed Murry's book *Son of Woman* in 1931.

Aldous Huxley and his wife Maria were occasional visitors at Villa Mirenda, and the Lawrences liked them, even if Lawrence cared little for Huxley's clever novels. Huxley was in Lawrence's view over-intellectualized (as Lawrence himself of course was, and this is one reason he fought against the condition in others); but Huxley paid him serious, open-minded attention when they argued about science, which to Lawrence had become one of the great menaces of the world. Huxley edited Lawrences's letters in 1932.

According to Forster, "Lawrence's novels are bound to be unusual. We usually ask of a novel, firstly, that its characters shall live; secondly, that it shall have some sort of unity, and if we apply either of these tests to his books they fail. In the earlier books, some of the people are alive because he was drawing more on his surroundings than he did later: George Saxton in *The White Peacock* was modelled on a young farmer he knew, and the mother in *Sons and Lovers* is his own mother. And all through his career he was capable of clever, malicious thumbnail sketches-the short story entitled 'Jimmy and the Desperate Woman' contains one of them. But he was not a true creator of character. And a similar doubt will beset you when you apply the second of the tests suggested above-the test of artistic unity. The plots are not well made, the books are not aesthetic wholes, yet there is a satisfied feeling at the close." One novel does survive the normal construction tests, and that is *The Plumed Serpent*. It is, on the face of it, a preposterous work about three people who dress up and pretend that the ancient gods of Mexico have returned to earth. But it is beautifully put together, the atmosphere increases with the story, both culminate.

F.R. Leavis in his work *Victorian Tradition* speaks of seven great English novelists and Lawrence is one of those seven writers. He was Lawrence's best advocate and critic. He published his first essay on Lawrence, emphasizing the correctness and relevance of Lawrence's criticism of modern industrial civilization. He wrote books like *D.H.L.* (Minority Press, 1930) and *D.H.L: Novelist* (Chatto and Windus, 1955).

T. S. Eliot had an unusual interest in Lawrence's myriad intellectual activities and he was a friend of Murry who was a friend of Mr. Lawrence. In fact, Eliot liked Murry's criticism of Lawrence. Eliot later reviewed Murry's book on Lawrence called *Son of Woman.* Eliot thinks Lawrence, throughout the rest of his life, was a strange mixture of sincerity or clairvoyance with self-deception or rather with the effort towards self-deception. Lawrence's subsequent history, and the history of his novels, is accordingly a record of his various attempts to kid himself into believing that he was right to be as he was, and that the rest of the world was wrong.

Eliot writes in "'A better illustration of Lawrence's 'ignorance', and a fault which corrupts his whole philosophy of human relations—which is hardly anything but a philosophy of human relations and unrelations—is his hopeless attempt to find some mode in which two persons—of the opposite sex, and then as a venture of despair, of the same sex—may be spiritually united. As Mr. Murry spares no pains to show, the whole history of Lawrence's life and of Lawrence's writings is the history of his craving for greater intimacy than is possible between human beings, a craving irritated to the point of frenzy by his unusual incapacity for being intimate at all. His struggle against over-intellectualized life is the history of his own over-intellectualized nature. Even in his travels to more primitive lands, he could never take the crude peoples simply for what they are; he must needs always be expecting something of them that they could not give, something peculiarly medicinal for himself. He was looking for it there, just as he looked within the men and women he knew, without finding it. Other men and women have needs of their own.

"There remains, however, one book, which I have not read, but which I judge from Mr. Murry's account to be worthy of the importance which Mr. Murry assigns to it: *Fantasia of the Unconscious*. It would appear that in this book Lawrence reached his culmination, and that his subsequent work marks chiefly decline and collapse."

He concludes, "One must, in considering a writer like Lawrence, confess what will be called one's prejudices, and leave the rest to the reader."

Chronology of D.H. Lawrence's Life

1885	D.H.Lawrence born at Eastwood, Nottinghamshire.
1898-1901	Attended Nottingham High School.
1901	Met Jessie Chambers ('Miriam').
1902-1906	Student teacher.
1904	Engaged to Jessie Chambers.
1906	First poems.
1906	Entered University College, Nottingham. Began *The White Peacock* (finished 1910, published 1911).
1907	First stories.
1908	Awarded teacher's certificate at Nottingham U.C.; went to teach in Croydon.
1910	Began *The Trespasser* (pubd. 1912). Broke with Jessie; became engaged to Louie Burrows; began *Paul Morel* (later *Sons and Lovers*, pubd. 1913). Death of mother.
1912	Illness: abandoned teaching career; returned to Eastwood; met Frieda von Richthofen Weekley, and eloped with her to Germany and Italy. Stories; poems pubd. in *Look! We Have Come Through* (1917), *The Widowing of Mrs Holroyd* (1914). Finished *Sons and Lovers*.
1913	Began *The Lost Girl* (*The Insurrection of Miss Houghton*). First versions of essays in *Twilight in Italy* (1916). Began *The Sisters* (first version of *Women in Love* and *The Rainbow*). Wrote 'The Prussian Officer,' title story of volume pubd. 1914.

1915 Returned to England in June. Wrote *Thomas Hardy*, worked on *The Sisters*.

1915 *The Rainbow* published and suppressed. Friendship with Russell. Wrote 'The Crown.' Tried to get passports for U.S.A.

1916 Cornwall. Quarrel with Russell. Wrote *Women in Love*.

1917 Wrote 'The Reality of Peace'. Began *Studies in Classic American Literature*. Was refused passports. Failed army medical examination. Persecuted by the army and expelled from Cornwall on suspicion of spying. Began *Aaron's Rod* (pubd. 1922).

1918 Wrote most of *Movements in European Literature* (1921). Play *Touch and Go*. 'Education of the People'. First version of *The Fox* (1923). Army medical examination described in *Kangaroo*.

1919 Stories for *England My England;* finished first draft *Aaron's Rod.* Went to Italy.

1920 Lived in Florence, Capri, and Taormina, Sicily. Sicilian poems of *Birds, Beasts and Flowers* (1923). Revised *Studies in Classic American Literature*. Finished *The Lost Girl*, worked on *Aaron's Rod.* Wrote *Psychoanalysis and the Unconscious* (1921) and fragmentary novel *Mr. Noon*.

1921 Visit to Sardinia, and wrote *Sea and Sardinia* (1921). *Fantasia of the Unconscious* (1922). Final version *Aaron's Rod; The Captain's Doll* and *The Ladybird*.

1922 Translating Sicilian novelist Verga; introduction to Maurice Magnus's *Memoirs of the Foreign Legion* (1924). Left for Ceylon, where the Lawrences stayed with the Brewsters; arrived in Australia in May. Wrote most of *Kangaroo* (1923). Arrived in Taos, New Mexico. Rewrote Mollie Skinner's *The Boy in the Bush* (1924).

1923	More of *Birds, Beasts and Flowers.* Final version of *Studies in Classic American Literature.*(1923). First draft *Plumed Serpent* (1926). Visited Mexico. Visited England and Europe.
1924	Saw Frederick Carter in Shropshire. Returned to Taos. Wrote pieces for *Mornings in Mexico* (1927). *The Woman Who Rode Away* (pubd. 1928). *St Mawr* (1925). *The Princess.* Began revision of *Quetzalcoatl* (*The Plumed Serpent*, 1926).
1925	Seriously ill in Mexico City. *The Flying Fish.* Final version *Plumed Serpent.* The play *David.* Essays on the novel. Returned to England, then to Germany and Italy.
1926	*The Virgin and the Gipsy* (1930). Stories. Settled in Villa Mirenda, near Florence. Last visit to England. Began *Lady Chatterley's Lover* (1928), wrote first two versions.
1927	Paintings. First part of *Escaped Cock* (*The Man Who Died*, 1929). Correspondence with Trigant Burrow. Began *Etruscan Places* (1932).
1928	Final version *Lady Chatterley's Lover.* Visit to Germany. Lived at Bandol, in South of France. Manuscript of *Pansies* seized by postal authorities. Finished *The Man Who Died.* Many articles; 'Introduction to These Paintings'.
1929	Visit to Majorca; Florence, Germany: return to Bandol. Seizure of paintings in London. *More Pansies* (1932). *My Skirmish with Jolly Roger* (later enlarged as *A Propos of Lady Chatterley's Lover* (1930)). *Nettles* (1930). *Tomography and Obscenity* (1929). *Apocalypse* (1931).
1930	Moved into sanatorium at Vence, 6 February. Died 2 March.

Annexure-II

D.H. Lawrence's Works

Novels

The White Peacock (1911), *The Trespasser* (1912), *Sons and Lovers* (1913), *The Rainbow* (1915), *Women in Love* (1920), *The Lost Girl* (1920), *Aaron's Rod* (1922), *Kangaroo* (1924), *The Boy in the Bush* (with M. L. Skinner, 1924), *The Plumed Serpent* (1926), *Lady Chatterley's Lover* (1928), [The two earlier versions are published as *The First Lady Chatterley* (1972) and *John Thomas and Lady Jane* (1972)], *Mr Noon* (1984)

Short Novels

Love Among the Haystacks, The Ladybird, The Fox, The Captain's Doll, The Man Who Died (The Escaped Cock), St Mawr, The Princess, The Virgin and the Gipsy, Sun (1926)

Short Stories

Lawrence published many independent books of short stories in his time and others brought out new collections of stories since then and the titles of them are as these: *Love among the Haystacks, England My England, The Woman Who Rode Away, The Prussian Officer and Other Stories, The Princess,* and *The Mortal Coil.* A complete list of his stories is as follows:

A Prelude, A Fragment of Stained Glass, The White Stocking, Goose Fair, Odour of Chrysanthemums, Daughters of the Vicar, Lessford's Rabbits, A Lesson and Tortoise, A Fly in the Ointment, The Old Adam, The Witch a la Mode, Delilah and Mr. Bircumshaw, Second Best, The Shadow in the Rose Garden, A Sick Collier, Strike Pay, Her Turn, The Miner at

Home, The Christening, A Modern Lover, The Shades of Spring, Love Among the Haystacks, A Chapel Among the Mountains, A Hay Hut Among the Mountains, Once, Bei Hennef, The Mortal Coil, The Thorn in the Flesh, The Prussian Officer (Honour and Arms), New Eve and Old Adam, The Primrose Path, The Thimble, England, My England, Samson and Delilah, The Horse Dealer's Daughter, The Blind Man, You Touched Me, Fanny and Annie, Tickets Please, Wintry Peacock, The Fox, Monkey Nuts, The Captain's Doll, The Countess Hannele, Baroness Mitchka, The Ladybird, Pan in America, The Overtone, None of that, The Princess, The Woman Who Rode Away, St Mawr, The Border Line, A Letter from Germany, The Last Laugh, Smile, The Blue Birds, The Man who Loved Islands, The Man who was through with the World, Things, Sun, The Virgin and Gipsy, The Man who Died, The Flying Fish, Rawdon's Roof, The Rocking Horse Winner, The Lovely Lady, The Blue Moccasins, Mother and Daughter,

Poetry

First published: *Love Poems and Others*, 1913; *Amores*, 1916; *Look! We Have Come Through*, 1917; *New Poems,* 1918; *Bay* 1919; *Tortoises*, 1921; *Birds, Beasts, and Flowers,* 1923; *Pansies*, 1929; *Nettles*, 1930; *Last Poems,* 1932; *Fire and Other Poems,* 1940; *The Complete Poems of D.H. Lawrence*, 1964.

Plays

A Collier's Friday Night (1906, 1909), *The Widowing of Mrs Holroyd* (1910, 1913), *The Merry-Go-Round* (1911), *The Married Man* (1912), *The Fight for Barbara* (1912), *The Daughter-in-Law* (1913), *Touch and Go* (1918), *Altitude* (1924), *Noah's Flood* (1925), and *David* (1925). *The Complete Plays of D.H. Lawrence* (1965); *The Complete Plays of D.H. Lawrence* (Heinemann, 1965, Viking, 1966).

Essays

The books *Fantasia of the Unconscious* (1922) and *Psychoanalysis and the Unconscious* (1921) published together contain the following: The Holy Family, Plexuses, Places and so on, Trees and babies and Papas and Mamas, The Five Senses, First Glimmerings of Mind, Education and Sex in Man, Woman and Child, The Birth of Sex, Parent Love, The Vicious Circle, Litany of Exhortations, Cosmological, Sleep and Dreams, The Lower Self

Travelogues

Twilight in Italy (1916), *Sea and Sardinia* (1921), *Etruscan Places* (1932), *Mornings in Mexico* (1927)

Criticism

Psychoanalysis and the Unconscious (1921); *Movements in European History* (1921); *Fantasia of the Unconscious* (1922); *Studies in Classic American Literature* (1923); *Reflections on the Death of a Porcupine* (1925); *Pornography and Obscenity* (1929); *Assorted Articles* (1930); *A Propos of Lady Chatterley's Lover* (1930); *Apocalypse* (1931); *Phoenix* (1936); *The Symbolic Meaning* (1962); *Phoenix* II (1968)

Paintings

The Paintings of D.H. Lawrence (1929)

Lawrence's Fame Outside Britain

No distinction has been made between Lawrence's reputation in Britain and America, since his work from the very first was published in both countries. In other countries, judging by translations, interest in his work began in the 1920s. The first of his novels to be translated into a foreign language was *The Rainbow,* which appeared in German in 1922. This was followed in 1925 by *Jack lm Buschland* (*The Boy in the Bush*), translated by Else Jaffe-Richthofen, the academic. Elder sister of Frieda Lawrence (nee Richthofen), who also translated *The Fox* (1926) and *The Woman Who Rode Away* (1928). Other translators produced German versions of *Sons and Lovers* (1925), *Women in Love* (1927), *Fantasia of the Unconscious* (1929), *Lady Chatterley* (1930), *St Mawr* (1931) and several other works between 1932-9.

Surprisingly, it was the Japanese who next paid attention to Lawrence, translating *Women in Love* (1923), *The Rainbow* (1924), *The Captain's Doll* (1924) and eighteen more items in Warren Roberts' list in the 1930s. Russian interest was also early (*Aaron's Rod* and *The Rainbow* both translated in 1925), but does not seem to have continued. The first French translation was *Le Renard* (*The Fox*), 1928, followed by *England, My England* (1930), *Sons and Lovers* (1931), *The Plumed Serpent* (1931), *Lady Chatterley's Lover* (1932), *St Mawr* (1932), *Women in Love* (1932), and, again, a long list of other works in the 1930s. Italian interest began, like the French, with *The Fox* (1929), and in 1933 five of the novels were translated: *The Trespasser, The White Peat:!ck, Sons and Lovers, St Mawr* and *The Lost Girl*. Under the editorship of the distinguished Italian biographer of Lawrence, Piero Nardi, the complete works have now been translated into Italian, including the otherwise unavailable second version of *Lady Chatterley's Lover* (translated by Carlo Izzo).

In other languages the most popular of Lawrence's books have been *Sons and Lovers*, translated into Swedish (1925), Roumanian (before 1930), Czech (1931), Spanish (1933), Croatian, Finnish and Hebrew (1934), and Danish and Norwegian (1935); and, as might be expected, *Lady Chatterley's Lover* into Czech, Danish, Polish and Spanish (1932), Hungarian (1933), and Hebrew and Portuguese (1938).

Annexure-I

A Select Bibliography

D.H. Lawrence's Works

Novels

The White Peacock, 1911. (Penguin).

The Trespasser, 1912. (Penguin).

Sons and Lovers, 1913. (Penguin; Viking Press)

The Rainbow, 1915. (Penguin; Viking).

Women in Love, 1920. (Penguin; Viking).

The Lost Girl, 1920. (Penguin; Viking).

Aaron's Rod, 1922. (Penguin; Viking).

Kangaroo, 1924. (Penguin; Viking).

The Boy in the Bush (with M. L. Skinner) 1924. (Penguin).

The Plumed Serpent, 1926. (Penguin; Viking).

Lady Chatterley's Lover, 1928. (Penguin; Viking).

[The two earlier versions are published as *The First Lady Chatterley* (1972) and *John Thomas and Lady Jane* (1972)]

Mr Noon (1984)

Short Novels

For the novelle, Viking's *Four Short Novels of D.H.*Lawrence includes *Love Among the Haystacks, The Ladybird, The Fox* and *The Captain's Doll.* Penguin's *Love Among the Haystacks* includes, along with the title story and some short stories, *The Man Who Died; The Ladybird* (Penguin) includes the novella of that title, with *The Fox* and *The Captain's Doll; St Mawr* and *The Virgin and the Gipsy* share a volume.

Short Stories

Lawrence's short stories are published complete in three volumes by Viking. The Penguin collections *Love Among the Haystacks, England My England, The Woman Who Rode Away, The Prussian Officer, The Princess* and *The Mortal Coil* together include all the short stories.

Plays

A Collier's Friday Night (1906, 1909), *The Widowing of Mrs Holroyd* (1910, 1913), *The Merry-Go-Round* (1911), *The Married Man* (1912), *The Fight for Barbara* (1912), *The Daughter-in-Law* (1913), *Touch and Go* (1918), *Altitude* (1924), *Noah's Flood* (1925), and *David* (1925). *The Complete Plays of D.H. Lawrence* (1965); *The Complete Plays of D.H. Lawrence* (Heinemann, 1965, Viking, 1966).

Poetry

First published: *Love Poems and Others*, 1913; *Amores*, 1916; *Look! We Have Come Through*, 1917; *New Poems*, 1918; *Bay* 1919; *Tortoises*, 1921; *Birds, Beasts, and Flowers*, 1923; *Pansies*, 1929; *Nettles*, 1930; *Last Poems*, 1932; *Fire and Other Poems*, 1940; *The Complete Poems of D. H. Lawrence*, 1964.

Travellogues

Twilight in Italy, 1916. (Penguin; Viking), *Sea and Sardinia*, (Penguin; Viking), *Mornings in Mexico*, 1927. (Penguin), *Etruscan Places*, 1932. (Penguin), *Mornings in Mexico*, 1927 (Viking).

Other Prose Writings

Phoenix: The Posthumous Papers of D.H. Lawrence, ed. Edward D. McDonald, 1936. (Heinemann; Viking).

Phoenix II: More Uncollected Writings, ed. Warren Roberts and Harry T. Moore, 1968. (Heinemann; Viking).

These volumes contain, among other essays, 'Pornography and Obscenity,' 'Study of Thomas Hardy,' 'John Galsworthy,' 'Introduction to These Paintings,' 'Education of the People,' 'The Reality of Peace,' 'Prologue to Women in Love,' The Crown' (originally published in *Reflections on the Death of a Porcupine* (1925), essays on the novel, and such important brief pieces as 'The State of Funk' and 'The Risen Lord.'

Movements in European History (by 'Lawrence H. Davison'), 1921. 2nd ed. of 1925 is under D.H. Lawrence's name. New edition with previously unpublished afterword, Oxford University Press, 1972.

Psychoanalysis and the Unconscious, 1921; *Fantasia and the Unconscious*, 1922. Published together with introduction by Philip Rieff, Viking Compass.

Studies in Classic American Literature, 1923. (Viking Compass.)

The earlier versions of these essays published as *The Symbolic Meaning*, ed. Armin Arnold, 1962.

Pornography and Obscenity, 1929. (In *Phoenix* I)

A Propos of Lady Chatterley's Lover, 1930 (first version, *My Skirmish With Jolly Roger*, 1929). (In *Phoenix II*; also reprinted, with *Pornography and Obscenity*, the 'Introduction to Pansies' and other relevant pieces, in *Sex, Literature and Censorship*, ed. Harry T. Moore (Viking Compass). *Apocalypse*, 1931. (Viking Compass.)

Penguin published *Selected Essays* and a selection from *Phoenix.*

There is a *Selected Literary Criticism,* ed. Anthony Beal (Mer-cury).

Letters

The Letters of D.H. Lawrence, ed. Aldous Huxley, 1932.

The Collected Letters of D.H. Lawrence, ed. Harry T. Moore, 1962 (Heinemann; Viking).

Bibliography

Barren Roberts, *A Bibliography of D.H. Lawrence,* 1963.

Biography

Harry T. Moore, *The Intelligent Heart,* 1954. (Penguin.)

Edward Nehls, *D.H. Lawrence: A Composite Biography* (three volumes, 1957, 1958, 1959).

Critical Works on Lawrence

Books

Aldington, Richard, *D.H.L., An Indiscretion,* Seattle, 1927.

_______*D.H.L.,* Chatto and Windus, 1930.

_______*Portrait of a Genius, But...,* Heinemann, 1950.

Arnold, Armin, *D.H.L. and America,* Linden Press, 1958.

Beal, Anthony, *D.H.L.,* Oliver and Boyd, 1961.

Boadella, David, *The Spiral Flame,* Ritter, Nottingham, 1956.

Brett, Dorothy, *L. and Brett,* Secker, 1933.

Brewster, Earl and Achsah, *D.H.L., Reminiscences and Correspondence,* Secker, 1934.

Bynner, Witter, *Journey with Genius,* John Day, N.Y., 1951; Nevin, 1953.

Corke, Helen, *L. and Apocalypse* Heinemann, 1933.

Carswell, Catherine, *The Savag, Pilgrimage,* Chatto and Windus, 1932.

Carter, Frederick, *D.H.L. and the Body Mystical,* Archer, 1932.

Clark, L. D., *Dark Night of the Body,* Texas, 1964.

Daleski, H. M., *The Forked Flame,* Faber and Faber, 1965.

Drain, Richard L., *Tradition and D.H.L.,* Groningen, 1960.

Draper, R. P. *D.H.L.,* Twayne, 1964.

E.T. (Jessie Chambers), *D.H.L., A Personal Record,* Cape, 1935.

Freeman, Mary, *D.H.L., A Basic Study of His Ideas,* Florida, 1955.

Goodheart, Eugene, *The Utopian Vision of D.H.L.*, Chicago, 1963.

Goodman, Richard, *Footnote to Lawrence*, White Owl Press, 1932.

Gregory, Horace, *Pilgrim of the Apocalypse*, Secker, 1934.

Hoffman, Frederick J. and Harry T. Moore, *The Achievement of D.H.L.*, Oklahoma, 1953.

Hoggart, Richard. *Introduction* to *Lady Chatterley's Lover*, Penguin, 1961.

Hough, Graham, *The Dark Sun*, Duckworth, 1956.

Kenmare, Dallas, *Fire-Bird, A Study of D.H.L.*, Barrie, 1951.

Kingsmill, Hugh, *D.H.L.*, Methuen, 1938.

Lawrence, Ada and Stuart Gelder, *Young Lorenzo, Early Life of D.H.L.*, Orioli, Florence, 1931.

Lawrence, Frieda, *Not I, But the Wind*, Heinemann, 1935.

Lawrence, Frieda, *The Memoirs and Correspondence*, ed. E.W. Tedlock, Heinemann, 1961.

Leavis, F. R., *D.H.L.*, Minority Press, Cambridge, 1930.

_______*D.H.L: Novelist*, Chatto and Windus, 1955.

Luahn, Mabel, *Lorenzo in Taos*, Secker, 1932.

Merrild, Knud., *A Poet and Two Painters*, Routledge, 1938.

Moore, Harry T., *The Life and Works of D.H.L.*, Allen and Unwin, 1951 (revised ed. Twayne, 1964).

_______*Poste Restante, A Lawrence Travel Calendar* California, 1956.

_______*The Intelligent Heart*, Heinemann, 1955.

_______*A D.H.L. Miscellany*, Carbondale, Illinois, 1959.

Murry, J. M., *Reminiscences of D.H.L.*, Cape, 1933.

_______*Love, Freedom and Society*, Cape, 1957.

_______*D.H.L.*, Minority Press, Cambridge, 1930.

_______*Son of Woman*, Cape, 1931.

Moynahan, Julian, *The Deed of Life*, Oxford, 1963.

Nehls, Edward, *D.H.L., A Composite Biography*, Wisconsin, 1957-9.

Nin, Anais, *D.H.L., An Unprofessional Study*, Titus Paris, 1932; Spearman, London, 1961.

Panichas, G. A., *Adventures in Consciousness: The Meaning of D.H.L.'s Religious Quest*, The Hague, 1964.

Pinto, V. de S., *D.H.L., Prophet of the Midlands*, Nottingham, 1951.

_______*D.H.L. After Thirty Years*, University of Nottingham, 1960.

Potter, Stephen, *D.H.L., A First Study*, Cape, 1930.

Rees, Richard, *Brave Men, A Study of D.H.L. and Simone Weil*, Gollancz, 1958.

Rolph, C. H., *The Trial of Lady Chatterley*, Penguin, 1961.

Seligmann, Herbert J., *D.H.L. An American Interpretation*, Seltzer, 1924.

Spilka, Mark, *The Love Ethic of D.H.L.*, Indiana, 1955.

Spilka, Mark, *D.H.L.*, Prentice-Hall, 1963.

Tedlock, E. W., *D.H.L., Artist and Rebel,* New Mexico, 1964.

Tindal, William York, *D.H.L. and Susan His Cow,* Columbia University, N.Y., 1939.

Tiverton, Father William (Martin Jarrett Kerr), *D.H.L. and Human Existence,* Rockliff, 1951.

Vivas, Eliseo, *D.H.L., The Failure and the Triumph of Art,* Northwestern U.P., 1960.

Weiss, Daniel A., *Oedipus in Nottingham,* Seattle, 1962.

West, Rebecca, *D.H.L.,* Secker, 1930.

West, Anthony, *D.H.L.,* Barker, 1950.

Widmer, Kingsley, *The Art of Perversity,* Washington, 1962.

Young, Kenneth, *D.H.L.,* Longmans Green, 1951.

Articles

Bennett, Arnold, 'D.H.L.'s Delusion,' *Evening Standard*, 10 April 1930.

Coombes, H., 'D.H.L. Placed,' *Scrutiny*, March 1949.

Danby, John F., 'D.H.L.,' *Cambridge Journal,* February 1951.

Eliot, T. S., 'Son of Woman,' *Criterion*, July 1931.

Grant, Douglas, 'England's Phoenix,' *Univ. of Toronto Quarterly*, XXVII (1958), 223.

Klingopulos, G.D. 'L.'s Criticism,' *Essays in Criticism*, July 1957.

Stewart, D., 'Immoral Books, *Lady Chatterley* and *The Shropshire Lad*,' *The European*, March 1953.

Traversi, Derek, 'Dr Leavis and the Case of D.H.L.,' *Month*, Mardi 1956.

Wilson, Angus, 'At the Heart of L.' *Encounter*, December 1955.

Adelman, G. 'Beyond the Pleasure Principle: An Analysis of D.H.L.'s The Prussian Officer,' *Studies in Short Fiction*, I, Fall 1963.

Aldington, Richard. 'A Wreath for L.,' *Encounter*, April 1960.

Armin, Arnold. 'D.H.L. and Thomas Mann,' *Comparative Literature,* XIII, i, 33-8.

Auden, W. H., 'D.H.L.' in *The Dyer's Hand,* Faber, 1963.

Baldanza, Frank. 'D.H.L.'s Song of Songs,' *Modern Fiction Studies,* 7 .

Bartlett, Norman. 'Aldous Huxley and D.H.L.,' *Australian Quarterly*, XXXVI, i, 76-84.

Beebe, Maurice. 'L.'s Sacred Fount: The Artist Theme of *Sons and Lovers,' Texas Studies in Literature and Language*, IV, 539-52.

Benedict, John. *'The Lady Chatterley's Lover* Case,' *American Mercury*, January 1960.

Bramley, J. A. 'The Challenge of D.H.L.,' *Hibbert Journal,* April 1960.

Branda, Eldon S. 'Textual Changes in *Women in Love*,' *Texas Studies in Literature and Language*, VI, 306-21.

Chamberlain, Robert L. 'Pussum, Minette, and the Afro-Nordic Symbol in L.'s *Women in Love*,' *PMLA*, September 1963.

Clements, A. L. 'The Quest for Self: D.H.L.'s *The Rainbow*,' *Thoth*, III, Spring 1962.

Corke, Helen. 'Concerning *The White Peacock*,' *Texas Quarterly*, Winter 1959.

Cornwell, Ethel F. 'The Sex Mysticism of D.H.L.' in *The Still Point*, Rutgers, 1962.

Cowan, James C. 'The Function of Allusions and Symbols in *The Man Who Died*,' *American Image*, XVII, 3.

Craig, G. Armour. 'D.H.L. on Thinghood and Selfhood,' *Massachusetts Review*, I, 56-60.

Cross, Barbara. 'L. and the Unbroken Circle,' *Perspective*, X, 3.

Dahlberg, Edward and Read, Herbert, on D.H.L. in *Truth is Afore Sacred*, Routledge and Kegan Paul, 1961.

Empson, William. 'Lady Chatterley Again,' *Essays in Criticism*, XIII, 101-4.

Engelberg, Edward. '*The Rainbow* as a Modern Bildungsroman,' *PMLA*, March 1963.

Englander, Ann. '*The Prussian Officer*: The Self Divided,' *Sewanee Review*, LXXI, 605-19.

Ford, George H. 'Shelley or Schiller? A Note on D.H.L. at Work,' *Texas Studies in Literature and Language*, IV, 154-6.

______ 'The Wedding Chapter of *Women in Love*,' *Texas Studies in Literature and Language*, VI, 134-47.

Foster, D. W. 'L., Sex and Religion,' *Theology*, January 1961.

Fraiberg, Louis. 'The Unattainable Self: *Sons and Lovers*,' in *Twelve Original Essays on Great English Novels*, ed. Shapiro, Detroit, 1960.

Fraiberg, Selma. 'Two Modem Incest Heroes,' *Partisan Review*, XXVIII, 5-6.

Garlington, Jack. 'L., with Misgivings,' *South Atlantic Quarterly*, Lix, 3.

Gifford, Henry. 'Anna, L. and the Law,' *Critical Quarterly*, Autumn, 1959.

______ 'The Defect of L.'s Poetry,' *Critical Quarterly*, Summer 1961.

Goldberg, S. L. '*The Rainbow:* Fiddle Bow and Sand,' *Essays in Criticism*, October 1961.

Gomme, Andor. 'L. the Poet, Achievement and Irrelevance,' *T.L.S.*, 26 August 1965.

Goodheart, E. 'L. and Christ,' *Partisan Review*, XXXI, i (Winter 1964).

______ 'L. and the Critics,' *Chicago Review*, XVI, iii (1963), 127-37.

Gordon, David J. 'D.H.L.'s Quarrel with Tragedy,' *Perspective*, Winter 1964.

Gregor, Ian. '*Lady Chatterley's Lover*,' in *The Moral and the Story*, Faber, 1962.

Gurko, Leo. '*The Lost Girl*: D.H.L. as a Dickens of the Midlands,' *PMLA*, LXXVIII, 601-5.

_______'*The Trespasser*: D.H.L.'s Neglected Novel,' College English, XXIV, 29-65.

_______'*Kangaroo*: D.H.L. in Transit,' *Modern Fiction Studies*, x, 4.

Guttmann, Allen. 'D.H.L.: The Politics of Irrationality,' *Wisconsin Studies in Contemporary Literature*, v, 151-63.

Harding, D. 'L. and the Unconscious,' *New Statesman*, LXII, 1961,788-90.

Hassall, Christopher. 'D.H.L. and the Etruscans,' *Essays by Diverse Hands*, vol. XXXI, ed. Green,. O.U.P. 1962.

Heilman, Robert B. 'Nomad, Monads, and the Mystique of the Soma,' *Sewanee Review*, LXVIII, 635-59.

Herbert, Sir Alan. 'Thoughts on *Lady Chatterley*,' *The Listener*, 10 November 1960.

Hogan, Robert. 'D.H.L. and His Critics,' *Essays in Criticism*, October 1959.

_______'L.'s Song of a Man Who Came Through,' *Explicator*, XVII, Item 51.

Jones, William M. 'Growth of a Symbol: The Sun in L. and Eudora Welty,' *University of Kansas City Review*, XXVI, 68-73.

Kaufmann, Stanley. '*Lady Chatterley* at Last,' *New Republic,* 25 May 1959.

Kazin, Alfred. 'Sons, Lovers and Mothers,' *Partisan Review,* Summer 1962.

_______ 'Lady Chatterley in America,' in *Colltemporaries*, Secker-Warburg, 1963.

Kendle, Burton S. 'D.H.L. The Man Who Misunderstood Gulliver,' *English Language Notes,* September 1964.

Kermode, Frank. 'L. in his Letters,' *New Statesman*, 23 March 1962.

Kerr, Fergus. 'Odious Corollaries in D.H.L.,' *Blackfriars*, October 1961.

Kessler, Jascha. 'D.H.L.'s Primitivism,' *Texas Studies in Literature and Language*, v, 467-88.

Knight, G. Wilson. 'L., Joyce and Powys,' *Essays in Criticism*, October 1961.

Knoepflmacher, V. C. 'The Rival Ladies: Mrs Ward's Lady Connie and L.'s *Lady Chatterley's Lover*,' *Victorian Studies*, December 1960.

Krishnamurthy, M. G. 'D.H.L.'s The Woman who Rode Away,' *The Literary Criterion*, Summer 1960.

Kuo, C. H. '*The Rainbow*,' *Explicator*, XIX, Item 60.

Leavis, F. R. 'L. Scholarship and L.,' *Sewanee Review,* Winter 1963.

Levy, Mervyn and Wilson, Colin. 'The Paintings of D.H.L.,' *Studio*, October 1962.

Lindsay, Jack. 'The Impact of Modernism on L.,' in *Paintings of D.H.L.*, ed. Levy, London, 1964.

Longville, Timothy. 'The Longest Journey: D.H.L.'s *Phoenix*,' *Critical Quarterly*, Spring 1962.

Lucas, B. 'Apropos of England, Atly England,' *Twentieth Century,* March 1961.

MacLeish, Archibald. Preface to 'Lady Chatterley's Lover,' Grove Press, 1959.

MacLennan, Hugh. 'The Defence of Lady Chatterley,' *Canadian Literature*, no. 6, 1960.

Magalaner, Marvin. 'D.H.L. Today,' *Commonweal*, LXX, 1960, 275-6.

Mandel, Oscar. 'Ignorance and Privacy' (on *Lady Chatterley's Lover), American Scholar*, XXIX, 509-19.

Martin, W. B. J. 'Significant Modern Writers-D.H.L.,' *Expository Times,* March 1960.

Maxwell, J. C. '*Lady Chatterley's Lover:* A Correction,' *Notes and Queries*, VIII, 110.

Merivale, Patricia. 'D.H.L. and the Modern Pan Myth,' *Texas Studies in Literature and Language,* VI, 297-305.

Michot, Paulette. 'D.H.L. A Belated Apology,' *Revue des Langues Vivantes*, IV, 1961,290-305.

Miller, James E. Jr. 'The Dance of Rapture,' in *Start with the Sun,* Nebraska, 1960.

Miller, Nolan. 'The Success and Failure of D.H.L.,' *Antioch Review*, XXII, 380-92.

Moore, Everett T. 'D.H.L. and the Censor-Morons,' *Bulletin of the American Library Assoc.* LIV, 1960,731-2.

Moore, Harry T., 'L. from All Sides,' *Kenyon Review*, xxv, 555-8.

_______ 'The Prose Style of D.H.L.,' *Langue et Litterature*, Paris, 1961.

Morris, James. 'Reflections on the Chatterley Case,' *N. Y. Times Mag.* 4 December 1960.

Moynahan, Julian. 'The Essence of D.H.L.,' *University* (Princeton), Summer-Fall 1963.

Myers, Neil. 'L. and the War,' *Criticism*, Winter 1962.

Newman, Paul B. 'D.H.L. and *The Golden Bough,' Kansas Magazine*, 1962, 79-86.

Nott, Kathleen, 'L. by Daylight,' *The Observer*, 13 November 1960.

Osgerby, J. R. 'D.H.L.'s *The White Peacock,' Use of English*, Summer 1962.

Pearsall, Robert B. 'The Second Art of D.H.L.' [his painting], *South Atlantic Quarterly*, LXIII, 457-67.

Peter, John. 'The Bottom of the Well' (on *Lady Chatterley's Lover*), *Essays in Criticism*, XII, 226-7, 445-7; XIII, 301-2.

Pinto, Vivian de Sola. 'Poet Without a Mask,' *Critical Quarterly*, Spring 1961.

_______ 'Mr Gifford and D.H.L.,' *Critical Quarterly*, Autumn 1961.

_______ 'L. and Frieda,' *English*, XIV, Spring 1963.

Requardt, Egon. 'D.H.L.'s *Sons and Lovers,*' Die Neueren Sprachen, 1961, 230-5.

Rieff, Philip. 'A Modem Mythmaker,' in *Myth and Mythmaking,* ed. Murray, Braziller, N.Y., 1960.

_______ 'Two Honest Men, Freud and D.H.L.,' *Listener*, 5 May 1960.

Roberts, Walter. 'After the Prophet: the Reputation of D.H.L.,' *Month*, April 1962.

Robinson, John. 'The Christian and Lady Chatterley,' *Time and Tide*, XII, 45.

Robson, W. W. '*Women in Love*,' in *The Modern Age,* Penguin, 1961.

Rosenthal, T. G. 'The Writer as Painter,' *The Listener*, 6 September 1962.

Rudikoff, Sonya. 'D.H.L. and Our Life Today: Rereading-*Lady Chatterley's Lover*,' *Commentary*, XXVIII, 408-13.

Ryals, Clyde de L. 'D.H.L.'s The Horse Dealer's Daughter,' *Literature and Psychology,* XII, 39-43.

Salgado, Gamini. 'D.H.L. as Literary Critic,' *London Magazine*, February 1960.

Sawyer, Paul W. 'The Religious Vision of D.H.L.,' *Crane Review,* Spring 1961.

Saxena, H. S. 'The Critical Writings of D.H.L.,' *Indian Journal of English Studies,* II (1961), 130-'7.

_______ 'D.H.L. and the Impressionistic Technique,' *Indian Journal of English Studies*, III (1961), 145-52.

Sharpe, Michael C. 'The Genesis of D.H.L.'s *The Trespasser*,' *Essays in Criticism,* January 1961.

Shonfield, Andrew. 'L.'s Other Censor,' *Encounter*, XVII (September 1961), 63-64.

Slate, Bernice. 'The Leaves of.D.H.L.,' in *Start with the Sun.*

Smith, L. E. W. 'Snake,' *Critical Survey*, Spring 1963.

Sparrow, John. 'On *Lady Chatterley's Lover*,' *Essays in Criticism*, XIII, 202-5, 303.

Spilka, Mark. 'Post-Leavis L. Critics,' *Modern Language Quarterly*, xxv, 212-17.

Stanley, F. R. 'The Artist as Pornographer,' *Literary Half-Yearly,* January 1963.

Stewart, J. I. M. 'D.H.L.' in *Eight Modern Writers*, Oxford 1963.

Tanner, Tony. 'The Man Who Lived,' *Spectator*, 23 March 1962.

Tenenbaum, Louis. 'Two Views of the Modern Italian: D.H.L. and Sean O'Faolain,' *Italica*, XXXVII, 1960, 118-25.

Tetsumura, Haruo. 'D.H.L.'s Mysticism: What the Moon Signifies,'*Hiroshima Studies in English Language and Literature,* IX (1963), i-ii, 51-65.

Thody, Philip. *'Lady Chatterley's Lover*: A Pyrrhic Victory,' *Threshold*, v, ii (Belfast).

Traschen, Isadore. 'Pure and Ironic Idealism. D.H.L.,' *South Atlantic Quarterly*, Spring 1960.

Vickery, John B. '*The Plumed Serpent* and the Eternal Paradox', *Criticism*, v, II 9-34.

Walsh, William. 'Ursula in *The Rainbow*,' and 'The Educational Ideas of D.H.L.', in *The Use of Imagination*, Chatto and Windus, 1959.

Way, Brian. 'Sex and Language-Obscene Words in D.H.L. and Henry Miller,' *New Left Review*, 27, Autumn 1964.

Werner, Alfred. 'L. and Pascin,' *Kenyon Review*, XXIII, 2.

West, Paul. 'D.H.L., Mystical Critic,' *Southern Review*, Winter 1965.

Whitaker, T. R. 'L.'s Western Path: *Mornings in Mexico*,' *Criticism*, III,

White, William. 'D.H.L. and Marquand,' *D.H.L. News and Notes*, II, i, 1962.

Wilde, Alan. 'The Illusion of St Mawr: Technique and Vision in D.H.L.'s Novel,' *PMLA*, March 1964.

Williams, Raymond. 'L. and Tolstoy,' *Critical Quarterly*, Spring 1960.

_______ 'Tolstoy, L and Tragedy,' *Kenyon Review*, Autumn 1963.

Wright, Raymond. 'L.'s Non-Human Analogues,' *Modem Language Notes*, LXXVI, 426-32.

Index